THE WINE WIDOW

Nicole Berthois is a peasant girl from a wine making village in Champagne. Philippe de Tramont is the young son of a village aristocrat and together they drunk the Tramont champagne cellars dry in an affair of reckless passion. In 1850's France their marriage can hardly be contemplated but marry they do to secure the future for their unborn child.

Their happiness is short-lived – Philippe dies tragically young. Nicole's pride triumphs over her grief, making the de Tramonts' name famous for its champagne along with her beauty in widow's weeds.

THE WINE WIDOW

THE
WINE WIDOW

by

Tessa Barclay

Magna Large Print Books
Long Preston, North Yorkshire,
BD23 4ND, England.

British Library Cataloguing in Publication Data.

Barclay, Tessa
    The wine widow.

    A catalogue record of this book is
    available from the British Library

    ISBN   0-7505-2011-6

First published in Great Britain in 1985 by W.H. Allen & Co.

Copyright © 1984 by Tessa Barclay

Cover illustration © Len Thurston by arrangement with
P.W.A. International Ltd.

The moral right of the author has been asserted

Published in Large Print 2003 by arrangement with
Tessa Barclay, care of Darley Anderson

Magna Large Print is an imprint of Library Magna Books Ltd.

Printed and bound in Great Britain by
T.J. (International) Ltd., Cornwall, PL28 8RW

Chapter One

The light from the shaded candle was only just enough to let Nicole see that the gathers of her petticoat were evenly spaced before she tied the waist tape. From the back of a chair she gently lifted her blouse of fine lawn, lightly starched. She let it slip over her head so that it floated round her young breasts encased in a bodice of thick decent cotton. Next came the black over-bodice cleverly trimmed with brown braid to accentuate her trim waist.

She tied the front lacing tight, so that from the shoulders the puffed sleeves of her blouse escaped like a fine white foam – like the foam from the champagne for which her district was famous.

Now she put on her best stockings, of fine brown thread, much darned and mended but so expertly done that the mends didn't show. Her mother was adept at the craft, had done special mending for the villagers until the crooking illness began to warp her fingers.

At the thought, Nicole gave a guilty glance towards the sleeping figure in the bed. She moved the candle a little further away so that its light should not disturb her mother. It was very early on a fine May morning, scarcely half-past four as yet, and if possible Madame Berthois should be allowed to sleep on until full daylight.

But already Nicole had been out to tend the goats that munched drowsily at the coarse new grass of their hillside field. She had milked them and moved their tethers so that they had fresh pasture enough for the time she would be away.

For Nicole was going to Rheims, for market day.

Market day! How she had longed for it. To get away from Calmady, if only for a few hours.

Nicole Berthois didn't dislike her village. Like many another in the Department of the Marne, it was neat, its main street well swept and its little square graced by a brisk and clear fountain over which a stone angel stood guard.

But the ragstone houses were faced with rough plaster left grey in the cool and often wet climate. The roofs too were grey, of durable slate. Villagers spent little money on the painting of woodwork – doors were generally plain oak or black-painted pine, and though some of the windows were graced with windowboxes there was little colour elsewhere.

In the great city, though, everything was

different. There were shops through whose window panes one could see fine silks, feathered bonnets, thin-soled shoes with pearl buttons. The cafes had awnings, sometimes red, sometimes emerald green, and under them on fine days sat ladies and gentlemen in fashionable clothes. There were beds of flowers, organ-grinders, street-singers.

Of course Nicole wasn't going to Rheims just to stare at the sights. No indeed, that would not have befitted her role as head of the Berthois family. There was business to be done today. She had cream cheeses to sell, and after that she must go to see Paulette at Madame Treignac's. From Paulette she would receive the wages earned by her elder sister for the spring quarter. The money would be safely tied in the chamois leather pouch which Nicole now tied about her waist before preparing to put on her skirt.

'Nicole!' came a cry of reproach from the bed.

Madame Berthois, awake, was struggling to sit up. Nicole hurried to help her, pushing the pillows into her back to ease the strains on the ailing joints. 'I didn't mean you to wake up yet, mama.'

'Evidently. Otherwise you wouldn't be putting on your coloured skirt.'

'Mama, I'm going to market–'

9

'If you were going to paradise itself, it would still be wrong to wear coloured clothes when you're still in mourning. Think shame on yourself, Nicci! Your father and your brother aren't dead a year yet.'

Nicole coloured at the reproof but her chin was stubborn as she turned back to the garment she'd been about to put on when her mother called out. 'Ten months' mourning is long enough,' she muttered.

'You know it must be at least a year! Father Raimond even said that for such a bereavement we ought to wear black a full eighteen months–'

'But you can't call a brown skirt so very bright–'

'It's cinnamon-colour! It's not even dark brown. I won't have it, Nicci–'

Nicci was fastening the buttons at the back. She smoothed the wide folds over her petticoat. 'I'm not going to take it off, Mama. I'm going to Rheims and it's a beautiful May morning. I refuse to go to market looking like a crow–'

'Good God, child, what does it matter what you look like? Who's going to care, except Paulette?'

'I might see Madame Treignac. I don't want her thinking we're a family of dull nobodies!' Nicole headed for the door of the bedroom knowing full well she could be out and away before ever her mother could struggle out of bed.

'Nicole!' cried Madame Berthois. 'You're not going to run off without even saying goodbye?'

At once her daughter turned and came back. After all, she was going to Rheims, a full eight miles away, a long journey by the market waggon which lumbered through the vineyard villages to collect peasants with produce and letters for the post office in the great cathedral city. Who could tell what might happen on the road? Over two hours' travel there and the same back – and one heard of such terrible accidents, coaches overturned on the terrible roads, footpads taking money and jewellery from passengers...

But then that was the coach passengers. No footpad was going to waste his time on the carter's waggon, for peasants had only farm produce or the money they had earned at market. All the same, one ought not to part without a kiss and a farewell, because life outside the village was always full of hazard, everyone knew that.

'Goodbye, Mama, I've left bread and milk on the kitchen table for your breakfast and there's soup by the side of the fire for dinner–'

'But you'll be home by then?' Madame Berthois said anxiously. 'I shan't eat till six o'clock.'

11

'Yes, yes,' soothed Nicole. But privately she had decided not to catch the afternoon waggon. On market days the carter had two vehicles on the road, and the second didn't leave Rheims to take the market-goers home until early evening once the long light evenings began.

They kissed and hugged. Madame Berthois had quite forgotten her disapproval of the cinnamon skirt. Her younger daughter, her mainstay, was off to the great city, too far for a sixteen-year-old to go unchaperoned but then, who was there to go with her? The Berthois family was reduced now to three womenfolk, and it was cause for gratitude to God that Nicole had so much good sense and courage. Without Nicole, Madame Berthois knew she would have been dead long ago – of hunger, of exhaustion, of sheer lack of desire to live.

Accident of circumstance had made Nicole Berthois head of her family. Her father and her brother, both fine sturdy men, had been carried off by a typhoid epidemic which struck the village in the previous summer. There had been some talk of bringing Paulette home from her work at the dressmaker in Rheims, but where was the sense of that? Though older, Paulette was timid and shy; moreover they needed the wages she could bring in with her exceptional talent for needlework.

When Paul and Robert Berthois died, the neighbours had done what they could to help. But many families in the district had been stricken by the sickness too, so even if Marie would have consented to marry off one of her daughters so as to have a hardworking son-in-law for the farm, it would have been impossible.

There had been no decision to let Nicole take charge. Somehow it just happened. But that was a hard life for a young girl, thought Marie – tending the goats and their few rows of vines, working for hire in the greater vineyards when the season called for labourers, looking after the house, tending a semi-invalid mother...

So now Marie sent her off to walk to the village crossroads to meet the market waggon, wishing her a happy day and praying inwardly that no trickster, no robber, would take advantage of her pretty little dove of a daughter.

The waggon was late. The waggon was always late. Nicole occupied herself in seeing that her precious cream cheeses in their little wicker containers were safe and moist in the wrapping of cabbage leaves, that her salt butter was neat and shapely in its precious paper package with the family name painstakingly lettered in indian ink. The produce from the Berthois farm was sought after in Rheims, but there could only be a limited supply and usually it had to be taken by a neighbour. That was a waste, because of course the neighbour had to be paid a commission.

But once a quarter, when Paulette's wages were due from Madame Treignac, Nicole made the trip to Rheims herself, and sold her produce proudly in the market place. After that, she would visit Paulette at Madame's dressmaking establishment, perhaps share the lunch that Madame provided for her employees, and go home the richer not only in money but in enjoyment.

The passengers on the waggon greeted her with pleasure. They made a space for her among the crates of ducks and the baskets of vegetables. In winter the waggon would be covered with a great canvas awning, but on such a fine day the great vehicle was open to the air. The passengers, when not forced to hang on like grim death as the wheels ground in and out of potholes, could look at the passing scene.

Nicole saw around her stretches of young vines, now in pale leaf. To her left were the vines bearing grapes which produced the vintage known as 'the mountain wine', after the Mountain of Rheims on whose slopes they grew. This 'mountain' would have made a Swiss farmer laugh – nowhere was it more than six hundred feet above the plain.

Yet it was imposing enough in the flat Marne landscape, with its thick cape of oak, beech and pine at the summit.

As the waggon toiled on, the fine new windmill at Verzenay became visible, built only thirty years ago in 1820 but already regarded as a famous landmark. The great sails were turning in the spring breeze. Beyond those spread fingers, the sky was azure and white, clouds sailing like galleons towards the west, towards distant places such as Lorraine and Germany, towards unknown worlds and adventure.

A cry from the other passengers called Nicole back from her daydreams. A sharp-eyed youngster had seen the first grey outline of a turret roof. The great cathedral at Rheims was coming into sight on the left. Everyone became busy wrapping shawls more tidily, tying lace caps more securely, exchanging wooden shoes for leather, unearthing baskets and containers buried under the belongings of others.

The route into the city lay past wool factories and the manufacturers of wine-growing equipment. At seven in the morning the workers were hurrying through the streets towards the factory gates. Cafe proprietors were sweeping the pavement in front of their shops. The early sun glistened on gilt shop signs, the high varnish of carriages, the tubs of iris bordering the entrances to the fine hotels.

Nicole was one of the first to jump down and hurry away, calling thanks to old Jouvet, the driver. She darted under the noses of the horses, who now stood tossing their manes and looking hopefully for a nosebag of fodder. Ahead of her at the end of the road lay the alley which led to the great square. She wanted to be early in choosing a place to set out her wares.

It was always strange to be in a square so vast. And the people around her spoke in a dialect different from her own. Not that Nicole Berthois was restricted to the patois of the Marne – certainly not. The Berthois family had always been a cut above the rest when it came to speaking the French of Paris.

Their superiority hadn't always endeared them to their fellow-villagers, and arose from a humanitarian act carried out by Nicole's great-grandfather at the time of the Revolution. Old Robert had given shelter to one of the monks of the Abbey of Haut-villiers, Brother Joseph. Nicole's grandfather grew up with this kindly and learned man, whose influence was strong throughout the Berthois family even two generations later. He had lived and died in their house, piously awaiting the restoration of his abbey.

The Berthois could read, which was by no means a universal talent in the Marne in

1850. They could write, not just their names but in current script and with good spelling. Taken together with the fact that the Berthois before the Revolution had been owners of quite a decent acreage and a house with four rooms, they were regarded as 'different' from the other villagers of Calmady. The fact that they were now desperately poor and hard-pressed didn't diminish the respect they were shown.

So now when housekeepers from wealthy families approached to buy her cream cheese and butter, Nicole was able to respond without awkwardness to their educated speech. She did brisk business. An hour after setting up her little stall, she had sold out.

It was still too early to go to Madame Treignac's if she were to share Paulette's midday lunch, so she set off for a stroll around the market. There were sellers of leather and wool yarn, basket-makers, silversmiths, purveyors of game and fresh vegetables, mushroom gatherers, a fortune-teller, a tooth-puller, and a muscular giant who broke iron manacles with one surge of his bulging biceps.

Nicole resisted the temptation to have her fortune told. She knew only too well what it would be: hard work, the care of her ailing mother, an arranged marriage with some older man who could take over the running of the farm. Though she accepted this future, she didn't like to dwell on it. Instead she wandered round the square, seeking free entertainment, occasionally grasping her lawn cap to keep it on her head in the fine spring wind.

The gentry were now beginning to arrive for the day's shopping. They came in their carriages from outlying estates, some of them wealthy bourgeois who had bought land cheap when the aristocracy were dispossessed, some aristocrats who had regained their possessions when the monarchy was restored. Nicole paused to watch a carriage which drew in to the kerb, a handsome caleche drawn by four horses and roomy enough inside for an entire family. But out of it stepped only a well-dressed elderly lady and a young man in the light-coloured morning suit considered right for country life.

As the lady was helped down from the carriage, she dropped her gloves. The footman retrieved one, but the other was kicked away by a hurrying passer-by. It came to rest a yard away from Nicole's feet.

She stooped to pick it up. At that moment a man's hand took hold of it too. For a moment both held fast, wondering who might be trying to take possession.

Philippe de Tramont raised his eyes to find himself head to head with an extremely pretty country girl. Her dark hair was held back in two thick loops that framed her forehead and covered her ears. On top was a little cap of embroidered lawn, caught back into two bone hairpins for safety. Sparkling dark brown eyes regarded him, rosy lips curved up in a smile.

'Thank you, mademoiselle,' he said, as she let the glove go into his hand.

'A pity to spoil it with market dirt,' she said, nodding towards the squashed cabbage leaves and dead flowers that littered the ground.

'Rheims is always so dirty on market day.'

'That can't be avoided, alas. We have to sell what we have as quickly as possible – no time to be tidy.'

'You're a stall-holder?'

She shook her head. 'I don't come often enough for that. I had only a few things to sell, and they've gone.'

'Philippe!' called Madame de Tramont, from the kerb by the carriage. 'Why are you wasting your time with that turnip of a common peasant girl? I'm waiting!'

The words floated to them above the hubbub in the square. Nicole coloured in resentment, Philippe coloured in embarrass-ment. 'My apologies, mademoiselle,' he said. 'My mother doesn't really mean–'

'Philippe! We have a lot to do!'

'You'd better go,' Nicole said, turning

away. 'You are summoned!'

Before he could detain her she had melted in among the passersby in the market. Intrigued at the thought of a peasant girl who could use a phrase such as 'you are summoned' and speak it like a lady of Paris, Philippe went to join his mother.

'You needn't have been so short-tempered, Mama. That girl saved your glove from being trampled underfoot.'

'Oh, did she indeed. And asked five sous as a reward, I daresay.'

'Mama, you got out of bed the wrong side this morning. Come along.' He offered his arm. 'Let's get on with the business of the day.' But as he escorted her along the pavement of the great square he was keeping watch for the thick brown hair in its cobwebby cap and the glimpse of a cinnamon-coloured skirt.

For her part, Nicole put them out of her mind. What good did it do to let insults rankle? The gentry, it was well known, had a high opinion of themselves and consequently misjudged others. And the lady who had called to the young gentleman was the most gentrified that Nicole had so far seen – tall, imposing, clad in a crinoline of dark brown grosgrain with a fur-trimmed mantle and topped with a very elegant capote hat.

Nicole's sister Paulette would have told her that the style was a little dated, that the fur on the mantle had been removed from some other garment to grace its present collar. In other words, either Madame de Tramont chose not to spend too much on fashion or she was not as rich as she liked to pretend.

The de Tramonts were, in fact, quite hard pushed for money. That was one of the reasons they had come to Rheims today. As everyone knew, the best way to bring money into a noble family was to marry well. Pourdume, the de Tramonts' lawyer, had been delicately negotiating with the parents of a young lady who wished to achieve a title.

The problem was, the de Tramonts didn't quite have a title.

Auguste de Tramont, eighth marquis of that line, had supported the Royalist cause wholeheartedly in 1789. The result was that he had to run for his life at the beginning of the Terror. His titles and his lands were swept away while he plotted in exile. When things began to cool down in France, Auguste returned with his son, but alas involved himself in Royalist plots against Napoleon, who wasn't inclined to treat such behaviour lightly. Auguste and Claude de Tramont were exiled once more.

When the monarchy was restored to France, the de Tramonts looked hopefully towards their homeland. Auguste had died, but Claude, now married, hoped to regain his estates and bring his young bride home in triumph. But endless legal wrangles ensued. Meanwhile Clothilde languished in London, growing more frustrated and embittered every day.

In 1820 Claude regained possession of the manor of Tramont, the country house on the lesser estate from which the family originally drew its name. The great estates in the south were lost forever. And most of the land around Tramont was gone too, snapped up by clever bourgeois and even some of the peasants who had enough money to buy when prices were low.

Clothilde wasn't pleased when she discovered she was to be mistress of a small wine-growing property in the Marne. She had imagined herself dwelling in a fine town house in Paris, attending court, occasionally travelling south to live *la vie champêtre* when it pleased her. Acquaintance with the British aristocracy had shown her that it was considered not only desirable but actually smart to live part of the time on one's country estate.

But to be condemned to live all the time in a ramshackle old house in the Marne! Worse yet, there was almost no money. If there had been any kind of income from the former great estates, she would have repaired the manor house and laid out pretty gardens.

But the only money came from the sale of the grapes from the few acres of vines – excellent vines, producing sought-after grapes fetching good prices. But that was *trade*.

Claude had come to terms with the situation long ago. The grinding experience of fighting the bureaucrats for his house and few fields had taught him that you had to make the best of what you had.

To Clothilde's horror, Claude went into the wine-making business.

He had good advice from his lawyer, who had many clients among the champagne-makers of the district. Mérimé Pourdume explained that to be a champagne-maker wasn't considered bourgeois. Great noblemen of the past had done it, the process had been discovered originally by the chief cellarer of a famous monastery, there was history and prestige behind it. Moreover, it was lucrative.

In the thirty years that ensued, Clothilde de Tramont never really reconciled herself to the idea that she was married to a wine-maker. It offended her that her daughter, Seraphine, had to accept a marriage with a minor English nobleman whose family she had come to know during the years of exile. When Clothilde's son Philippe was born, rather late in her marriage, she begged Claude to leave 'trade' so as not to bring a stigma on the boy. But Claude had continued his struggle to learn the business of champagne-making until the day he died, three years ago.

Now Clothilde herself and Philippe were supposed to run the firm of Tramont de Tramont, champagne-makers. Clothilde had never cared to learn anything about it and Philippe had scant ability where business was concerned.

Luckily they had a fine chief cellarman, who knew more about champagne than the Tramont family were ever likely to learn. In his capable hands the small firm managed to make a profit, whereby the workers were paid and a balance was left over so that mother and son could live in comfort.

But the only way to restore the glories of the de Tramont family was for Philippe to make a splendid marriage. And somehow that wasn't proving quite so easy as Clothilde had envisaged.

While these two went for an anxious discussion with M. Pourdume, Nicole Berthois amused herself in the streets and alleys of Rheims. Though she had anxieties of her own, today she banished them. When she went at last to Madame Treignac's to ask for Paulette, she was on the crest of a wave of happiness – she had seen handsome and fashionable people, watched glossy horses and carriages, listened to a street band, and generally enjoyed herself without the expense of a single sou.

The storeman came out of his room full of cloth bales to inspect her when she stepped inside the back door from the cobbled courtyard. 'Oh, it's you, Nicole. You can go straight up. I think the girls are still working but they should break for lunch any moment now.'

He stood to watch the twinkle of slim ankles under cinnamon skirts as she ran upstairs. Nicole, perfectly aware of the fact, twirled about at the first landing so that he could have a glimpse of brown thread stockings above good leather shoes before she started on the second flight which took her out of sight.

Paulette had heard her footsteps. She came out of the big attic workshop on the third floor. 'Nicole, you'll have to sit quiet for a few minutes. Madame hasn't closed for the lunch hour yet, she has a customer.'

Nicole followed her sister into the workshop. It was a fine airy room – draughty, in cold weather – with skylights to give perfect illumination for the seamstresses and embroideresses. Eight girls were seated at tables, with work spread out before them, some still busy, some beginning to fold the garments into their muslin protective wrappings in preparation for the meal. Lunch was eaten at the work bench. Not the slightest crumb or spot of soup must touch the dresses, or there would be fines and stoppages of pay and scoldings.

'Who's in the showroom, then?' Nicole inquired after she'd kissed and hugged her sister.

'Don't know. Who is it, Francoise – d'you know?'

'The bottle-green moiré, isn't it? It's one of your own, surely, Paulette – they came to fetch it first thing this morning, remember?'

'Oh, her,' Paulette said with a shrug. Anyone who ordered a gown in March and left it until early May before having it fitted was unworthy of consideration.

It seemed that lunch wouldn't be served for at least another half hour. After Nicole had brought her sister up to date with news of the farm, Paulette followed suit with little incidents from her life at the dressmaker's. Nicole found it all terribly strange: imagine spending all your day shut up in an upstairs room, with only a view over roofs for diversion, and only the gossip from the workroom and the showroom to talk about.

Nevertheless it was intriguing. Rich women came and went through the grandiose front door. Downstairs in the fitting room some fine lady was surveying herself in the big gilt mirrors.

'Could we go down and take a look, Paulie?'

'What!'

'I'd like to see the showroom. From the outside, you can see fine velvet curtains. Couldn't we look?'

'But Madame's there, with the customer...'

'Go on, take her,' the other girls urged. 'You can stay behind the big draft screen that shields the passage door. Go on, Paulie, let your country mouse of a sister see how the city people live!'

Laughing and yet a little scared, Paulette led Nicole down the stairs up which she had just come. On the first floor they went through a door and along a short passage; Madame Treignac and her husband lived here, in two rooms far less splendid than the showroom. They went down a carpeted stairway to the ground floor, where Paulette softly opened a bit mahogany door.

Immediately the tops of the stately windows and their velvet hangings could be seen over the tapestry screen that stood in front of the door. Nicole was about to peep round it when a rustle of movement and a cough made her stop. She drew back in alarm. By craning their necks the girls could just see, reflected in one of the mirrors that graced the room and reflected light, a trousered leg and an elegant boot polished like glass.

'A husband!' breathed Paulette in Nicole's ear.

Nicole stifled a giggle. Poor man, doomed to wait while his wife was pushed and prodded in the fitting room on the other side.

The door of that room was thrown open with a bang. Madame Treignac could be heard uttering soothing cries.

'Nonsense, nonsense, the gown looks terrible!' stormed an angry voice.

Nicole recognised it at once. It belonged to the lady who had referred to her as a common peasant girl.

'Philippe, give me your opinion. There is something utterly wrong about this gown, now isn't there?'

Indeed there was. By a trick of reflections in mirrors, the girls behind the screen could see Clothilde de Tramont in her almost-completed gown.

'She's put on weight since she ordered it,' Paulette whispered to her sister. 'My word, it's a mess.'

'You'll have to let it out,' Nicole replied.

'Can't. It's cut too strictly.'

'Well, you'll have to let in a piece.'

'Can't do that either. I'll tell you why – Madame used up the rest of the bale to make a semi-mourning dress for little Mademoiselle Lubec. Her mother didn't want to put her into black, you see, and rather than miss a sale, Madame remembered the end of the piece used for Madame

28

de Tramont.'

'Dear me,' Nicole murmured with amusement. 'What a problem. She'll have to tell Madame de Tramont she's got too fat.'

'Are you out of your mind?' said Paulette in a muffled shriek, which was luckily drowned in the noisy complaints of the customer.

Philippe, bored out of his mind by a half hour wait with not even a newspaper to look at, was trying to help Madame Treignac convince his mother that the gown fitted beautifully. 'It's fashionable to be nipped in at the waist, surely?' he remarked.

'Nipped in? I feel as if I'm encased in armour. I can't breathe! I tell you, you've done something silly with this gown since I was measured for it–'

'No, no, madame, I assure you–'

'One thing is certain! I'm not paying good money for a disgraceful piece of work like this!'

'The gown is beautifully made, madame. Only the finest workmanship, I assure you. And when you have worn it once or twice, it will seem easier–'

'Do you take me for a fool? If I tried to go out to an afternoon engagement in this dress, I would have a fainting fit.'

'Mama, truly, it looks fine. You must allow for the fact that the material is new and stiff–'

'Stiff? Stiff? Silk shouldn't feel like board! I can feel it pressing against my ribs to such an extent I can't draw breath. Look at my face – it's giving me an apoplexy!'

An impulse of mischief, prompted by a wish to pay back the slighting remark in the Grand Square, caused Nicole to step from behind the screen.

'The gown is a disaster, Madame,' she told Clothilde de Tramont calmly. 'It's too tight because your figure has changed since you were measured. That's why you're going red in the face.'

Chapter Two

The silence that followed Nicole's remark was ominous. It was broken by Paulette. She gave a little squeak of terror and threw her apron of crash linen over her face. Philippe gave a little gurgle of stifled laughter. Madame Treignac, her angular face going white with shock, drew a careful breath.

'Changed?' echoed Clothilde, recovering from the surprise of Nicole's sudden intervention. 'Nothing of the kind! My figure is just as it always was!'

Now Nicole saw what she had done. Out of a silly impulse of revenge, she would lose a customer for Madame Treignac and her sister's job. Her quick wits flew to her aid.

'Ah, madame,' she said in a tone of sympathetic understanding, 'the head of a great household such as yours cannot afford the time to think of herself. You have the servants to control, parties and outings to arrange, correspondence to attend to.' Here Nicole's imagination ran out. She really couldn't think of much more that a wealthy woman could have to do. 'In the midst of all this,' she went on, 'is it surprising that you

31

are unaware that a more majestic outline has developed?'

'More majestic,' echoed Madame Treignac in a faint, hopeful murmur. 'A fine figure of a woman, as the saying goes.'

'Indeed,' Nicole agreed, 'very much in the fashion. But alas it does mean that the dress is now too tight.'

'Too tight,' said Clothilde de Tramont. 'Of course, that's what's wrong with it. That's why my upper arms feel as if they were gripped in a vice – the sleeves are cutting into them.'

'I believe the dress *is* a little too tight,' Madame Treignac said.

'Why didn't you say so?' demanded Clothilde in vexation, ignoring the fact that she had been making a great fuss only a few minutes ago over the suggestion her figure had changed. 'Absurd creature. Well, then...' She turned this way and that to view herself in the mirror. 'The bodice must be let out.'

'Let out,' gasped Paulette, looking ready to throw her apron over her face again, though she had just emerged.

'Yes, certainly, let out. Who are you, in any case?'

'I'm ... ah ... madame, I'm the seamstress who cut and made the dress.'

'Then you know just how to do it. I shall expect to return this afternoon for a new fitting of the bodice—'

'Impossible,' whispered Paulette.

'Impossible? How impossible, young woman?'

'Because … ah, you see … the seams were cut very fine, to ensure a trim fit.'

'Cut very fine? What does that mean?'

It means, thought Nicole, that there isn't enough material on the seams to let out. Oh dear… She cast a glance of sympathy at Paulette.

Paulette faltered out just that information to Clothilde, who frowned for a moment but then waved a ringed hand dismissively. 'I suppose then, two pieces must be let in at the sides. That can be done without spoiling the cut?'

Oh yes, thought Nicole, if there were any fabric left to use. But alas Madame Treignac had sold about one-third of the piece of moiré silk paid for by Clothilde to make a dress for someone else's child.

'Madame de Tramont,' Nicole said quickly, 'although of course it would be perfectly simple to put two new pieces into the bodice, don't you think that would make the shape unduly dull? That would mean, let me see – eight plain seams at the front not counting the fastening. Don't you agree it would be much better to enhance the line rather than have a plain alteration? Insertions of fine embroidery edged with

33

braid – how very elegant that would look!'

'Very elegant,' echoed Madame Treignac in a voice of sudden gratitude. 'Yes, indeed, only today I have received a parcel of new braid from Paris – there is a very handsome one with steel beading that glints grey and green. How splendid it would look if one put it in here, and here...' Her slim fingers flickered over the moiré silk, putting little chalk marks to suggest the placing.

'And embroidery?' urged Clothilde.

'Paulette could make the embroidery insertions,' Nicole said, taking her sister in a firm grasp and propelling her forward. 'Suppose she were to do green eyelet work on black silk–'

'Or brown,' Madame Treignac put in, 'or dark blue...'

'Or, since summer is coming, beige would be very suitable,' Paulette said, plucking up courage to look into Clothilde's thoughtful face.

'Beige ... beige...'

'No, madame,' Nicole said, shaking her head. 'The colour of the gown is sumptuous, one shouldn't detract the eye by adding too much contrast. No, if you'll take my advice, you'll have black or brown.'

'Perhaps you're right. Perhaps ... yes, I think, black, Madame Treignac. Black embroidery insertions with black braid edged with beading... I believe I will look very well.' She turned, portly and good-humoured now. 'And how much is all this extra work going to cost me?'

'Oh, a mere nothing, madame, I assure you! This way, madame, let us try the braid against the bodice before you take it off.' The dressmaker led her customer away to the fitting room, with Paulette in her train.

Nicole was left with Philippe de Tramont. 'That was quick thinking,' he remarked with a grin.

'Oh, us common peasant girls can think too, you know,' Nicole said, turning away with a shrug.

'Ah, so that's where I've seen you before! It was you in the square this morning.' He bowed. 'I'm delighted to meet you again. I'm Philippe de Tramont.'

'And I'm Nicole Berthois.'

'Well, Nicole Berthois, I wish we had you at home to deflect Mama's bad temper now and again...'

'You're very kind, sir, but I have a mother of my own to claim my attention.'

'Are you from hereabouts?' he inquired, partly to detain her and partly because he was puzzled. She wasn't speaking in the local dialect. She wasn't like most pretty country girls, difficult to understand when she spoke and a bore when she didn't.

Nicole saw a tall, slender young man with fairish brown hair worn rather long – had she been more in touch with fashion she would have understood that this stamped him 'poetic'. His hands, which he used to emphasize occasional words, showed that he had never done a day's hard work in his life.

To Nicole he was strange and exotic as a bird of paradise. It was infinitely flattering to see that her liked her, even admired her. But she knew this was only a passing encounter for when Madame Treignac came back Nicole must make herself scarce. Madame had met Nicole several times, had no objection to her visits to her sister and even the clandestine sharing of a midday meal or two. But she certainly wouldn't feel friendly towards the girl who had almost precipitated a disaster with a wealthy customer.

She told Philippe she came from the village next to the manor house estate, that several inhabitants of the village were employed by the Tramont champagne house. He asked if she would like employment. She told him she had in fact sometimes worked on his rows of vines. They were delighted with the idea that they had already been in contact, even if in some remote fashion.

But then back swept Clothilde de Tramont in her street gown and fur-trimmed mantle, ready to be taken to the best hotel for a meal before setting out on the other matters of business that brought them to Rheims. 'Come along, Philippe, we've wasted enough time here. Ah … you, child!'

Nicole, quietly slipping towards the screen that shielded the big door, paused. She hardly knew what to expect – a scolding for daring to interfere in the affairs of the gentry? 'You have some sense, it seems,' Clothilde said with an approval that was somewhat grim. 'Here, you deserve some reward.'

She held out a coin. Nicole drew back, about to tell her she didn't expect to be tipped like a coachman. But then she recollected that the extra fifty centimes could be used to advantage in the Berthois housekeeping, and that to refuse it might precipitate another scene. 'Thank you, madame,' she said with a curtsy. As she took the money she allowed her glance to flicker towards Philippe. He looked apologetic, she let her mouth tremble in the beginnings of a smile.

Then she had left the room, with Paulette ahead of her carrying the troublesome gown in its shroud of protective muslin.

'*Never* do a thing like that again, Nicci!' Paulette cried when they were safely up to the first landing. 'Madame can't make up her mind whether to be grateful or infuriated!'

Nicole shrugged. 'It all turned out all

right. Why the fuss?' But she knew very well. Peasants didn't make critical remarks about the gentry. There might have been a revolution to establish liberty, equality and fraternity, but it had very little effect in the countryside of France. Even in Paris, the memory of those heady days had faded.

The midday meal was being served as they reached the workrooms. The gowns and mantles were carefully covered with cotton sheeting. Eight girls, the storekeeper, the errand boy and Nicole drank the soup. Madame Treignac's maid and coachman ate in splendour in the kitchen attached to the living quarters.

The story of Madame de Tramont's gown had somehow reached them already. 'My word, Nicci, you took a big risk, speaking out like that! Why did you do it?'

She couldn't tell them that she'd wanted to assert herself after being dismissed by Madame de Tramont as a nothing. She laughed and bit into the chunk of crusty bread. 'If a thing needs to be said, why not say it?' she remarked. And that was all they could get out of her.

It would be untrue to say that she never gave Philippe de Tramont another thought. He came into her mind now and then as she worked through her day's tasks – as she sprayed the Berthois vines with her own special mixture against mildew and cochinelle larvae, as she hoed between the rows, as she tended the goats, and more especially as she went into the village to work for some other small vineyardist. On those walks she would look at the carriages which occasionally went by, wondering if Philippe de Tramont would be in one.

She didn't see him again until July, a frantically busy month for the wine villages. She and a few others from Calmady stole time off to go to Rheims, in order to see the nephew of the great Napoleon.

Louis Napoleon wanted to have himself elected Emperor-Consul. He had gained the rank of President two years previously, but those who knew about such things maintained that he wanted a more imposing title.

To further this aim, the President appeared at big events all over France. To encourage the country people to attend, his supporters spent money hiring carts and conveyances. Who wouldn't seize the chance of a free ride into Rheims to see a great man review a local regiment? Delighted at the idea, Nicole put on her best clothes once again – with no protest from her mother this time – and clambered aboard the cask-cart decked with bunting.

It was a fine enough day, warm, sunny, but with heavy clouds often concealing the sun – in fact a typical July day in the Department of the Marne. The old men shook their heads and predicted rain. The shopkeepers and businessmen who had paid for seats in the stands had brought umbrellas, and some of the country folk had their broadbrimmed hats or pieces of oiled linen to protect their heads.

Nicole had no hat or shawl. She was blithely certain it would be a fine day. So when the clouds broke overhead to send down a cascade of heavy, thundery drops, she ran for shelter.

The nearest doorway was that of a lawyer's office. She huddled under its stone canopy, wishing the doors would open so that she could slip through into the hall or the concierge's office.

As if in answer to her prayer, the double doors parted. Out came Philippe de Tramont, unfurling an umbrella. Nicole, about to whisk past him, drew back. 'Oh, m'sieu...!'

'What? Oh, it's you!' He stopped in the doorway, examining her, smiling, pleased at the encounter. 'My word, you're wet! Have you fallen in the river?'

'No need of that, the river is coming to us,' she said in a rueful tone, holding her hand out into the pouring rain.

'Have you been to the review?'

She nodded. 'But you have not?'

'Oh no!' He laughed aloud. 'No, no, the de

Tramonts cannot show any interest in the descendants of the ogre Napoleon. Mama would die of shock at the mere idea. No, I've been to see the family lawyer.' He didn't add that yet one more tentative approach towards a marriage had come to nothing. At twenty-one Philippe felt no great distress at being spared an arranged marriage so far.

But that wasn't the kind of thing you told a pretty girl who was smiling up from under a drenched lawn cap. 'Tell me, mademoiselle, what are your plans now?'

'Plans? Good gracious, my plan was to have a good time listening to the band and watching the soldiers, and then I was to be driven home again in the cask-cart.'

'So now that the review has been more or less ruined, you are free?'

'I suppose so.'

'Let me offer you a glass of wine. I'm sure you need it, to ward off a chill after being soaked through.'

'No, thank you, m'sieu.' Nicole couldn't see how it could be done. He couldn't take her to one of the fine cafes and sit down with her – he in his fine summer suit and silk cravat, she in her country-girl's clothes. And he wouldn't want to patronise the sort of homely little cafe that the peasants used.

'Oh, please permit me. I owe you at least that much, after you averted a near-catastrophe the last time we met.'

'But I was paid for that,' she reminded him, with a wrinkle of the nose.

'That, too – I should like to make amends for that. Please let me offer you some refreshment.'

'But ... where could we go?'

'To the Market Cafe?'

Well, that was quite a good idea. It was some distance away but it was the kind of place that had customers of all kinds – merchants, farmers, wine-growers and wine-dealers, housewives, visitors from out of town, and such stall-holders from the market as felt they could afford to celebrate the day's takings.

They set off together along the pavement, which was awash with rain. Philippe held the umbrella so as to protect her from the downpour. It was a most unusual feeling to be escorted in this polite fashion. The men of Calmady rarely had occasion to try out their good manners on the womenfolk, for most of the time they were working together in the vineyards or the wine-cellars. Only now and then, at a village celebration, would courtesy seem natural – and then, alas, it was usually a way of getting a girl into a corner to steal a kiss while her mother wasn't looking.

Philippe had been in the Market Cafe only once, to meet a wine-dealer from Paris. He didn't greatly care for it but he understood

Nicole would be more at ease among its plain wooden furniture and checked cloths than in the Cafe du Dome with its gilt chairs. She was an attractive girl, pretty and lively – but nothing could come of this little *tête-a-tête* except an hour's amusement on a wet day in Rheims.

Naturally, since they belonged to the Champagne district, Philippe ordered champagne when they sat down. Nicole was flattered that he chose a good wine and with it gateau: it was as if he regarded her as a guest at his mother's house, where the ladies were served sweet champagne and cake at about this hour in the afternoon.

There was a formula, more or less, for making a good impression with a girl. You told her she was very pretty, then by and by came around to saying you would die if she didn't give you a kiss, or let you hold her hand, or whatever you thought would find a chink in her armour.

With Nicole, however, it didn't happen. She laughed when he told her she was pretty and to his astonishment replied that he was quite goodlooking. Then she somehow turned the conversation so that he was talking about himself. She had a genuine curiosity to know what he did with himself all day.

'I write plays,' he told her.

'You do what?'

'Write plays. For the theatre.'

'The theatre!' She was impressed, no doubt of it. She studied him with her sparkling brown eyes, a little frown gathering between her brows. 'What's it like in a theatre?'

'You've never been to one?'

'Never. I've seen the street performers in Rheims, of course, and sometimes a company of actors comes to the village but they perform in the village hall, which I suppose is...' Her voice died away as she thought about it. 'Are your plays put on in Paris? How many have been performed? Oh, when anyone gives me a newspaper from now on, I'll look for your name!'

'We-ell...' He twirled his wine-glass about on the cloth. 'The fact is, I've never had one accepted so far. But–' as he saw the disappointment momentarily glinting in her eyes– 'I shall!'

She agreed that of course his plays would be performed but he had the feeling she was saying it out of politeness. He felt it was imperative to impress her with his talents. He told her the plot of the play he was working on, explained the intrigues and influences that kept the work of young playwrights off the stage.

Although it all sounded like another world, Nicole was genuinely sympathetic. It must be terribly frustrating to have talent and yet be unable to make anyone listen. She knew the feeling. She had ambitions herself – secret, absurd ambitions that she had never dared confide to anyone. There were things she could do that needed more scope than a few rows of vines and a stretch of chalky hillside.

An hour flew by while she listened to his quick sketches of interviews with lofty theatrical managers, play-readings where all the actors mistook the sense of the words, times of hope when a play was under consideration, times of despair when it was returned as too unusual or too difficult.

'It only means they don't have sense enough to understand it,' she soothed. 'You shouldn't let it upset you.'

'It's easy for you to say that,' he replied, as if she were his equal and quite accustomed to dealing with such disappointments. 'It puts me in the doldrums for weeks, a thing like that! And then my mother gets annoyed and accuses me of wasting my time – which is true I suppose, for I don't really spend as much time in the wine cellars as I should.'

'Well, that's understandable. Making champagne is a great art. But it doesn't happen to be the one that interests you.' She sighed. 'I'd love to read one of your plays.'

He almost exclaimed, 'You can read?' but checked himself. This remarkable girl… She spoke French that was almost Parisian, she understood all he had told her about the theatre world. Why shouldn't she be able to read? She was a cut above every other country girl he'd ever encountered and, if it came to that, above most of the girls of good family. Few of them had shown any interest in his play-writing and not one had wished to read one.

He asked: 'Have you ever read a play? It's not like an ordinary book, you know.'

'I've read Racine.'

'Racine!' This time he couldn't hide his astonishment. How could this little vineyard-girl ever have come to handle a book of the plays of Racine, France's great tragedian?

'We have quite a few books in our house,' Nicole explained. 'They belonged to Brother Joseph.'

'And who, pray, is Brother Joseph?'

'Oh, that's a long story. My family took him in years ago – you know, when the monasteries were broken up and the monks had to find ordinary work or go to prison? My grandfather used to say Brother Joseph turned up in Calmady with twenty books tied up in a blanket and no shoes on his feet. *His* father – that's my great-grandfather – took pity on him. And found he had a great bargain, for Brother Joseph knew a lot about the vines, and could read and write…'

'I see,' said Philippe. He felt a dawning admiration. This girl had a family history, quite different of course from his own but just as interesting. It had never struck him before that peasant families could have a history.

Outside the drums of the 4th Regiment of the Marne could be heard beating time as the men marched off parade. The review had continued despite the wet weather and a much-reduced audience. Louis Napoleon had stood gravely in his dark blue and gold uniform, at the salute in the pouring rain, to prove to his people that he would never fail in his duty.

'I must go,' said Nicole, patting her still-damp cap into place and tucking up some curling tendrils of hair. 'I have to go back on the cart that brought us from Calmady, which is waiting for us by the basket factory, if Etienne hasn't gone off with the other drivers to play cards.'

'Oh, but you must let me drive you home!'

She was astounded at the offer and, to tell the truth, so was he. One didn't make such offers to peasant girls. One might suggest such a thing to an older woman of one's acquaintance, or to a young lady whose home lay nearby (so that there could be nothing compromising in the incident). But to be seen driving a girl in peasant blouse and skirt...

Then he recalled that, as the weather was wet, he could have the hood up on the curricle. As they whisked by on the heavy, uneven road, who would be able to peer inside at his passenger?

Nicole was thinking about something different. What a commotion it would cause at home if she was handed down from a gentleman's carriage! She thought of her mother's surprise and disapproval. No, though it would be delightful to sample the charms of a private conveyance, she must refuse.

'I had better not,' she said with real regret. 'In the first place, they'd go looking for me if I didn't join the party in the cask-cart. And then … you see … my mother…'

'Ah yes.' He understood perfectly. 'Let me at least escort you to the waiting place – you'll get soaked again without an umbrella.'

'Well, all right… Perhaps just to the corner of the building.' Then she could say a grateful goodbye and escape without any of her fellow villagers seeing her companion. She dreaded the teasing and gossip that might ensue if they knew anything about today's events.

'Just as you wish.'

Outside the rain was much less heavy. She could quite easily have said she could manage in the shelter of the buildings. But she somehow found she didn't want to part from him any earlier than she had to. He was so … so *different*. And so kind. Though he was a gentleman, she'd felt no embarrassment in his company.

At the far end of the street in which the basket factory stood, she paused to bid farewell. He took her hand. '*Au revoir*,' he said, raising it to kiss.

'Oh, I doubt we shall see each other again, m'sieu–'

'Of course we shall! I'm going to bring you a copy of one of my plays to read–'

'No, no!' Not to the house. Apart from the risks her mother would foresee in friendship with the son of the de Tramont family, there were the reproaches for wasting time on reading. Her mother didn't disapprove of reading, although she herself had never learned, but she felt that one should use the talent only for the newspapers and worthy volumes about the lives of saints.

'But I thought you were interested?' He was hurt. And when she saw his disappointment she relented at once.

'I really should love to read your play, m'sieu. I meant that. But you see, if you come to the house...'

'Could we meet? Is there a moment when you would be free to spend some time with me? I should like to read some of the scenes aloud to you. You know, my plays aren't in verse, like Racine – they need a certain amount of understanding in the way they're read.'

'I see. Well, of course, Monsieur de Tramont, I have a lot to do. Running a farm, even a small one like ours, takes up a lot of time.'

'Of course. How selfish I am–'

'But in the evening, m'sieu... About nine o'clock?'

'You're free then? That's splendid! We dine early at the manor house, you see. I could come out – where could we meet?'

She had no idea. There were lanes and corners where village lovers could find solitude, but those were hardly suitable for a play-reading.

'I know!' cried Philippe. 'There's a ruined summerhouse on the edge of our land–'

'Oh yes, I know it, the one where the honeysuckle has reached the roof–'

'That's it, the Jacobins pulled the building down–'

She could have told him that the villagers of Calmady had taken a lot of the stone away for their own building purposes during the long years when the ownership of the estate was in dispute. But it was true, the original wrecking had been carried out by vengeful gangs in the first days of the Revolution, so she'd been told.

'Shall we meet there? Tomorrow? At nine?'

'Not tomorrow, m'sieu – I'll have to catch up with the work after taking today off. But next day–'

He shook his head, sighing. 'That's Sunday. It's difficult for me to get away on Sunday – we go to Mass at the Cathedral and the whole day is thrown into commotion...'

She said nothing. Perhaps after all it had only been a passing fancy on his part.

'Monday? Would you be able to come on Monday evening?'

Now she smiled. She didn't know how much pleasure she allowed to show in that smile. 'Yes, I could manage Monday.'

'Then that's a promise. Monday at nine. I'll bring *Duel of Wits* to read to you – it has some very good things in it.'

'I look forward to it.'

He stood watching her as she hurried down the street towards the factory that stood on the far corner. It wasn't just that she was pretty. The carriage of her head, the eager briskness of her tread...

Suddenly he felt that Monday was a long way away.

Nicole had more to occupy her than Philippe, but even so she thought about the coming meeting with happy expectancy. She went about the daily round singing to herself. From her wooden armchair by the window, her mother looked out to watch her comings and goings, and wondered to herself. Could the child have met some handsome young vineyardist in the party that went to Rheims? If so, how long before he came a-visiting? And if he didn't come, how long before the songs died on the girl's lips?

It was part of Nicole's routine to go out after the day's work was ended to take a last look at the goats. Sometimes, particularly in wet weather, they trampled their patch of pasture into a chalky mud. Last thing at night she would re-tether them if necessary, and spend a little time wandering around the little domain, breathing in the scent of the wild thyme on the nearby slopes and the meadow rue by the river.

Her mother generally went to sleep soon after eight at night, but would wake when she heard the door open and close on Nicole's return. A murmured exchange soothed her back to sleep. It never occurred to her to ask the time nor to query Nicole's doings.

On the Monday, Nicole made no change to her working clothes except to hide her good shoes under her apron when she went out. When she had looked to the goats, she walked along a hill path to the edge of the farm, sat down on a bank to exchange wooden clogs for leather shoes, and then jumped down into the lane. A scramble up the bank on the far side, a brisk walk through wooded grounds easily entered through gaps in the ruined walls, and she could see the roof of the summerhouse below her.

The villagers called it 'the temple', for it had originally been built in the Greek style as an amusement for a former marquis. Now there was nothing to be seen from the distance but a hummock of wild honey-suckle, with an occasional glimpse of white marble shining through in the evening sunshine. As she drew near, Philippe stepped out. He waved, came to greet her. 'I was afraid you weren't coming!'

'Why? I'm not late, am I?' She had no watch, but the old clock in the cottage kitchen kept good time and she knew well how long it took to walk from her home to any point in the landscape.

'No, no, of course not, I just thought you might have changed your mind.' He held her hand to guide her into the shady interior of the summerhouse. The air was heavy with the scent of the blossoms.

He asked if she'd got home safely on the cask-cart, told her an amusing little incident about his own drive home. He seated her on a marble bench. A copy of his play was lying there. 'You read from the text,' he said, 'and I'll say the words.'

'You know it so well?'

'I wrote it! Here, it's this page.' He turned over the script before handing it to her.

She was startled to find it was handwritten.

She had expected a printed book. Somehow there was something very personal, almost physical, in holding in her hands his own handiwork. She felt herself blushing as if in some strange way it was a caress.

The scene he repeated was between a man and a woman, the man arguing in favour of adventure, of going out to face the world, the woman attempting to state a case against it because she knew that, if he left, she would lose him. Gradually the dialogue grew more passionate. At last the woman betrayed her feelings: 'Ah, Sebastien, if you go, how empty you will leave my world!'

Nicole gave a half-sob of sympathy. Philippe paused. 'You like it?' he asked with eagerness, sitting down beside her.

'Oh, it's wonderful!' she cried, putting a hand on his sleeve to press it in emphasis.

The next moment she was in his arms.

Chapter Three

Nicole recovered first from this momentary madness. She pushed herself free from Philippe's embrace, her fists against his chest.

'No, no, we mustn't–'

'But yes we must, darling–' His lips were against her hair, he was pulling her back towards him.

'No, you know this is silly–'

'How can you say that? Nicole!' At his use of her first name, she stared up at him, brown eyes swimming in sudden tears. He saw that she was wavering and went on quickly, 'It was meant to be, wasn't it? We met and met again. And now we know we're in love–'

'No, it's not love! And we're as far apart as geese and swans so how can you–'

'If you mean because our families–'

'Yes, our families, our families! We live in different worlds–'

'But that's just convention, Nicole. Besides, we're not in the eighteenth century any more – people can be valued for what they really are and you're so special–'

His naive liberalism was so genuine that she checked the bitter laugh on her lips.

'Philippe, look at this.' She took one of his hands from her shoulders and held it alongside her own. His was soft and white. Hers was hard and brown. 'That's what I mean when I say we're from different worlds. As people ... yes, perhaps we have much in common, perhaps we could understand each other. But you're a gentleman and I'm a peasant, and...' She broke off.

'All right, let us accept that. I'm a gentleman, you're a peasant. What of it? We're in love, despite that.'

To her, the case she had stated was self-evident. Gentlemen of course pursued the local girls, and nothing good ever came of it. Whether there was love, or merely a flirtation ending in an affair, the result was always the same. There came a time of parting, the girl was paid off according to the good nature of the man – and according to how much her good name had suffered.

Nicole moved away in a kind of muffled anger. 'I have to go home now.'

'No, not yet!'

'I must, Philippe. It's late. I have to be up in the morning early.'

'But you're upset, unhappy. Don't go like that. Tell me you love me. Tell me you're happy because we've been lucky enough to find each other.'

Stifling a sigh, she said, 'I'm happy to have known you. In a way it's an honour to have had your interest, that you liked me enough to read me some of your work. But that's the end of it, Philippe.'

'What?' He grabbed her as she was about to slip out through the tangle of honeysuckle into the growing dusk of the July night. 'It can't end like this! We've got to meet again!'

'No, Philippe, it's gone too far as it is. I should never have come here in the first place.'

'Don't say that! Promise you'll come again tomorrow night.'

'No.' She shook her head, unclasping his fingers from her arm. 'No, this is goodbye, my dear.'

'But why? Why? You love me, I know you do – I felt it the moment you came into my arms.'

'No I don't. That was … well, it was a mistake. I don't know why I let it happen…'

'Nicole, promise you'll come tomorrow night.'

'No, I told you. I can't come.'

He stood staring at her, his eyes burning in his pale face. She was about to turn away in finality when he said: 'I'll be here tomorrow night. At the same time, here, waiting for you. And you will come.'

'No, I won't.'

'You will, you will. You won't be able to bear the thought of leaving me here, aching with longing for you.' He summoned a half-smile. "'If you don't come, Nicole, how empty you will leave my world.'"

He spoke the line with an actor's passion, but he meant every word. In the dimness there was a glistening of tears as she darted away from him into the tangled wilderness of the old woodlands.

All next day she tried to shut her mind to the memory. But when a rainy evening set in, with clouds rushing across the sky, her mood of determination died away. She was depressed, close to tears. Her mother asked if she was unwell. 'I'm all right, Mama. This weather is enough to make anyone miserable.'

But a rainy day had never before made Nicole Berthois as miserable as this.

Nine o'clock came. Madame Berthois had gone to bed and was asleep. Stoically Nicole sat down with some mending. The ticking of the old wall clock measured out the seconds. At almost half past nine she got up, put on her cloak. She must make her nightly round to see that all was well.

She had no intention of taking the path that would lead her to the de Tramont land. Yet when she had seen to the livestock and walked along the vine rows, she found herself going in that direction. At the lane she paused. She knew if she jumped down the bank and up the other side, she was committed.

She wasn't going to go. In any case, even if Philippe had come to the trysting place, he would have gone home by now. It was almost ten at night. And he wouldn't have come in the first place because it had been raining hard at nine.

She would just go out of curiosity, to assure herself that he had never come to the rendezvous. It would show that he was like all the rest of the aristos, unwilling to put himself to any inconvenience in pursuit of his *amours*.

She jumped down into the lane, climbed the bank, walked through the dripping woods. Her cloak was by now soaked through, her bare feet in their clogs were cold. She was angry with herself for getting into this state, she was angry with Philippe for trifling with her, she hated the wet landscape, the dripping trees, the bushes whose leaves lashed at her cheeks as she pushed her way through.

When she reached the temple there was not a sound, not a movement. Just as she'd expected. It had been all talk, all nonsense. She wheeled about to hurry home. The bushes rustled loudly at her action.

'Nicole?'

His voice swept away all her doubts and confusion. She ran into the ruined building. He seized her and held her close. 'Nicole, I thought you weren't coming!'

'I'm sorry, forgive me! I didn't mean to make you wait!'

'Nicole, Nicole! My angel. Oh, I've been in torment all day, wondering if you really meant what you said last night!'

'I meant it, Philippe. I meant it *then*. But now... Oh, now, nothing else matters.'

They kissed and embraced. He realised she was soaked through, untied the strings of her cloak and spread it to dry on the marble bench. She was shivering, with cold and reaction. He gathered her in his arms, warming her with his body.

And then, as naturally as if it had always been intended, they made love. Without reservation they gave themselves to each other, in the shadows of the summerhouse, with the sound of the rain for music and the blown leaves of a hundred summers for a bed.

Thereafter they met as often as they could, but it was never easy. Without ever discussing reasons, they knew their affair must be kept secret.

Theirs was a courtship the rest of the villagers would have thought very strange. They didn't walk sedately to church side by side nor sit awkwardly in the best parlour with the parents looking on, stealing kisses and caresses in moments when no one was looking. Instead they spent long hours in each other's arms, murmuring their secrets, voicing their innermost thoughts.

Or, to tell the truth, Philippe did the talking. Nicole found him so strange and wonderful that she scarcely dared to interrupt. She understood that he had a poet's visions: she was thrilled and flattered that he bothered to share them with her. He would tell her about Paris, about the bohemian friends his mother disapproved of so severely. He described the theatre, he recited Corneille and Moliere. When she intervened now and again to ask what the women were like he would give vague descriptions – and she was secretly delighted, because it meant he had never really been in love before.

No one else in Calmady would have understood. Nicole didn't even tell Paulette, until then her usual confidante. It wasn't that she feared Paulette would betray them, it was simply that she knew her sister would be terrified at what she was doing.

It was strange about Paulette – so like Nicole in appearance, pretty, neat and trim, and yet everything spoiled by an inborn timidity. In a social gathering, Paulette would dissolve into embarrassed giggles when spoken to. In business matters, she would tremble visibly if she had to disagree over anything. Her wages at Madame Treignac, negotiated by her father when she first went as an apprentice, were never likely to be increased by any effort of hers. Dearly though Nicole loved her sister, she would never discuss Philippe with her. The mere mention of the de Tramont name would cause Paulette to go white.

Philippe was free more often than Nicole. He was not very interested in the wine business, didn't feel himself bound to give it his attention because their chief of cellar, Jean-Baptiste Labaud, could be relied upon to see to everything. His chief interest lay in the theatre. Madame de Tramont considered the theatre if not wicked, then certainly frivolous. But she had almost given up scolding her son about it.

Yet even Philippe had to take some part in the work of the de Tramont vineyard as August progressed. The last spraying of the vines had to take place, at least a whole month before the grapes would be picked. Then came another trimming of the leaves, then the last hoeing to keep the weeds from drinking up the rain which the grapes needed so much to fill them out.

For this last task, every able-bodied man, woman and child in the district was called out on the various vineyards. The work had to be done painstakingly by hand. Philippe learned, to his dismay and chagrin, that Nicole was to be employed on the work on his vines.

He was outraged. 'I won't have it! You

aren't going to stoop and scrape on my land – it's medieval – I couldn't bear the thought!'

'But, Philippe, I need the money,' she replied with a sigh.

'I'll give you the money! I'll give you what you'd earn if you did the actual labour, but I can't bear the thought of–'

'And how will you explain that to Jean-Baptiste? How will you explain paying wages to someone who doesn't appear each morning?'

'I'll think of a way–'

'And my mother? What will she say when I stay at home working on our own vine-rows when I should be up at the manor house?'

'Nicole, I simply will not allow you to work like a slave on my land–'

She put an arm around him and laid her cheek against his shoulder. 'My love, I understand how you feel. It makes you uncomfortable–'

'Uncomfortable!'

'But it must be, it really must. To change the routine so completely would only cause comment. Jean-Baptiste is no fool, you know. If you start discussing special arrangements for me, he'll quickly guess our secret.'

Nicole had a high respect for Jean-Baptiste. Like herself, he was something of a notable in Calmady. He could read and write and calculate, even without paper and pencil to write down the figures. He had always done well as a worker for others, and when Claude de Tramont needed a steady man to oversee his cellars it was Jean-Baptiste's name that his lawyer came up with.

Jean-Baptiste had given up a good job to take on the role of chief of cellar for the de Tramonts, at lower wages and with somewhat shaky prospects – for who could tell whether the de Tramont blend of champagne would be successful? But all had gone well, weather and vintage permitting. The Tramont brand of champagne sold to capacity. Indeed, it was well-known that if only the family had more cellarage, they could increase their business almost as much as they wished.

The growing, making and selling of champagne obsessed the people of Calmady and all the other villages of the Champagne district. They knew or could guess how much each firm was making. The great champagne houses were of course household names throughout Europe – Moet, Ruinart, Heidsieck. To the people who made their living by tending the vines and blending their wines, their fame was in the air they breathed, the bread they put in their mouths.

The smaller firms, too, were a source of

constant interest. Who knew when one of the smaller houses might not, with luck or guidance, take the path to greatness? The choice of the right grapes for the blend, the perfect care needed during the maturing and working of the wine, and something else – perhaps intuition, perhaps salesmanship – all these could come together at one of the lesser estates to produce a great champagne.

Everyone in Calmady knew that the growing success of the Tramont champagne was due to Jean-Baptiste Labaud. The villagers greeted him with the humorous respect that masked something like awe.

'Well, then, Jean-Baptiste, how much money have you piled up for the great lady, eh? Earned enough for her to buy back her title yet?'

Jean-Baptiste, tall, bony, dark-browed, shrugged off such remarks. 'All I know about is wine,' he would say.

His wife was also respected in the village. Jean-Baptiste had married young, had three young children. Everyone in Calmady agreed that they were a credit to their mother, bonny, well-shod, and as far as one could tell, likely to do well in the world if they inherited their father's abilities.

Nicole thought well of Jean-Baptiste. He was as important in his way as the mayor of the village, or the priest. It always pleased her if he singled her out for some responsible task when she reported for work at the de Tramont vineyard. In a way, she would have been sorry to miss the opportunity of being under his supervision, had Philippe remained adamant about not having her work on the estate.

'Well, then, so there you are, young Nicole,' Jean-Baptiste grunted when she presented herself as usual on the first morning of the hoeing period. 'Prettier than ever, if that's possible.'

'Thank you, Jean-Baptiste. And you're taller than ever, I declare.'

'Huh. Men don't grow after the age of twenty – except outwards.' He consulted a list he had in front of him in his little portable shed on the edge of the vine rows. 'You'll be on the north edge, working on the Prelous rows.' The Prelous were the family from whom de Tramont had bought those particular vines. Nothing was ever forgotten that had to do with the growing of grapes. Almost every row was known by some name or nickname.

He nodded towards the pile of shallow baskets, which were for the weeds when they had been picked from the earth. Nicole moved off, collected a basket.

'Nicole!'

'Yes?' She went back at his call.

'Everything all right in your family?'

'Yes, why?'

'Are you worried about your mother? She never seems to come to the village any more.'

'No, the rheumatism has got into her hip joints now, Jean-Baptiste. It wears her out just to go to the end of the garden.'

They both knew it was inevitable that the disease should progress in this way. It was common among the villagers, brought on perhaps by the continual kneeling, stooping and trudging through the clay soil of the Marne district.

'Anything I can do?'

She shook her head. What was to be done, even by Jean-Baptiste?

When her day's work was done for the de Tramonts, there was still her own work on the Berthois farm. Her mother could manage to hobble out to keep an eye on the goats from time to time, but the milking morning and evening was Nicole's task, and then there were the vegetables to tend and their own vines to hoe.

Exhaustion cut down her meetings with Philippe. She would fall into bed each night and stagger out again in the mornings, with no energy left over for secret walks to the ruined temple or the joys of love.

Yet in the end the longing became too great. Momentary contacts as Philippe surveyed his workers in company with Jean-Baptiste, secret smiles when no one else was looking – these became insufficient.

'Come tonight to the temple, Nicole,' Philippe whispered as she walked past him to empty her basket of weeds on the heap at the end of her row.

She walked away without comment. But the yearning in her face was his answer.

That night, when she had finished the farm chores, she was wringing with sweat in the sultry August heat. She drew a bucket of water from the well to splash in and cool herself. Then in a mood of sudden defiance, she fetched her good clothes from the chest in the bedroom and there, in the kitchen, she began to put them on.

She had already helped her mother to bed. Marie called drowsily from her pillow: 'What are you doing, Nicci?'

'I'm just washing off some of the grime, Mama. It's been a hard day.'

'All right, dear. Don't be long coming to bed.'

'I think I'll sit outside and read for a while, Mama. I'm too tired to sleep.'

Marie Berthois understood easily enough. Sometimes when the body had come to the end of physical resources, nervous energy took over. And after that, time was needed to unwind before sleep would come. Men sought relaxation in a pipe and a drink, women would sometimes find it in sewing or the tending of window plants.

Her clever little Nicole would find it, of course, in reading. 'Don't strain your eyes when it gets too dark,' she warned, but then dropped off into the paradise of painfree sleep.

Nicole sat for half an hour with a book on the bench outside the cottage door. Then she tiptoed away to take the path towards her own particular paradise.

Philippe had been there for hours. He had slipped away from the house the moment his mother settled down to cards with the housekeeper. Seeing him go, Clothilde de Tramont had said to herself: 'Some village girl, I suppose. Well, when we find him a suitable wife, all that will be at an end.'

When Nicole came into the temple, Philippe was overwhelmed. 'How beautiful you look! It's just like the first time I saw you!'

She flew into his arms. If he was surprised at the passion and urgency of her love-making, he was delighted too. Fierce at first, they came later to a long, tender interlude, filled with caresses and whispers and little jokes. Then they lay in each others arms, happy almost beyond words.

'"Behold thou art fair, my love,"' quoted Philippe, '"behold thou art fair!"'

She knew he loved these little word games of exchanged quotations. '"I am my beloved's, and his desire is towards me,"' she responded.

'"Thy breasts shall be as clusters of the vine".'

'"And the roof of thy mouth the best wine for my beloved..."'

They fell asleep with the sultry night for a coverlet.

When Nicole awoke it was to find daylight seeping in among the leaves of the thick honeysuckle. 'My God!' she cried, sitting up. 'It's after dawn!'

'What?' muttered Philippe, trying to awaken. He had seldom been up at dawn, except on hunting mornings.

'Philippe, it's daytime. I must get home. My mother–'

She had sprung up, was darting about the temple collecting scattered garments. Her limbs gleamed like ivory except where the sun had tanned her hands and wrists, and her neck down to the deep cleft between her breasts.

'No, darling, don't hurry away,' Philippe exclaimed. He caught her hands as she was about to slip her fine cotton chemise over her head. 'Don't go yet.'

'But I must, Philippe. You don't understand! The day's begun–'

'Not for me, not yet, not yet,' he whispered, locking her in his arms.

She meant to fight free, but this was the last moment, the last precious moment, before they had to part. Who could tell when they might find an opportunity to be together again? She let the world of everyday things slip from her like the discarded chemise. In its place came a whirl of passion that caught them up, joyous, intense, inevitable.

As she ran home she didn't care if her mother was awake and ready to cross-question here. She would make up some story to protect Philippe, she'd say she'd been with one of the migrant workers from the city who were beginning to arrive for the grape harvest. Her mother would be shocked but it didn't matter.

Marie had awakened earlier and called for her. But there had been no reply. She had dozed off again meanwhile. Nicole was able to slip indoors, take off the telltale finery, bundle it up in a work basket for future bestowal in its chest in the bedroom. Then she donned her working clothes of blue blouse and bodice, thick black skirt, and clogs. By the time Marie Berthois woke again, her daughter was tending coffee on the kitchen fire.

'Nicci, where were you? I called about an hour ago.'

'I was probably over the far side of the hill. One of the goats got loose.'

Nothing more was made of it. Her luck had held.

Yet she began to doubt that in the days that followed. She knew the cycle of her own body as well as she knew the cycle of farm work and vine culture.

She was expecting a baby.

The dawning realisation obsessed her. Her mother remarked that she'd become careless and inattentive but she couldn't alter her attitude. She was wondering how to tell Philippe, and what his reaction would be.

She could make a good guess. He would be upset, but would promise to make provision for the child so that it would never know want. Neither, however, would it ever be acknowledged by its father.

Well, that was how these things were. Her mother would be dismayed, there would be a short scandal, her hopes of making a good marriage to some worthy man would be damaged for a while.

Marriage to some worthy man... How impossible that had become. She knew in her heart that if she were left to bring up Philippe's child, she could never marry anyone else and let that man be stepfather to the baby. The baby belonged to herself and Philippe – no one else.

At last there came an opportunity to meet at their trysting place. This time she didn't risk changing from her working clothes. She came in a mood that was a mixture of apprehension and determination.

'What's the matter, my darling?' Philippe asked as she came in. 'Is something troubling you?'

Now was the opening to tell him. But she couldn't, not yet. This might be the very last time they would be together, for once he heard the news his feelings towards her might change.

'It's nothing,' she said with forced lightness. 'The vines are a little affected by yesterday's rain, that's all.'

'Oh, the vines, the vines – let's forget about the vines!'

When at last she lay in his arms, full of tenderness towards him for the pleasure he had given her, she caressed his cheek with her palm. 'Philippe, I have something very important to tell you.'

'Indeed? About the vines, no doubt.'

'No, be serious, darling. It's about us.'

'I'm all attention.'

'Philippe, I'm going to have a baby.'

There was a silence. His brows drew together. He stared at her.

'I know it's a shock—'

'A shock?' He threw his arms about her and held her close. 'It's wonderful! A baby? Our baby?'

She nodded, against his chest. 'It was that last time ... you remember, Philippe...'

'That's just how such a wonderful night

should be blessed – with a child of our own. How long have you known?'

'A week or two. Nothing need be decided for the moment, because it will be some time before there's any sign that I'm carrying a child–'

'What has that to do with it? We must get married at once.'

'Married?' She was so taken aback that she actually jerked away from him.

'Yes, of course, married. A baby needs parents, doesn't it?'

'But Philippe – the difference between our families–'

'Oh, that! Nonsense!' But then he paused. 'Well, of course, my mother isn't going to be very pleased. No, that's true. It's always been part of her plan that I should marry a rich girl.' He gave Nicole a smiling glance. 'I suppose you haven't got a sockful of gold hidden away in a mattress?'

'If only I had!'

'No, I thought not. And even a sockful wouldn't be quite enough, I fear. Mama has been looking for a rich girl from the bourgeoisie, but they're not so easy to catch. She might just possibly say yes to a rich peasant girl, but I think it would have to be a mountain of money.'

'And then there's her family pride–'

'Oh, I don't think that's so important. Of course she'd ideally like to have the family allied to some other aristocratic clan, but they don't have the cash these days. Living in exile as a child taught Mama that having a roof over your head and soup in the pot is more important than blue blood – what she wants from my supposed marriage is security.'

'She won't get that if you marry me, Philippe. She'll never agree.'

'No, she won't,' he admitted. 'All right – we'll elope.'

'Elope!'

'Yes, run away and get married. We can marry as soon as we're safely out of her reach – once we've left the Marne, for instance.'

'But where would we go?' she asked, at a loss at these sudden vast horizons.

'Paris, of course! It's an ideal place to hide from angry relations.'

'But … Philippe, what would we live on?'

As usual, Philippe in his enthusiasm had bounded ahead of what was practical. 'Well, that's a difficulty. I don't have any money of my own, you know, only the salary I get for managing the estate. My father left the property to Mama in his will – he knew she needed to own the place, for security.'

Nicole could make no suggestion. His flow of ideas was leaving her breathless.

'I tell you what!' he exclaimed. 'I could contact some of my theatrical friends!

Perhaps I could get one of my plays put on. It's time I started taking my writing seriously.'

'Would that make much money, dear?'

He had no idea. There were rich playwrights, that he knew – Sardou, for instance, had plenty of money. But then Philippe had no desire to write like Sardou.

'We'll manage somehow, my darling. The first thing is to get to Paris and get married before Mama can intervene.'

'Philippe, you've spoken a great deal about your mother. What about mine?'

He was startled. To tell the truth, he'd forgotten Nicole had a mother. 'What about her?' he asked, perplexed.

'She hasn't anyone but me. She can't get about without help. If I go, who will look after her? Who will run the farm?'

'Oh, lord…' He had heard Nicole speak of her mother's ailment. And there was no one else except the sister he had glimpsed in the showroom in Rheims, who had made so little impression he couldn't even remember her features. 'What about Paulette?'

'She doesn't understand the vines. And besides, she'd get swindled in any business deals.'

Nicole had thought on beyond Philippe's idea. If she left Calmady, in the end her mother would have to offer to share the profits of the farm with some hardheaded villager. But that didn't solve the problem of someone to keep house and care for her. If she had to pay for that too, there wouldn't be enough money.

They discussed the dilemma for some time. Then she said, 'I must go, Philippe, it's getting late. We don't need to solve it tonight, there's time enough.'

He was unwilling to let her go and for the first time over-ruled her embargo about escorting her to the door. It was dark, a bird piped in the bushes after being disturbed by their passing.

'Goodnight, wife,' he murmured as he gave her a last kiss.

'Goodnight, my husband.'

As the September days drew on and the grape harvest was about to begin, Nicole's thoughts were elsewhere. When she went to the village to read the announcement of the vintage dates, one for red grapes and one for white, she scarcely heard the discussion and comments of the other vineyardists. As she bent, knelt, and stooped among the low-trained vines, her brain was busy with her problem. What could be done to ensure that she and Philippe could marry and bring up their child?

A chance encounter with Jean-Baptiste Labaud gave her the answer. They were walking back from the Tramont vines towards the village one evening in a group of workers when he fell into step at her side.

'Well then, young Nicole, you've worked hard today.'

'So has everyone else.'

'True enough, and plenty yet to do.' He jerked his head back towards the estate they were leaving. 'Some good grapes on the Tramont vines. And I've advised Monsieur de Tramont to buy yours and Bestulet's and Lavauge's.'

'The Lavauge vines have done very well – more bunches than I've ever seen.'

'Aye, and fine grapes, fine grapes. Ah, we'll make good champagne this year, I feel it in my bones.' He laughed. 'The only problem is, where are we going to put it all, eh?'

'In bottles, Jean-Baptiste, in bottles – where else?' called someone from the edge of the group.

'Aye, and where shall we keep the bottles, eh? Under the beds?'

This old joke was greeted with the usual laughter. It was supposed to be a token of ineptitude to keep bottled wine under the bed, for lack of good cellarage.

When at last the grapes were all safely in the press house, Nicole had thought her problem through to a solution – or at least, to the possibility of a solution. She had decided to face Clothilde de Tramont with the news that she and Philippe were about to marry. She hoped something she had to offer would reconcile Madame de Tramont to the match in the end.

But the first interview would need careful stage-managing.

Chapter Four

When Nicole disclosed the first stages of her plan to Philippe, he was aghast.

'Confront my mother? Nicole! The idea is grotesque!'

'In what way?' she asked, with a calmness that astonished him.

'Well ... she would be very angry ... she would...'

'She would what? She can't prevent us from marrying, Philippe. You are of age, after all.'

The conversation was taking place in the shelter of the vat house on the Tramont estate. The juice from the grapes harvested earlier in the month had been transferred to the vats from the press house, which stood higher up the slope. The transient workers had moved on elsewhere, but the juice intended for the de Tramont champagne now stood in a great round wooden vat, waiting for the main impurities – twigs, pips, grains of dust – to fall to the bottom: and when fermentation began, the permanent labour force would begin the long process of turning the juices into champagne.

Philippe was so taken aback by Nicole's suggestion that he was at a loss for words. Nicole, anxious and apprehensive, mistook his hesitation. 'You do want us to get married, Philippe? You didn't just say that in the warmth of the moment?'

'Of course I do! You know I do!' But truth to tell, there was more charm in the idea of a romantic elopement to Paris than in confronting an irate Madame de Tramont.

He had taken both Nicole's hands as he spoke. He put them to his lips now, kissing the knuckles gently. 'Do you really think you know how to handle Mama?' he asked in perplexity.

'I'm not sure. I only saw her that one time, in the dressmaker's. But I have something to offer her, Philippe – and if, as you say, she is interested in money, this may be just the thing to convince her.'

'But you said you had no money, Nicole–'

'This is something better than money.'

He was shaking his head. 'What? All you have is a few acres of hillside, a farmhouse, some vines and some goats.'

'Yes, you've summed it up. But there's a gem hidden there, my love–'

'A gem?' Now he was worried. Had the beginning of her pregnancy caused his darling to become light-headed? Romantic poetry was full of the sad tales of young women who went romantically mad in such situations. 'Nicole, are you sure you aren't under some delusion?'

She laughed, taking her hands from his grasp and putting them on her hips. 'Do I look deluded? Do I look as if I didn't know how many grapes make five? No, I have thought about this very seriously and the wonder is that I never thought of it before. It ought to make all the difference to the family fortunes of the Berthois.'

'Tell me about this gem, then.'

'No, Philippe. I want it all to come as a tremendous surprise to your mother.' The fact was that, cross-questioned, she felt it was just possible Philippe might give something away to Madame de Tramont. She knew, from what he had told her, that his mother was a very formidable lady.

Philippe's open, eager features were overcast with anxiety. 'What do you want me to do?'

'Tell your mother that I want an interview with her. Don't say why – just make an appointment. Don't arrange it for any day this week – I have to get a dress made.'

'A dress?'

'Of course! You don't think I'm going to introduce myself as a future daughter-in-law wearing peasant clothes? That would wreck our chances from the outset. No, I'm going to Rheims tomorrow, to ask Paulette to make me a dress – nothing elaborate, just something neat and plain. Well, she won't have time to do anything fancy, will she – but in any case I can't afford braid and lace. When I tell her what it's for, I'm sure she'll give up all her Sunday to make it and so I hope to have it by Tuesday at latest.'

All at once Philippe began to see the funny side of the whole affair. His sweetheart – his fiancée, as he ought to think of her now – was making plans to beard the lion in its den. And how did she intend to do it? With a pistol? With a net and trident? Not at all – womanlike, she was going to have a new dress.

He gathered her to him, chuckling, and kissed her. She pushed him away. 'Philippe! Someone might see!'

'If you were afraid of that, you ought not to have come looking for me in broad daylight–'

'It's all right to be talking to you, we could say it was about the grapes you bought. By the way, you still haven't paid for them, Philippe.'

Now he was helpless with laughter. 'My adorable girl, I believe you can handle my mother. I now have complete confidence in this scheme, whatever it is. Anyone who can remember a small debt in the middle of a conversation about getting married must be level-headed–'

'It's not a small debt to me,' she

reproached him. 'In any case I need the money to pay for the dress.'

He put his hand in his breast pocket, took out his pocket-book, and handed her a banknote without even looking to see how much it was for. Nicole, unaccustomed to such easy ways with money, examined it. Ten francs. That was enough for the kind of gown she had in mind.

'Thank you,' she said, going on tiptoe to give him a little kiss on the cheek. 'And now, don't pay that debt. Let it lie. So if your mother wants to know why I'm coming to see her, you can say it's about money owing.'

She was gone next moment. He stood watching her vanish among the outbuildings which (in his mother's opinion) disfigured the back of the manor house property. Here the wine was made and under them the wine was stored.

From the cask house window, which was almost at ground level, Jean-Baptiste had witnessed their parting: the giving of something into Nicole's hands, the quick kiss as she turned to go.

Jean-Baptiste drew back with a sharply indrawn breath. His assistant, turning casks to see if they were wholesome to receive the juice for fermentation, looked up. 'Hurt yourself? There's some old nails want knocking in on that windowframe.'

Jean-Baptiste shrugged and turned back to examine the casks Louis was hauling round, grunting with exertion. He'd only gone to the window to glance out at the weather, wondering if the September sunshine would take the temperature up too high for the new grape juice in the vat house. He had never expected to spy on the two lovers – for lovers they were, he knew it without having to have it said in so many words.

Well, then… This usual beginning to any thought or opinion rose to his mind. Well, then, good luck to them, poor things, he thought. Especially to poor little Nicole Berthois. She wasn't the kind to give herself lightly to anybody and if she loved that one, it was a doomed love. Jean-Baptiste could only hope the liaison would die a natural death before the girl found herself with a baby on her knee. Bad, that would be. Bad for the family – might kill poor Marie Berthois – but worst of all for poor, bright, clever little Nicole.

When her sister came demanding to have a dress – a *dress* – made quickly, and when she explained why, Paulette Berthois was ready to die of fright. 'To visit Madame de Tramont? Are you mad? What for?'

'To tell her I'm expecting a baby by her son.'

That was even worse. She fell upon Nicole, she sobbed and cried, she besought her to visit a woman who lived in an alley of the city and could supply a mixture of herbs which would solve Nicole's problem at once, without any need to speak to the terrible Madame de Tramont.

Nicole was outraged. Get rid of her baby – hers and Philippe's? 'You don't understand, Paulie. We're going to be married–'

'Marry Philippe de Tramont? Don't be silly!'

'It's not the least silly! He loves me and I love him and we're getting married.'

But after she got home to wait for her new gown and plan the details of her campaign, that certainty began to ooze away. Madame de Tramont had so many resources – she could go to lawyers and businessmen, confer, learn how to cheat Nicole out of the great asset that was to open the way for her marriage to Philippe...

Just to make sure she had got everything about her idea correct, Nicole consulted the books and papers that had belonged to Brother Joseph. That quiet and saintly man had interested himself in everything to do with the family who had given him shelter. He had walked every inch of their land, and of the village too. He had been interested in geological strata, weather conditions, archaeological remains, local history. He had kept accounts in his notebooks of everything to do with the district he regarded as his home, and there they were still, in his sharp, plain, monastic script.

Evening after evening, when her work was done, Nicole pored over the notebooks of Brother Joseph. As far as she could tell, everything was as she had thought. She was safe in her belief. She could bargain with Madame de Tramont in the sure knowledge no one could take away the half-forgotten blessing that belonged to the Berthois family.

The new gown arrived by the carrier's cart, a package that threw Marie Berthois almost into panic. 'What is it? Who is sending us parcels from Rheims?' Unable to read the label, she had no idea that it came from the dressmaking establishment of Madame Treignac.

Even when that was explained to her, it made no sense. 'Madame Treignac is sending something to us?'

'No, Mama, it comes from Paulie. It's a dress she's been making for me in her spare time.'

'A dress?' Marie was totally astounded. 'A dress?'

'Yes, Mama, and look – a bonnet too, and gloves.'

'*Gloves?*' If the sky had fallen in upon her, Marie couldn't have been more amazed.

Never in her whole life had she worn gloves, nor had she seen any member of her family with them. The fact that Paulette, off in the higher reaches of society in Rheims, often wore gloves had never occurred to her.

'Why?' asked Madame Berthois, baffled. 'Daughter, what does it all mean?' She caught at the one fact she was sure of. 'It must have cost a *fortune,* clothes from Rheims…'

'Yes, Mama. But it's an investment.'

'An investment?' To Madame Berthois, an investment meant buying land or rows of vines. 'Clothes are an investment? Have you gone mad?'

Nicole made a little gesture asking for patience. She settled her mother comfortably in her wooden armchair with an extra cushion at her painful hipjoint. Then she knelt by her side, taking one twisted hand in both of hers. 'Mama, I have something to tell you. Don't be upset or worried by it. Listen to the end.'

But that was impossible. Marie Berthois cried out in alarm at almost the first words of explanation, so the story had to be suspended while Nicole ran for smelling salts and a glass of brandy. It took all day to explain and reassure her mother – and even when at nightfall they went to bed, she heard her sobbing with fear and anxiety.

Doubts assailed her as she lay exhausted

yet sleepless. Was she right in what she was doing? Her mother was so terrified... Yet she *must* take the risk, she *must* dare – or wreck three lives, her own and Philippe's and the child that was to be born to them.

It wasn't vanity that had caused Nicole to ask Paulette to buy gloves for her. She needed them to hide her work-roughened hands. She wanted to make as good an impression as she could on Madame de Tramont, so the less she looked like a 'common country girl' the better.

She tried on the clothes next evening. Her mother delayed going to bed so as to watch. She sat speechless as her daughter came from the bedroom into the kitchen, taking small steps like a lady, holding her gloved hands lightly clasped in front of her.

'Nicole...!'

'Do I look nice? Will I make a good impression?'

'On whom, for the love of God?'

'On Madame de Tramont.'

Her mother could find no words to utter. She was stricken, terrified, amazed – yet impressed. Who was this elegant little figure in the gown of pale grey dimity striped with palest rose? Whose face was that under the bonnet of ruched grey ribbon? After Nicole had helped her to bed that night, Marie Berthois didn't sleep. Her mind was too full of what she had seen and what she had been told.

The great day came. Nicole had asked Philippe to arrange the appointment for the afternoon, so that she could spend the latter part of the morning scrubbing off the grime of the daily chores. It was a fine autumn day as she walked by way of her secret path to the ruined temple and from there through the woodlands to the grand drive of the manor house. She must of course be seen walking up the drive – it would never do to arrive via the footpaths and lanes at the back door.

Clothilde de Tramont was expecting her, but for what she hardly knew. Philippe had said, 'Mademoiselle Berthois requests an interview, Mama.'

'Indeed? What about?' When Philippe shrugged and spread his hands, she went on: 'Have we paid for her grapes yet?'

'Not yet.'

'Well, if she's coming to argue for more money, it will be a wasted journey.'

If she had been expecting an equal, Clothilde would have ordered sweet champagne to be put on ice and a plum tart to be baked, as refreshment. This girl from the village would expect no such thing, naturally. Clothilde closed the periodical she was reading when the housekeeper announced the arrival of the visitor, turning to watch the girl come into the drawingroom.

If Marie Berthois had been startled at the appearance of her daughter in her new clothes, Clothilde was equally so. At first sight, one would have said this was a young lady come a-calling. The simple, well-designed gown, the neat bonnet, the well-polished leather shoes, the grey gloves...

Nicole Berthois? From the village? Impossible. Yet when Clothilde began the interview by speaking her name, the girl curtseyed.

'Yes, madame. Thank you for letting me see you.'

Nicole was trembling. The ordeal was greater than she had expected. The room in which she was now standing was the biggest she'd ever been in – it seemed to her like a church, with its great high ceiling and paintings on the walls.

And to say truth, Madame de Tramont looked as forbidding as the parish priest when he was about to deliver one of his sermons against the sins of the flesh. She sat in a tapestry covered armchair, her magazine half-closed in her hands. That was a sign that she didn't expect the interview to last long.

Nicole had rehearsed the words she would use a hundred times. But now her tongue stuck to the roof of her mouth. She swallowed convulsively, and her throat hurt. If only she could exchange a glance, a saving glance, with Philippe.

But he was standing behind her, having met her in the hall and followed when the housekeeper announced her to his mother.

'Well, young woman? You wanted to speak to me?'

'Yes, madame. I…. I…'

'What? I suppose it is something important otherwise you wouldn't come here in your best clothes – though if it's to make a fresh bargain about the grapes, your working clothes would have been adequate.'

'It's not about the grapes, madame.'

'No? Then what? Do speak up. I have other things to do this afternoon.'

'Yes, madame. I… We…'

'We? Who is we? You mean your family?'

Nicole found she couldn't say a word. Everything had gone out of her head except terror before this brusque, imposing lady. Her heart was thumping wildly, threatening to burst out of the bodice of the new dimity gown.

'When Nicole says we,' Philippe intervened, 'she means herself and me.'

'Eh?' cried Clothilde inelegantly.

'Nicole and I are in love. We want to–'

'Be quiet!' His mother had started up from her chair. 'I won't have such nonsense–'

'It's not nonsense, Mama. Nicole has come to be introduced to you and–'

Philippe was trying to make the best of the

disaster he saw about to ensue. He had no idea what Nicole had intended to say. He invented the idea of being introduced, though the moment he said it he knew it was a mistake.

'Introduced? Are you insane? The de Tramonts do not accept introductions to peasant families! Why, Philippe – what has got into you? You should have more sense! As if I would–'

'Mama, you must accept the fact that Nicole and I–'

'I accept nothing!' She stopped for a moment. So this was the girl he'd been slipping off to during the summer! Ah, well, now it was out in the open. She gave Nicole a hard look. 'Ha. You've come to cause trouble, I suppose. Is it money? If you think I'm going to give you money–'

'No, madame,' Nicole said, finding her voice at last. Now everything was easier. Philippe had spoken, had come to stand at her side. Now she didn't feel dwarfed and outclassed. 'I have not come to demand money. On the contrary, I have come to offer money – or something better – to you.'

Clothilde had been assembling her weapons to use against this saucy girl. But at Nicole's words it was as if the weapons had been knocked from her hand. Moreover, she hardly knew what kind of fight she was involved in.

'What do you say? Offer *me* something?'

'Yes, Madame. First,' said Nicole, 'let me explain the situation. Philippe and I have been falling in love for some months and now I am expecting his child–'

'Oh heavens! Oh, dear heavens!' Clothilde felt about blindly for the arms of her chair and sank into it.

'Don't be upset, madame. It's something to be happy about. You will have a grandchild–'

'No!'

'But yes–'

'I will not acknowledge any illegitimate child to be my grandchild–'

'The child won't be illegitimate, Mama,' said Philippe. 'Nicole and I are going to be married.'

'Don't be absurd–'

'Nicole and I are going to be married. We've made up our minds. If you refuse to accept it, then she and I can go away–'

'No, Philippe, you know we decided that was impossible,' Nicole said, taking his hand and pressing it to warn him not to say things that would complicate her argument. 'No, you belong here at the Manoir de Tramont and I belong in Calmady. This is our home, and our baby should be born here–'

'Never!' cried Clothilde, almost bursting into angry tears. 'Never, never!'

'Don't take up a position you can't retreat

from,' Nicole warned gently. 'Listen to what I have to say. You will find it interesting.'

Clothilde stared at her. Who was she, this well-dressed child from nowhere, who came to speak to her in such terms? And who spoke, moreover, in precise, clear accents, not a bit like the local patois.

'Madame, first let me speak of myself. You don't know me but I am of a good family–'

'A good family!' snorted Clothilde.

'Indeed, yes – the Berthois have been in Calmady as long as the de Tramonts. We have been through hard times, just as you have. But the Berthois weren't so lucky, or so persistent – we didn't get our land back.'

'Your land! A few hilly fields–!'

'Perhaps, but they contain something important. I'll come to that in a moment. Madame, my family is a good one, I'm not entirely without assets myself – I believe I'm intelligent and I'm a hard worker–'

'A hard worker! What are you talking about? The de Tramonts are not interested in labourers from the fields!'

'No, but about the vines, you're interested? About the vines, and the making of the champagne? For after all, that is what we depend on for our livelihood.'

'If you are about to say, mademoiselle, that you have been brought up with winemaking, don't trouble. So had almost every person in the neighbourhood. I have

95

an excellent chief of cellar in Labaud and an eagle-eyed supervisor of the vineyard in Compiain. There is nothing you could offer that would be important to me–'

'Indeed there is! I have a special knowledge–'

'Knowledge! An ignorant little village girl? What knowledge could you have?'

'I can tell you where there is almost unlimited and perfect cellarage.'

For the first time, Clothilde's interest exceeded her indignation. Cellarage ... in the making of champagne, almost nothing was so important as cellarage.

Clothilde relied on Labaud to choose the right grapes at harvest time. Sometimes they came from one vineyard, sometimes he selected from several, and usually the Tramont vines figured largely. After pressing, the juice was blended and went into the casks for the first fermentation.

But in champagne the second stage was crucial. After the wine had been put into bottles a second fermentation took place, encouraged by the vintner's art. It was essential to have plenty of cool space to store the bottles. A degree or so too warm, and the bottles would explode. In the past, the Tramont cellars had lost as much as sixty per cent of their year's work when the temperature played havoc with their plans.

Seeing that Clothilde was intrigued, Nicole

pressed the point. 'I came here today to ask your blessing on the marriage of myself and your son. I don't come empty-handed. I can give you an inestimable benefit for the making of Tramont champagne. I know, madame – everyone knows – that your wine is in great demand, that you could double what you sell if only you could ensure the safety of the second fermentation and even enlarge your output. I can give you the place in which that can be done. But the condition is the marriage.'

It was an ultimatum and, as Nicole expected, Clothilde reacted at once. 'No impossible! Impossible!'

'Think about it, madame. Take time to examine the prospect – a great increase in your income so that you could repair the house properly, restore the gardens, do other things of importance to you.'

She saw the other woman hesitate. She had no idea that there was a project very dear to Clothilde's heart: she wanted to reclaim the title of Marquis de Tramont for Philippe. It could be done, but only by the hiring of experts in that branch of the law, and making friends in high places – even bribing a few people. Lack of money had hampered all her attempts so far.

But if what this girl said was true...

'No,' she said, shaking her head with utmost vigour to assure herself she really meant it.

'Speak to Jean-Baptiste Labaud–'

'What! Is he in this with you? Is it a plot?'

'Not at all, madame. Jean-Baptiste has no idea of what I am proposing to you today–'

'Come, come, Mama,' Philippe put in, going to her and taking her hand reassuringly, 'you are not surrounded by deceivers! You know Labaud is an honest man. Ask his opinion of what Nicole has been saying–'

'Ha!' cried his mother. 'Deceivers! *You* have deceived me, my son!'

'That's a harsh thing to say, Mother. I fell in love – did you expect me to run to you with the news I'd lost my heart to a girl you'd disapprove of? We've come to you now, openly and honestly – and let me tell you, Nicole's proposal to you is generous. Don't you see that if you turn your back on her, she could go to someone else with her information?'

Clothilde shrugged. There was always buying and selling of information among the winemakers. The girl might get a few hundred francs by pointing out the cellarage to some other firm but it would be no great advantage to her to do so. A fee of a few hundred francs...

All the same, Clothilde very much wanted to know where the cellars were.

'If you wish to inspect the place, madame,'

Nicole said, as if reading her thoughts, 'I will take you. You won't be buying a pig in a poke.' With that Nicole, who had never been asked to sit down, made a movement to leave.

Philippe went with her to the door. 'Philippe!' his mother reproached.

'Mama, I must escort my fiancée home.'

'I forbid it! I want you to remain here so that I can speak to you—'

'I'm sorry, Mama, but that will have to wait.' If the truth were told, he was burning to know more about Nicole's plans. He now knew her well enough to understand that she had made only the first moves – she would wait for his mother to respond and then the next scene would unfold. It was like some play that he was writing, except that he didn't know how the drama would proceed.

'No, darling, I don't want you to know anything. She might worm it out of you,' said Nicole. 'I want her to get the full impact of the place when she sees it. Urge her to speak to Jean-Baptiste – he will certainly want to see what's available. Get her to bring him with her. Even if she can't understand the marvel I'm going to show her, Jean-Baptiste will.'

They parted at her cottage door. Marie Berthois, for the first time, limped to the threshold to be introduced. 'How do you do, sir,' she said, attempting a curtsey.

'Oh, Madame Berthois, please – don't–' He caught her by the arms as she bobbed clumsily. 'You mustn't do that. We are going to be relations.'

She smiled, shook her head, and wiped away a tear that crept down her pale cheek. 'I hope so, m'sieu, I do indeed. But it's all so frightening to me.'

'Don't be frightened,' Philippe said. 'Have faith in Nicole. I have.'

When he got home, Clothilde pounced on him at once. 'Well? Where is this place with all the cellars? Probably we could see the owner without the need for Mademoiselle Berthois to introduce us–'

Philippe laughed. 'I have no idea, Mama. I think Nicole foresaw that you would ask just that question so she didn't tell me.'

'She doesn't confide in you? And this is the girl you wish to marry!'

'My dear mother, if you will guarantee not to try to trick her out of her advantage, no doubt Nicole will confide in both of us.'

'Trick her! Who are you to speak of trickery to me? You brought that girl here so that she could trick her way–'

'Mama, please try to direct your antagonism correctly. I pursued Nicole, I made love to her and now I want to marry her. No trickery is involved in our intention to get married.'

Clothilde looked as if she might exclaim: 'Over my dead body!' But for the moment she decided to withdraw from her attitude of unrelenting antagonism to the marriage, for curiosity about the cellars was very strong.

'Ring the bell, Philippe. Send for Labaud.'

Smiling to himself, Philippe did as he was bid. Of course Annette, the housemaid, was agog at what was going on. The household had been astounded to see Nicole Berthois present herself at the front door in a very fetching gown and bonnet. Lingering in the hall, Annette had been able to hear raised voices – or at least, Madame's raised voice. Once she thought she caught the word 'marriage'.

Then the young master had actually gone out with Nicole's arm through his. They had walked along together side by side, just like any lady and gentleman. Unbelievable! Madame had been pacing about her drawingroom during Monsieur's short absence and now – for what reason? – she was summoning Jean-Baptiste. What could Jean-Baptiste have to do with a love affair between Monsieur and the Berthois girl?

Jean-Baptiste already knew most of this. The kitchen gossip had been relayed by the coachman to the vineyard supervisor, Compiain, who in his turn had mused about it to Jean-Baptiste.

Jean-Baptiste went into the drawingroom, having carefully wiped his feet on the hall mat and taken off his cap. Madame was sitting in her usual chair. Monsieur was standing by a window, so that his face was in shadow. But his attitude was alert and perhaps a little anxious.

'Labaud, our champagne is going well so far this season?'

'Of course, madame.' What a question. As if he would let anything go wrong with the champagne at this stage. It was later, at the second fermentation in bottle, that the trouble arose.

'Labaud, we have often said that the house of Tramont could sell much more champagne if only there were space to blend and store it?'

'That's so, madame.'

'Have you ever looked about for more cellar space?'

'Oh, certainly, madame. I've walked the estate with a tape-measure, trying to see where we could dig out a decent-sized cellar. But the soil isn't particularly suitable hereabouts, unfortunately. You see, madame, when your ancestors built this house, they never imagined themselves going in for winemaking on a big scale so they built where the soil was suitable for easy gardening and so forth. But as to digging out cellars...'

'It could be done, however?'

'Oh, undoubtedly. But at great cost. The vaults would have to be lined with stone, which would have to be brought to the site. I think it might be fifteen, twenty years before you recouped the cost.'

'Good heavens!'

'Oh yes, madame. Cellarage is no easy matter.'

He heard Monsieur Philippe make a sound almost like a chuckle. But he didn't turn his head to look at him, his attention was on Madame.

'Ah … Labaud … have you heard of ample cellarage available elsewhere in the district?'

Jean-Baptiste was truly puzzled. Why was Madame asking these questions? She was in general uninterested in the business, except to see that the accounts were properly kept. If she were to be honest, she knew almost nothing about the various processes of making champagne. And as to being interested in the cellars! – he had tried time and again to get her to spend money simply to make the manor house cellars less difficult to work in. The existing cellars weren't deep enough, they had uneven floors, the matter of making the wine racks stand steady involved wedges of wood which could warp in the damp…

'Madame de Tramont, there's nothing available nearer than the banks of the

Marne – and that's a long way to transport pressed juice, because all kinds of things can get into it while it's travelling, and besides...' He was going to say travelling upsets fine grape juice, but he broke off. She would think that fanciful.

'The cellars near the Marne are available,' he went on, 'because they get swamped in water when the Marne is in flood. They are used – I don't say it's impossible to use them. But people tend to lease them for as short a time as possible, simply as a make-do until they can get something better.'

'I see.'

There was a long pause. Jean-Baptiste glanced at the son, thinking that he might now take up the conversation. But Philippe remained silent. Either his mother would discuss Nicole's offer with Labaud, or she wouldn't. It was no use interfering.

'Labaud,' said Madame de Tramont, getting up and moving to a bureau where she sought about as if for a letter, 'do you know of any cellarage Nicole Berthois might have access to?'

Ah! Well, then, thought Jean-Baptiste, so this is what it's about! The gossip about Nicole's visit and the use of the word marriage in tones of loud indignation by Madame de Tramont made sense now.

'I know Mademoiselle Berthois,' Jean-Baptiste said. 'A very well-thought-of family in the village.'

'But does she know people in, for instance, Epernay? Rheims?'

'She has a sister working in a dress shop in Rheims,' suggested Jean-Baptiste.

'Oh, dear heaven... A peasant girl with a sister a dressmaker...'

'If Nicole says she knows of cellars for champagne,' Jean-Baptiste said, taking the plunge, 'it's true. I don't know where they might be, but if she says they exist, they do.'

Madame swept round so that her back was to him. She didn't want him to see her face as annoyance, frustration and curiosity fought there.

'Mademoiselle Berthois has suggested that we look at some cellars she knows of,' she said over her shoulder. 'We will go as soon as possible – I wish you to come with me. My son will make the arrangements.'

'Yes, madame.'

As Jean-Baptiste went out, Philippe followed him. 'I've already discussed it with Nicole. She says it's best to see the cellars in the morning – something to do with the light, but I don't understand what. We are to be at her farm tomorrow at ten-thirty.'

'Just as you say, m'sieu. We'll be going on somewhere else, I take it – shall we be on foot?'

'Oh, no, I imagine my mother will want to use the carriage.' Because it would be more impressive, he meant, but he didn't say it out loud.

The following morning, an early autumn day of amber sunshine, they drove to the outskirts of the Berthois small-holding. The track up to the door would be too rough for the big old carriage so from the edge of the property they walked up the slope.

Nicole was awaiting them. Today she was in her working clothes of blue cotton and clogs, but everything about her was neat and trim. She led them along a path across the little pasture to a stretch of chalky hillside clothed with a few gorse bushes and thin grass. From here Clothilde half-expected to be blindfolded and led by some roundabout route to some old building, but not at all.

A great flat stone lay on the hillside, as if left there among the debris of some earlier geological upheaval. Only someone interested in rocks and stones could have pointed out that it was quite different from the chalk of the district.

A set of iron bars lay nearby. Nicole pointed to them. 'Please, Jean-Baptiste – and you too, Philippe – help me lever the stone aside.'

Jean-Baptiste frowned, but picked up a lever. Philippe had been about to stare at his sweetheart in the fear that she had at last taken leave of her senses, but seeing Jean-

Baptiste obey, did the same. Clothilde stood by in utter amazement.

With grunts and groans they shifted the stone. It was heavy, and refused at first to budge, but when Jean-Baptiste put his back into it, first it parted from the rough thin fringe of turf and then it began to move sideways. Seeing that Jean-Baptiste took it all in earnest, Philippe pushed too.

In a moment it became clear that there was an opening under the stone. Jean-Baptiste made a sound of surprised understanding.

Nicole picked up and lit a lantern that had been standing by a gorse bush. 'Come, madame,' she said to Clothilde, offering her hand.

And to Madame de Tramont's astonishment, she found herself being ushered towards a staircase of deep steps, cut in the chalk, leading down.

Chapter Five

Madame de Tramont was frightened. 'What is it?' she whispered through suddenly parched lips. 'A tomb?'

'No madame,' said Nicole, 'you will find no dead bodies. It is quite empty.' She began to descend slowly, holding the lantern in front of her but steadying herself with one hand against the side of the staircase.

Madame de Tramont, ashamed to be less courageous than this child, moved forward. Her son stepped in front, went down a few steps, then held up his hand to guide her. Jean-Baptiste came last.

'Take care,' warned Nicole. 'The steps are well made but there may be lichen – even in the dark, some plants can grow.'

She was speaking with great calmness, but if the truth were known her heart was thumping wildly. It was years and years since she'd made this trip to the under-world. She was nearly as frightened as Clothilde. But she couldn't let it show. She must remain in command while she opened to her future mother-in-law the wonders existing below her feet.

The descent was long, or seemed so. The steps were rather deep for a woman's stride but were in perfect condition except for one or two tiny grey plants here and there. There was even a niche cut in the wall at hand level, to act as a bannister rail.

Nicole felt level ground under her feet. She reported to those who followed: 'I'm at floor level. Please stay where you are for a moment. I'll walk a few paces to light the area.'

She did so. From above, Philippe watched the light of her little lantern move a yard or two. It lit up her head and shoulders but little more. 'Nicole, take care–!'

'I'm all right, Philippe. Stay there. There ought to be candles.' She moved carefully forward on the rough floor, hand out-stretched until it met a little alcove. There she found a candlestick with a candle in it, and beside it a bundle of candles tied with string. She lit the first candle from her lantern, leaving it in the alcove. Immediately more of the cavern sprang to life.

There was a long white wall soaring off into the distance on her left. As Philippe joined her, she handed him a lighted candle. 'Walk to the right,' she requested. When he did so, another wall disappearing into the distance became visible.

Clothilde had been ushered down the last few steps by Jean-Baptiste. She joined her son and Nicole. From behind her Jean-Baptiste said, 'When did you last come down, Nicole?'

'Not since I was a little girl. I remember my father and grandfather levered the stone aside – it was a hot day in August and they made it an excuse to drink a great deal of marc. But when they got down here, they sobered up.'

'They let you come down?'

'Oh, I was dying to come down and see what it was like. I remember Paulie wouldn't come – she sat on the hillside crying, because she thought we were going to Hell.'

'But what is this place?' cried Clothilde in perplexity. 'How does it come to be here – because one can see it isn't a natural cave, the walls and floor are too regular.'

'It was made by the Romans, Madame,' said Nicole.

Clothilde gave a snort of annoyance. 'Come, don't tell fairytales. Who dug out this cavern?'

'She's telling you the truth, madame,' Jean-Baptiste put in. 'The firm of Ruinart Pere et Fils have just such a series of caves near Rheims. They were dug out by the Romans to build the original city of Rheims – I forget what it was called–'

'Durocortorum,' supplied Nicole.

'Durocortorum? Where do you get that

name? How do you come to know such things, child?' cried Madame de Tramont, baffled and impressed despite herself.

'My family took in a monk from Hautvilliers at the time of the Terror, madame,' Nicole explained. 'He was interested in such things. It was he who found this cellar, and the others that open from it.' She directed her lantern towards the wall at the left. 'There is a passage there which goes into another cavern – I haven't been in there, I wasn't brave enough for that, the only time I came down here.'

'But at the time of the Terror? The good man has been dead these many years – how did you know of it?'

'Brother Joseph kept a sort of journal. We still have it, also the books he brought with him from the abbey and his rosary.'

'And you could read it, this journal?'

'Yes, madame, and my father and grandfather too. I went back to it to re-read the information about this set of caves. Brother Joseph says they are all shaped like a pyramid with the summit of the pyramid at the surface where the stone is set. This is because, if it gets wet, clay cracks and dissolves. So the openings were made very small and rectangular, and then the slaves who quarried it worked outwards while hanging from some kind of chair, I believe.'

'Slaves!' cried Philippe in horror.

'Yes, Philippe, it must have been very dreadful, to work in such conditions. But you see, it was work well done – the clay was removed, and the stone cove was put back each day – I suppose they had pulleys stationed at the top of each opening in those days. Then when the space below ground became big enough, they cut a staircase.'

'Incredible!'

'No, madame, I have been in those taken over as cellars by the Ruinarts, and I assure you that fundamentally their cellars are just like this,' Jean-Baptiste said. 'They of course spent money to make them suitable – each clay-pit has been levelled and the walls made smooth to the height where the bottles lie. They have put in lighting brackets and proper staircases and so forth, but the effect is the same – the Ruinart champagne is cellared in the steady, constant temperature of a succession of claypits.'

'By heaven, if it's good enough for the Ruinarts, it ought to be good enough for us!' Philippe exclaimed.

'Very impressive. I ... I must admit you have surprised me, Mademoiselle Berthois. And now, if you don't mind, I should like to go above ground again. I find ... I find I am not comfortable in this underground chasm. I find it oppressive.'

'I understand, madame,' Nicole said

sympathetically. 'My father always said he didn't like it either.'

It took much longer to get up the staircase than down. Madame de Tramont had to pause several times to rest, and be almost carried up the last few steps by her son. Once in the open air, she sat down on the flat stone to regain her breath and her composure.

Nicole emerged last, having put out the candles and restored them to the spot where her father had left them on his last visit so long ago. Without being asked, Jean-Baptiste at once set to work to lever the cover back into position, a task in which he was joined by Philippe.

'And now tell me, mademoiselle,' said Clothilde, 'why have you done nothing with these cellars up to now?'

'What should we have done?' Nicole replied. 'We didn't know they were here until Brother Joseph worked out that they existed, from some old books he had consulted. Even then, times were bad – it didn't do for a villager to begin showing himself too clever, too ambitious. That way, enemies could report you to the Tribune and you ended up in prison. And then, later, when Brother Joseph had died, my grandfather didn't exactly know how to use the pits. We don't make enough wine ourselves for it to be worth our while remodelling the pits and

113

besides – it will cost money, not as much as digging anew but still, it would have cost more than my grandfather had.'

'Does anyone else know of them?'

'No, madame. We've never spoken of it. My father came to ensure that all was well, perhaps once every five years or so. I think the last time was about two years ago, when my brother Robert was still alive.'

'Well,' said Clothilde. 'This requires some thought.'

'Of course, madame. And now if you have recovered, please come to the house where my mother would like to offer refreshments.'

Clothilde would have given an automatic refusal, but she needed something to help get her home. She was unused to physical exertion: the climb up from the caves had exhausted her. Besides, she had had a shock.

She had half expected to be shown some neglected building in which she would have shown some interest, but afterwards would have made her own arrangements about leasing or buying. What she had seen was something quite different, something that couldn't be touched without the help of Nicole Berthois.

When they reached the house, Madame Berthois was waiting for them. Knowing no better, she invited them all in. And Jean-Baptiste decided not to be delicate about it and linger outside to admire the view. He had a natural curiosity to know all that was going on, so he went in with his employer to be a guest at this very awkward party.

Marie hobbled about with her stick, offering chairs to the guests. A bottle of wine in a pail of cool water stood on the table, which was covered with the special-occasion cloth of white linen edged with deep rough lace. There were also little cakes, made mainly of honey and hazelnuts, a specialty which Marie used to make for the birthdays of her children.

'This is a very good wine, madame,' Jean-Baptiste said after a sip. It was a fine, rather sharp, still champagne.

'Thank you, Jean-Baptiste, you know it's our own. But we don't make much, how can we, now there's only Nicole to attend to the vintage.'

'No, of course you sell almost all your grapes to us. But I compliment you. This wine has been well produced.'

'And the little cakes are delicious,' Philippe added, hoping to warm the glacial silence of his mother. 'When you come to live at the manor house, you must teach our cook how to make them.'

'Oh, no, m'sieu! Oh, don't suggest such things!'

'But why not? I agree Madame Grelliot is a bit of an ogre but she would be glad to

115

have the recipe for–'

'Oh, I didn't mean that, m'sieu. I meant, don't speak of living at the manor! I couldn't do it, really I couldn't–'

'But of course you can! In fact, it must–'

'No, really, Monsieur Philippe, I know you mean well, but truly I couldn't ever think of living in a house like that. Nicole tells me the rooms are so big that practically the whole of our house would go into one, and then there are servants – I know you have six or seven, and I shouldn't know what to say to them–'

'But all that would become natural–'

'No, it wouldn't, you don't understand, Monsieur Philippe! I've lived in this house since I was married, and I just shouldn't be comfortable anywhere else. Besides, I hear there are many staircases at the manor house. I can't go up and down staircases. And carpets – I'd trip over carpets. No, I must insist, m'sieu, you must realise I shall stay here even if you and Nicole marry.'

Clothilde was vexed to have the marriage even mentioned in front of Labaud. Yet she found herself thinking: Now *there* speaks a woman of sense – without even realising that in this thought she admitted the possibility of the marriage taking place. She said, speaking for the first time, 'I will have a little more wine, if it is not too much trouble.'

'Oh, certainly, madame. Nicole, pray refill madame's glass. And offer her another cake.'

'Thank you, no cake, I find them a little too sweet with the wine. So, madame, I hear your family had a priest living with them in days gone by.'

'Yes, so I've been told. I of course only know of it by hearsay. Very awkward it must have been, don't you think so, madame? A priest, you know... The menfolk must have had to curb their tongues sometimes, I imagine.'

Philippe laughed, Jean-Baptiste grinned quietly to himself and sipped his champagne. Nicole began to relax a little.

All day she had been strung up like a violin. She had scarcely slept all night, had risen long before daylight to get rid of the farm chores so as to have the morning free for the visit to the chalkpit.

She had been worried, too, about the chalkpit. Years had gone by since she last saw it. Although in his notes Brother Joseph remarked that the place remained dry and secure at all times, she had been afraid she would find a wet, mouldering grotto with slippery steps down which Madame de Tramont would refuse to go.

The place had lived up to Brother Joseph's description. She now had full confidence that there were, as he noted, at least four other pits opening off the one to which they knew the upper entrance. The fact that Jean-Baptiste had been able to support her information from his own knowledge had cheered her enormously.

She could see that Madame de Tramont was impressed. It now remained to turn that advantage into practical terms for the marriage.

Clothilde had bestirred herself enough to say to Marie: 'And these cellars, madame – have you seen them?'

'What, me, madame? Nothing would induce me to go near them. I'll tell you what, madame – if they had not been found by a monk, I'd say they were works of the devil! But then...' She recalled that her daughter had begged her to take care what she said, that the caves were important in bargaining for the marriage between herself and Philippe. 'What I always say, madame, is handsome is as handsome does, and if the caves are used for a good purpose, then that's all right.'

It was time to go. Clothilde felt up to the walk to her carriage, and she needed to get home to think over what she'd seen. 'Thank you for the hospitality, madame,' she said, but without offering her hand as she left.

'A pleasure, madame,' said Marie, holding on to the door jamb so that she could curtsey. 'What an amiable lady,' she whispered to her daughter as Clothilde went down the path.

'Oh, very,' said Nicole in dry tones as she followed her.

At the carriage Clothilde was handed in. When Jean-Baptiste stood back to let the young master climb in, Philippe shook his head. 'I'll stay on awhile, Mama. See you later.'

Jean-Baptiste, with some dismay, got in. He sat opposite his employer. The fact that he had put on his best suit for the carriage ride didn't help him feel at ease in this *tête-à-tête*.

The coachman, who had spent an interesting hour or so standing on top of the coach watching the group move about the hillside and then enter the farmhouse, took off the brake and set the big horses in motion. When they had made a lumbering turn on to the main road, Madame de Tramont said: 'You thought well of the cellarage, Labraud?'

'Oh, I did, madame! You wouldn't find its equal for miles in any direction.'

'But money would have to be spent – they couldn't be used as they are.'

'No, we should have to dress the walls and floor to make them even and easier to clean. And we should have to put up barns or sheds at the opening to hold gantries and so forth. It would cost something. But there would be no difficulty to raising the money, madame. The bank would be only too glad to advance it against security of that kind.'

'You think so?'

'You'd naturally consult Monsieur Pourdume. But I think he would agree.'

Now she found it an advantage that Labaud had heard the marriage spoken of. 'The condition, of course, is that I allow my son to take Nicole as his wife.'

'Indeed, madame?'

'I don't believe I can do that.'

'Ahem... Well, then, madame... Your son could fare further and do worse. Nicole Berthois is a good, clever girl, from a family that has always been respected in Calmady.'

'Respected?' She raised her eyebrows.

'Oh yes, madame. In a way, they're part of the village aristocracy. They're having hard times now, I agree, losing all their menfolk in the typhoid last year. And the land that was ceded to them in the re-shuffle after the Revolution isn't of the best. Yet they don't go begging for help, they stand on their own feet.'

'The girl certainly has character...'

'Yes, clever and independent–'

She gave a great sigh. 'Independence is not what one seeks in a daughter-in-law, Labaud.'

'What then, madame? Money, good looks? Nicole's a pretty girl, and if she now exploits those chalkpits she'll have money enough to find herself an excellent match.'

'Not enough to entitle her to marry into the de Tramont family, Labaud!'

Jean-Baptiste hesitated. He chose his words carefully. 'That of course is a family matter, Madame de Tramont, on which I have no right to express an opinion. But I can speak with authority about the cellarage. Not even Mademoiselle Darlannier could bring a dowry like that!'

Mademoiselle Darlannier was the last in the line of young ladies found by Monsieur Pourdume as a possible match for Philippe. Normally it would have made Clothilde indignant to think that Jean-Baptiste knew so much about the family's private affairs, but other things held her attention at present.

'Mademoiselle Darlannier at least has some breeding!'

'Do you think so, madame?' Jean-Baptiste said with an air of surprise. 'Her father was a waggoner at Veuvillot. He used to drink in the Market Tavern in Rheims with mine, before he began to make his fortune as a haulage contractor. Her mother, if I remember aright, is Josephine Reboul as was – well thought of for her butter-making.'

'What?' Clothhilde said faintly.

'You see, Madame de Tramont – Mademoiselle Darlannier is only one generation away from what Nicole is.'

'Monsieur Pourdume said nothing to me of all that!'

'He would have, no doubt,' soothed Jean-Baptiste, 'had the match looked like going forward.' He broke off there. It was well-known on the estate that Jacques Darlannier had refused the match in blunt fashion. He'd declared that for his money he expected to get more than the non-existent title of a *ci-devant* marquis and a champagne firm that was only just making its way.

There was a pause while the imposing travelling carriage swayed on its way along the dusty road. 'But it would cause so much *talk*, a marriage like that.'

There was no use denying that. 'Well, then... They're going to get married whether or not you agree,' he said, abandoning diplomacy. 'Monsieur Philippe is of age, and once Nicole begins to offer the chalkpits to other firms they'll have money enough to set them up on their own. It's true, isn't it, madame – none of the other matches came to anything? From now on, would he look at anyone else?'

'Oh, dear God...'

'Isn't it best to resign yourself, madame? Make the best of a bad job?'

'If my poor husband were alive, he would know how to deal with this!'

Jean-Baptiste greatly doubted that, but he kept the thought hidden behind his dark, angular features. 'The first thing to do is talk it over with Monsieur Pourdume. I am almost sure he'll recommend the marriage. Madame, I assure you – the girl is going to make the fortune of the de Tramonts!'

As he finished speaking, he felt a little like a knight who had been sent to joust for his lady and had carried off the guerdon. But, in less fanciful terms, he had done his best for pretty, bright little Nicole Berthois, of whom he'd always been fond and whom he'd come to admire since she entered womanhood.

Madame de Tramont made the journey to Rheims next day to take the advice of Monsieur Pourdume. That gentleman was astounded at what he heard, but quickly took in all the facts. After a very short time his anxiety, which he hid from Madame, was that by her antagonism she would drive this prize of a girl away from the de Tramonts. With property like that at her command, Nicole Berthois could get a handsome husband anywhere, together with a mother-in-law who'd be much more agreeable to her than Madame de Tramont.

At the end of the week Clothilde de Tramont sent for Nicole. Nicole put on her new gown, her bonnet, her gloves and her leather shoes. When she was ushered into the drawing-room, Clothilde inclined her head. Philippe, standing by his mother's armchair, went at once to place a chair for his fiancée. At that moment Nicole knew they had won: she would have been made to remain standing if it was a rejection.

Clothilde said without preliminaries, 'I have consulted my lawyer and the papers can be drawn up as soon as you care to go with us to the office in Rheims. Do you have title deeds to the chalkpits?'

'No, madame. But of course I can prevent anyone from entering them if they have to cross Berthois land, so that gives me tenure.'

Clothilde swallowed. Had this child been reading a law book?

'You are not the owner, of course. The owner is your mother.'

'My mother gives me full title to do what I choose.'

'Oh, she does. Then … I believe there are no obstacles.'

'You have won, Nicole,' Philippe said with admiration. He was standing by her chair. He stooped to pick up her gloved hand and implant a kiss on it. 'Mama, will you give us your blessing?'

'I … er … I…'

Nicole smiled. 'Perhaps that will come later, Philippe. I ask less than that, madame. I ask only that you give us your permission.'

Clothilde eyed her. No denying the quality in the girl. Where did it come from? Could there possibly be some aristocratic love-child back in the family somewhere? Looked at objectively, Nicole Berthois at this moment seemed a very suitable candidate to be the young Madame de Tramont. All the same, Clothilde had difficulty saying the words.

'I give my permission for the marriage.'

Chapter Six

The wedding ceremonies, both civil and religious, were quiet. Nicole wore her new gown of pale grey dimity striped with soft rose, her new bonnet and gloves and good shoes. To these she added, for the day, a shawl of fine lace that was a family heirloom.

Madame de Tramont could have offered the Tramont family lace, but did not. When she saw Nicole in the soft folds of the Berthois shawl, she was sorry she had been so grudging. The girl looked really lovely, framed in the spider's web of cream dentelle.

Philippe took his bride to Paris, where he fell in love with her all over again as he watched her wonder and enthusiasm at the splendours of the city.

Paris was so big! She'd thought it would be perhaps twice the size of Rheims, but it was bigger, much, much bigger. And that fact alone was a lesson unconsciously learned. Calmady, the Champagne region, even the Department of the Marne – these weren't as important as she'd imagined. There were greater things, farther horizons.

For the first time she understood what it meant when wine-makers talked about exporting their products. It meant carrying the wine to these great centres of wealth and influence. It was more than just selling what you made – it was becoming part of the heartbeat of civilisation.

'One day I will take you to London,' he said. 'Perhaps London is an even finer city, because for the last hundred years they have been putting up good buildings whereas we have been knocking ours down!'

He took her to the Left Bank haunts he used to tell her about. They were cafés full of cigarette smoke, noise, and the smell of oil paint and grease paint – for most of the clientèle were artists or theatre people. At first she was shocked and a little scared at the freedom of the talk, but she soon learned to enjoy the conversation, though she took little part. The habitués came from all walks of life originally: from them she painlessly learned an ease of manner that was to serve her well in times to come. They for their part were kind to her, a shy country girl who could suddenly speak with authority on a subject that interested them all – good wine.

He took her to the theatre. She was entranced. This was the world her husband longed to enter; now that she saw a real play, she understood why. Philippe told her she mustn't admire Sardou, so she didn't, but she enjoyed his work for all that. The great theatrical moments he contrived, the beautiful actresses who played in his pieces – they were all easy to appreciate. If she found Shakespeare and the opera less friendly she told herself she would understand it all when she became accustomed to them.

But there were other delights. He must buy her trousseau, he insisted. She had been married with only one gown suitable for town wear: now he took command and carried her off to the dressmaker, the milliner, the shoemaker, the *lingiste*.

Paulette had warned her to buy only light colours and plain designs. 'Those are suitable for a bride–'

'But no one will know I'm newly married.'

'They'll know,' her sister said, with a hidden envy of that glowing happiness which couldn't be concealed.

On the whole the disdainful saleswomen at the fashion houses were kind to the little country mouse. She had married money – not a great fortune, of course, but a decent enough income. And the name was aristocratic. And she was a pretty little thing with her ringleted dark hair and longlashed eyes. They were disposed to be helpful.

So the shopping expeditions, which could have been terrifying, became great fun.

Philippe played his part well, giving opinions on shoe trimmings and the value of a bonnet as against a toque. It wasn't unusual for the Parisian male to take part in choosing his wife's clothes, but for Philippe it was a new amusement.

The greatest pleasure of all was the *lingiste*. In the showroom, garments of soft georgette, voile, broderie anglaise, fine lawn, lace and silk hung from display stands. When she first saw them, Nicole hid her face against her husband's sleeve in embarrassment.

'Come now, dearest... It's quite all right. You must have pretty things to wear under all those lovely gowns. Come now, choose...'

'But, Philippe ... I can't ... I've never...' She'd never had anything finer than soft cotton against her skin. She didn't know how to choose between these filmy fabrics, some imported from as far away as China.

Gently, Philippe and the salesgirl coaxed her into making the first choice. After that it was easier. She picked out a nightgown of shell-pink ninon, a negligee of matching satin trimmed with beige and pale green ribbons, boudoir caps of lace and muslin, a chemise of crêpe de chine edged with picot lace...

The items in their wrappings of tissue paper were delivered to their hotel that evening. After dinner they had a wonderful time while Nicole tried everything on – and Philippe helped her take it off again. They laughed and played among the finery like children. Yet when, in the early hours of the morning, they stood side by side to watch the grey dawn come up over Notre Dame, the frippery lay around their ankles like a tide of pale mists, unregarded while they shared yet another moment of complete understanding.

It had never occurred to Nicole that she would be unwilling to return home. But when it was time to leave Paris she felt a momentary heartache. She understood that she was leaving something behind for ever – the right to carelessness, the days of sheer enjoyment. She was to look back on her honeymoon as an enchanted time, a time when love and only love was important.

Before the wedding she had signed all the necessary papers concerning the cellarage. She had also arranged for a monthly income to be made available to her mother, for whom she found a distant relative to act as housekeeper companion. Marie Berthois, staggered at the good fortune of having money come in regularly, at once set about putting something aside as a dowry for her elder daughter Paulette, only to find it unnecessary – within two months Nicole had arranged a suitable marriage for Paulette.

The man was Auguste Fournier, with whom Paulette had become acquainted in Rheims although he came from Rethel in the Ardennes. He had a respectable small building firm, inherited from his father. If you compared him with Philippe, thought Nicole, he was a nothing. But Paulette seemed to like him and he seemed to want Paulette, if only there were some money to go with her.

Nicole was well aware that it was a terrible vexation to Madame de Tramont to be related to a dressmaker's drudge. Nicole had toyed with the idea of arranging for a sum of money to buy a partnership for Paulette in the Treignac shop, but perhaps that wouldn't have pleased Madame de Tramont and besides, Paulette wanted to be married. She was older than Nicole. Now her younger sister was married, it was embarrassing to be a spinster still.

So it was arranged, Paulette went to Rethel to live, Marie Berthois was tucked away in her cottage unlikely to be the least nuisance to the Tramonts, and all that Clothilde had to do was get used to her daughter-in-law living in the house.

Surprisingly enough, this proved easy. The young couple were so in love that they couldn't bear to be parted. They were seldom about to fret Clothilde's nerves.

Nicole went with Philippe about the

131

estate, looking at the vines, examining the wine in the existing cellar, watching the adaptation of the new vaults on the Berthois farm. When there was nothing that called for his attention, he would walk hand in hand with his young wife among the chestnut trees in their autumn splendour or, as the weather grew colder and rainier, he would take her to his study. There he would write, pausing to read out anything he thought exceptionally good. Nicole would sit by with her needlework, always ready to listen and approve.

The baby, a girl, was born in May, early enough to make the wiseacres of the neighbourhood smile about a seven month child, but late enough to safeguard Nicole's reputation. They called her Alys, after Clothilde's mother. The following year there was another child, also a girl – to Clothilde's disappointment, for she dearly wanted a grandson to carry on the de Tramont name. The younger daughter was called Delphine, in honour of no family member but merely because it was the name of the heroine in the play Philippe was presently writing.

Nicole had felt herself subtly being changed by her new life. She drank in 'refinement' from merely living with the de Tramonts. Aghast at the outset when she saw the array of cutlery and glasses used by the rich, she bided her time, watched what

Philippe did, and followed suit: when she came back from her honeymoon in Paris she had learned which knife to use for what.

Entertaining had at first been an ordeal. Since Clothilde was still the head of the household, it was she who invited the guests and arranged the menus. But Nicole had to play her part in entertaining the guests.

She rather endeared herself to her mother-in-law by admitting she was scared before their first evening party. 'I shan't know what to say to them, madame.'

'My young friend, you need say scarcely anything. Ask about health, family, or business welfare – these three topics have stood me in good stead for more than fifty years.'

It was good advice. Only occasionally did Nicole come across a conversationalist who was determined to put her in her place, and when she met such a one she bore it with good grace. After all, she was still not yet twenty, had never 'come out', came from simple parentage: it was only natural that those with no manners should try to take advantage.

An unexpected event, outside the household of the manor of Tramont, brought Clothilde closer to Nicole than she ever expected. Her only daughter, Seraphine, died in childbirth in England. Clothilde was overset with an unexpected grief. She hadn't seen Seraphine in over eight years, and now reproached herself for not having made the uncomfortable journey to Lincolnshire.

'Madame, you couldn't have known. Don't blame yourself,' soothed Nicole.

'But she had had two miscarriages already. I should have been more concerned. Nicole, I have not been a good mother–'

'You have, indeed you have. You have a fine son, a credit to your upbringing.'

Clothilde smiled through her tears. 'You are biased,' she said. 'You only say that because you love Philippe.'

Afterwards both women were struck by the phrase. It was the first time Clothilde had admitted openly that Nicole had married Philippe purely for love, and not to aggrandize herself.

It took several weeks for Clothilde to recover her equilibrium. But then she began to think of her own self-reproach. 'She had not been a good mother' … it was her duty to ensure that Philippe inherited the title which was his by right. She simply wasn't doing enough to recover it for him.

'Nicole,' she said one morning as they strolled on the parterre edged with roses, 'I have decided to remove to Paris.'

'Madame?'

'Er … I am right in thinking the business is doing well? We could afford an apartment there?'

'Most assuredly, madame,' Nicole agreed. For some months now, since the birth of Delphine and the necessary handing over of the baby to the care of the nurse – a thing that could never have happened had she still been a peasant girl and which Nicole half regretted – she had been filling in some empty hours by taking part in the making of the wine.

This became more important to her as Philippe began to make more frequent visits to Paris. He had three plays finished now, was negotiating to get at least one of them put on. It was his reports of the life there that had made his mother realise how provincial they were here in Calmady.

What chance did Clothilde have, out in the sticks, of influencing the important men who could say yes or no to the necessary court cases, read the vital documentation, set in train the actual re-establishment of the marquisate? She began to think that the lawyers she employed probably didn't even read the letters she sent. They had many such clients, eager to regain past glories.

She explained all this to Nicole. The younger woman listened with attention. If she had been asked for an honest opinion she'd have said she thought it a waste of time and money – what did it matter if Philippe were the Marquis de Tramont or plain Monsieur? Yet it mattered to

Clothilde, and after her grief over Seraphine Nicole knew that beneath the imposing self-importance there was a vulnerable woman.

'Tramont Champagne can certainly afford to buy an apartment in Paris,' she said. 'We would of course talk it over with Monsieur Pourdume but he would agree, I know.' Monsieur Pourdume had got into the habit of agreeing with Nicole. In general, he found she talked good sense.

It seemed a great upheaval at the time. But after Clothilde's removal to the capital, life soon resumed its even tenor at the manor house. When Philippe went to town he was able to stay comfortably at his mother's apartment instead of in some bohemian tavern where his theatrical friends would encourage him to drink too much. Clothilde wrote regularly, long letters, rather dull in style, but full of news about Parisian life, fashion, and, of course, the progress of her court case.

Nicole found herself busy. There was an unexpectedly good grape harvest the year Clothilde went away, and the making of the first pressing and then the careful preparation for the second fermentation were full of suspense.

'This might turn out to be a notable vintage,' said Jean-Baptiste Labaud as he leaned over a vat in the pressing house. 'All we need is a week of cool weather and a north wind.'

'Jean-Baptiste, you are the only man I know who thinks the direction of the wind matters!'

'Well then, madame... You know as well as I do that the south wind generally brings infection...' He fell silent, his attention on the vats.

It always made Nicole uncomfortable to have Jean-Baptiste call her 'madame'. She had known him all her life and until her marriage he'd always called her Nicole or Nicci.

Yet she understood his reasons. There was a gulf between them now, which must be respected.

The transition to being a 'lady' meant giving up many of the easy ways of her earlier life. People to whom she had been a familiar figure now had to treat her with some distance. The household staff had come to terms with this quite soon, because under Madame de Tramont's eagle eye they dared not do otherwise. After two years with Nicole as the younger Madame de Tramont, they had accepted her role, even now that Clothilde had removed to Paris.

But the workers on the estate and in the vaults were less easy to impress. 'What, little Nicci, giving us instructions? What does he know? Anyhow, *she's* not the manager of the firm, it's her husband.'

But everyone knew that the real manager of the firm was Jean-Baptiste. It was his knowledge and experience that produced the wine which was now in such great demand. It was his verdict on the amount to make, the blends to choose, the timing and routines, which really mattered.

As to the young Madame de Tramont, she might imagine she had a role to play, but she'd better think again. True, she'd grown up with the vines, but so had every inhabitant of the champagne region. They knew as much as she did about the culture and harvesting of the grapes so she needn't think she could go around giving orders.

If they had stopped to think it over they would have realised that Nicole gave few orders to do with the actual grapes. It was the processes in-cellar that she was interesting herself in.

The making of champagne, a long laborious process, had always been known to her. Throughout her girlhood she had of course visited many cellars, although none on the scale over which she now held sway. But living with it from day to day was different. Slowly she began to see ways in which the processes could be improved.

Almost two hundred years had gone by since Dom Perignon first invented the champagne method, the method which turned the good, still wine of Champagne into the sparkling drink that captured the hearts of the world. During that time traditions had grown up, habits that were now accepted not only as unchangeable but also as beyond criticism.

Each stage of the work had its name and its appointed time in the cycle of wine production. The first separation of the wine from the lees in the casks, the collection of the wines needed to begin the blending, the second separation of the wine, the rest period, the actual preparation of the blend, the last racking for separation, the transfer to the bottling vat, the addition of the mixture of wine and sugar needed to help the second fermentation... All of these were done in order, with a sort of ceremony that emphasised their importance.

And of course they were important – vital, to the production of a fine wine. Yet as Nicole watched the workers moving about the vaults she couldn't help feeling that there were methods that could be improved.

There was a lot of wastage of wine. It seemed inevitable. When the wine was bottled and then stacked for the second fermentation, there were breakages, seepages, faulty corking. Then during the re-stacking – and this had to be done at the beginning of the ageing process and at least once more during the succeeding year – accidents occurred. Before the bottles were re-stacked they had to be twirled to move the sediment through the wine, and in the course of that, breakages were bound to happen.

But the process which irritated Nicole most had to do with waste of time, rather than of wine. It was the one known as the *remuage*. It consisted of collecting the sediment together; the object of course was to separate it so as to produce an absolutely crystal clear wine, through which one could watch the bubbles rise as if through sunshine.

Often, when Philippe was away and sometimes when he was at home, Nicole would go into the vaults at night. She would roam the alleys between the piles of bottles, examining them in the light of her upheld lamp, sniffing the air for any change in the scent which would tell her of seepage from badly-inserted corks.

There they lay, the bottles that contained the fortune of the de Tramont family. There they must lie until the sediment had settled, after which the wine would be decanted into other bottles. All this took time, and the loss of effervescence during the change from one bottle to another was really wounding to Nicole. What was the use of spending so much time and effort in making a wine beautifully fizzy if you then let half the fizz escape in order to get rid of the sediment?

She began picking up a bottle or two regularly, moving it to watch the sediment slide down the side. Surely it must be possible to get rid of those dregs without having to move the wine to another bottle?

The lump of impurities would lie inside the bottle, on the curve of its wall. It would stay there unless the bottle was moved. Could one somehow scoop it out?

But what tool, what utensil could be used? Nothing would go inside and hook out the lump. Besides, whatever implement you used, it might alter the taste of the wine.

No, it had to be done without harm to the wine. And the problem was, that the bottles lay on their side and the sediment collected on the lower curve of the bottle. Careful turning ensured that it collected in one small mass. But once there ... so what?

Nicole and her experimental group of bottles became like antagonists. She would go to them in the dark of the night and stare. 'You are like old men with the cough,' she muttered to them. 'You have phlegm in your chest but you won't let it go! Foolish, stubborn things...! You know you would be better in every way if you spat out that lump!'

Weeks went by while she kept returning to the matter. Philippe, busy polishing his latest play, scarcely noticed her pre-occupation. When she tried to discuss this technical

141

problem with him he shook his head. 'Oh, darling, you know that Labaud understands all that. Leave it to him.'

But even Jean-Baptiste could think of no way to part good wine from bad without decanting. 'It's always been one of our chief problems, madame. It's like the weather – you have to put up with it.'

'I don't see why,' she replied with a stubborn lift of her chin. 'The Good Lord gave us brains to solve problems, not submit to them.'

'Well, then, madame … I wish you luck.'

The idea came to her when she was taking Alys for a walk. It was a chilly day in September and Alys had a cold. Nurse had been unwilling to let her go out at all, but the toddler was fretful after being kept indoors for days. She was well wrapped up. In her little woollen coat, leather leggings, woollen bonnet and a shawl tied crossways over her chest, she was well protected from the raw weather. She trotted at Mama's side, calling to the little terrier Toto.

At the pond, which in the great days had been a handsome lake, they stopped to feed the mallards. Nicole had brought bread for the purpose. Alys obediently threw crumbs to them, but as often happened, she munched a piece herself when she thought Mama wasn't looking.

'Alys! Anyone would think we starved you!

Spit that out this minute!'

Alys shook her head and chewed vigorously. She had encountered a chunk of crust that, offered at home, would have been instantly refused. But stolen from the food intended for the ducks, it had a special flavour.

'Alys!' scolded her mother, advancing upon her.

Intending to wail in protest, Alys opened her mouth wide. The crust went down the wrong way, she began to cough, and within seconds was red in the face and gasping for breath.

'Darling! Oh, silly child! Stop howling! Lean forward. Lean forward, Alys!'

Through her gasps and tears, Alys heard the command and obeyed. Nicole thumped her hard on the back, the chunk of bread flew out into the water, to be eagerly snatched by unfastidious ducks.

'There, sweetheart, there, it's all right now,' Nicole comforted, wiping the little girl's nose and drying her tears.

Alys clung to her mother's serge skirt. 'Mama, Mama! The nasty bread stickted in my throat!'

'Yes, dear, I know, but it came out, didn't it! Whoosh!' Nicole cried, enacting the curve of the bread as it fell into the pond. 'Whoosh! And the duck ate it.'

'Yes, naughty duck, eat my bread.'

Recovering, Alys was inclined to kick the duck who had got the better of the crust that had nearly choked her.

Nicole prevented her, then led her on to look for nuts in the woodland. It was as they were heading for home, and she was re-enacting the scene in her head to tell it to Philippe later, that she was struck by her inspiration.

'That's it!' she cried. 'That's it, Alys!'

'What, Mama? What?'

'The *remuage*, Alys! That's how to do it!'

'What, Mama? What we goin' to do?'

'Never mind, my darling. But you're a very, very clever girl! You've solved a problem not even Jean-Baptiste could handle.'

'A clever girl,' Alys agreed with satisfaction, nodding. 'Cleverer than Delphine.'

'Of course, bigger and cleverer,' said Nicole, hugging her.

But it was easier to see the solution than to bring it about in the *remuage*.

Like Alys's chunk of bread, the sediment in the champagne bottle had clogged together. If it could be got to a point in the neck of the bottle, it could be ejected – perhaps not by anything so violent as a thump on the back, but surely the force of the champagne itself must act, as Alys's cough had done?

Night after night she went into the cellars

144

to experiment. She dared not do it during the daytime when the workmen were about, for she knew they would stare, and mutter, and be disapproving. But alone in the night hours she tried placing the bottle in various positions of incline to get the lees down to the neck. And in the end she saw how to do it.

She had a table made, pierced with holes. Into the holes she inserted the necks of the bottles. She examined them each day. 'Ha,' muttered the cellarman, 'what's the point? The sediment will only fall back when the wine has to be decanted.'

But no. She learned how, by a quick flick of the wrist, to make the lees slide down to the cork and stay there. After that, a swift removal of the cork, then a little jet of champagne from its own effervescence rocketed the sediment out into a container. One suddenly little explosion like a gunshot and then the cork was put back. Almost no wine was lost. The lees were gone. The champagne was clear.

It took months of trial and error. Her wrists ached, her fingers became hardened from the continual working of the corks and the metal clips that held them in place.

But when at last she showed the technique to Jean-Baptiste, she knew it worked. She knew that men with stronger wrists and much experience would make a better job of uncorking and recorking than she ever could. What she had done was to establish the principle – that the sediment could be got down to the neck of the bottle for easy removal, in spite of everything that tradition had taught.

'Well then, madame…' Jean-Baptiste said when he had watched her take ten bottles from her special table and successfully eject the sediment. 'That's quite an invention. You ought to patent it.'

She never did so. But the table with holes, later modified, became known throughout the Champagne region as the de Tramont Table.

Chapter Seven

Nicole couldn't help being pleased by the respect from the wine-workers that followed her 'invention'. But a greater thrill was about to befall the de Tramont family.

Philippe's latest play was to receive a performance.

'Oh, sweetheart, I am *so* pleased for you! At last, a theatrical manager with some taste! When is it to be?'

Philippe hugged his wife. 'It won't be until March, I expect. Verilat has a play waiting to be staged, and the one that's playing at the moment is doing well, so mine takes third place, you see–'

'But that's absurd! Your play is so good – it deserves preference–'

'Don't you think you're perhaps a little bit biased, Nicci?' he teased.

'Not a bit! I've read a great many of the modern plays and I've actually seen – how many? – three, no, four–'

'Well, dear, that hardly makes you an expert. All the same, I do hope Verilat will get ahead with casting the parts and having the costumes made.'

The play was set in Ancient Syria and was

based on the story of Berenice, for whom Antiochus divorced his existing wife. Philippe had chosen to see Berenice as victim of a hundred plots, the whole thing ending in terrible tragedy when the king's first wife regained power. Nicole, on hearing Philippe read it out to her, had been brought to the verge of tears.

The trip to Paris for the first performance began to be a great project. Nicole, who hadn't seen her sister Paulette for almost six months, invited her to come to the capital for the event.

'Thank you a thousand times for your suggestion, dear sister,' wrote Paulette, 'but things aren't going too well with Auguste's business just at present, so I couldn't afford it.'

Nonsense, was Nicole's response. Of course Paulette must come as her guest. She must first come to Calmady to visit Mama, who wasn't too well these days, and then she could leave little Edmond with Nanny and Nicole's two little girls while the sisters went to Paris for a shopping spree. 'I need some new clothes, Paulette, and you know I'm never sure of my own taste. So I should really value your presence as an advisor, and besides I must have a special gown for the first night...'

So it was settled. Paulette arrived at the manor house, looking somewhat strained

148

and thin. 'I think that husband of hers was a bad bargain,' Philippe confided to Nicole as they prepared for bed that night. 'Do you think he is good to her?'

Nicole paused in the brushing of her thick chestnut hair. 'I think Auguste is as good as he knows how to be,' she sighed. 'He's not a man of much delicacy, I fear... And Paulette has always been timid and shy. Also, darling, I don't think his business is going too well.'

'Good lord,' exclaimed Philippe. 'If a man can't make money in the year the Emperor gets married, when can he?'

'Oh, my love,' Nicole said in laughing protest. 'We're lucky – we're in the wine business – of course champagne is in demand to celebrate at banquets and great occasions. But as for buildings... I don't know if anyone's so quick to say, I'll found a school in honour of the Empress as they are to say, I'll give a banquet.'

Philippe had lost interest in the topic. He came to his wife's side and ran his hand over the long curling tresses that shone in the candlelight. 'Never mind about Paulette and her marriage,' he said, 'let's do a little celebrating of our own.'

They all set off in good time to allow a week in Paris before the opening night. This was to give Philippe the opportunity to supervise the last few rehearsals, and so that Nicole and Paulette could have new dresses made. They went in the stage coach, The Parish Flyer, so that the journey took less than two days with an overnight stop at Meaux.

There wasn't room enough in Madame de Tramont's apartment near the Grand Palais, so Paulette was accommodated at a respectable hotel nearby – greatly impressed by what she saw as luxury. This also served the purpose of keeping her separated from Madame, who could never forget that this young woman had been her dressmaker.

It was a time of high enjoyment. Paulette was encouraged to shop for herself and Nicole without regard to expense. 'Are you sure, Nicci? This silk is awfully expensive...'

But Nicole knew how substantial the profits had been from this year's sales of champagne. 'Be brave, Paulette! If you like it, buy it!'

Philippe too was happy. He came home at odd hours of the day and night reporting that the actors were doing full justice to his ringing speeches. The actress cast as Berenice was extremely beautiful, the actor playing Antiochus had a real spade shaped beard, the scheming Laodice had a voice like velvet. 'It will go extremely well,' he said. 'Certainly no fault can be found with the cast – if only my lines are as good as the people who speak them...'

'My son,' Clothilde rebuked, 'you are a de

Tramont – if you cannot express yourself with dignity and eloquence, who can?'

Philippe exchanged a secret smile with Nicole. His mother would never understand. But he was pleased that she was proud of his success as a playwright.

The two new gowns were delivered on the morning of the great day. Nicole had instructed her sister to come to the apartment so that they could dress together and help each other with the accessories – fans, new gloves, flowers for the corsage and the hair. Paulette's gown was of shot silk with a neckline decorously filled in with gauze trimmed with ruched lace. Nicole's, which displayed her pretty shoulders, was of peach pink with flounces edged in brown-dyed Chantilly, to be covered by a brown and pink merino opera cloak.

When the two girls came out of the bedroom to join Philippe and his mother, even Madame de Tramont exclaimed in admiration. 'My dear children, how very nice you look!'

'Thank you, madame,' Nicole said with a little curtsey. 'We want to do justice to our playwright.'

Philippe had ordered orchids for the two girls. He smiled to see them pinned to the bosom of the dress and in Nicole's case, nestling in her hair. He felt buoyant, expectant. It seemed to him that since meeting Nicole, life had been very good to him.

He had ordered an exceptionally fine meal at one of the best restaurants, with appropriate wines ending, of course, in champagne to accompany the dessert. But the only person who enjoyed the food was Paulette. She, usually so nervy, was relatively unconcerned: her role had been fulfilled, Nicole's new clothes were being made and the gown for tonight was a triumph.

'I propose a toast,' said Madame de Tramont as the champagne was carefully poured by the attentive and knowledgeable waiter. 'To Philippe de Tramont, whose varied talents have caused the triumph of our champagne in the world's markets, and an expected triumph tonight.'

'Oh, Mama, *absit omen!*' her son cried. 'It's tempting Providence to speak of a triumph tonight!'

Privately Paulette, who was no fool, thought it absurd to speak of a triumph for Philippe in the world of champagne. Although she didn't live in Calmady, she knew enough of what went on to understand that her clever young sister was to be credited with Champagne Tramont's success. Without the dowry of her cellarage, and without the attention she paid to the work, Tramont would still be one of the respected lesser brands.

But she raised her glass with a smile, and saw that Nicole did too, without reservation. She sighed inwardly. It must be wonderful to be so in love with one's husband, she thought. Auguste ... Auguste was a good man, a suitable partner for a girl like herself. And yet ... all she could give him was respect and affection. And all he could give her was a decent home and a handsome little boy. Love seemed something she must do without – except the love between herself and her child.

They went to the Theatre Claudel in a four-wheeled cab. The service in the restaurant had been so leisurely and full of little extra flourishes that they were really rather late. It was the custom for the author to arrive, on the contrary, a little early, to receive the good wishes of friends among the audience. It seemed Philippe would have to forego this. The curtain might be about to go up, only awaiting his arrival for the signal to be given.

They were shown to the velvet-and-gold box. It seemed to Nicole that the usher who guided them and provided them with programmes seemed a little worried, but she thought nothing of it. The theatre was reasonably full: Parisians enjoyed first nights, where there was plenty of opportunity to display taste and discrimination by applauding good lines and booing poor performances. But an unknown author couldn't expect the same attention as the established dramatists, so there were some empty seats.

They settled on their gilt chairs. Philippe took out his watch and consulted it. Curtain time had gone by ten minutes ago. He leaned over to wave to a group of friends in the stalls, draped his mother's fur stole around her shoulders to shield her from the draught, fidgeted, coughed.

'I hope nothing has gone wrong.'

'Oh, my dear, what could go wrong?' Nicole soothed.

'A million things. The scenery – you know, ancient Syrian temples are heavy things – and then there was the problem of Berenice's wig–'

'My son, delays are frequent on theatre first nights,' his mother intervened. 'You know it is a time of nerves for the actors too.'

'Yes, yes… But Verilat said this morning they were all very confident…'

The delay lengthened. The happy buzz of conversation in the stalls and gallery began to give way to a tone of annoyance. Then a slow handclap began.

'Come on, Verilat! I know it's from the Syrian era but you should have got it here by now!'

'Truget drunk again? Put him on, drunk

154

or sober!'

'Verilat, Verilat, if you've lost the play give us op-er-a!' chanted one wag, pleased with his wit and eager to hear the sound of his own voice.

It was taken up goodnaturedly for a while, but then irritation got the upper hand. 'Come on, Verilat! We'll come up and get you if you don't start soon!'

Philippe had been on his feet for some time, edgily moving from the front of the box to its door, wondering whether to go backstage but certain that the moment he left, the curtain would go up. He was turning for the door again.

'Philippe!' Nicole cried, catching his jacket.

He turned back. The heavy red velvet curtains had parted. André Verilat stood in the gap.

'Ladies and gentlemen,' he began, with an agonised glance towards Philippe's box.

'Ahh!' groaned the audience. They expected to hear one of the actors had been taken ill and, if it proved to be the great beauty playing Berenice, her substitute would have a hard time from them.

'I regret to inform you—'

'Get on with it! Who's died?'

'To inform you ... that there will be no performance. The play is temporarily withdrawn.'

'Withdrawn?' gasped Philippe.

'Withdrawn?' echoed the womenfolk, in dismay and perplexity.

'I regret—'

'Tickets! We paid for our tickets!'

'Withdrawn? Is it so bad!'

'Down with Verilat!'

'Those patrons who have paid for tickets,' the manager went on, raising his sonorous voice to make himself heard, 'will have the money refunded at the box office. I apologise for the disappointment, which is not of my making.'

'Withdrawn?' said Philippe, in a lost voice. 'How can it be withdrawn? And without my consent?'

'Go and find out, Philippe,' urged Nicole.

'No, my boy, stay with us,' Madame de Tramont said, looking with anxiety at the turbulence breaking out below, and glimpsing a rain of small coins and sweetmeats from the gods above.

'Madame, he must find out what has happened,' said Nicole. 'He must go. We are safe enough here. This will die down in a moment. Go, Philippe.'

He stared at her as if he hardly knew her, then nodded. 'Stay here until I come for you. I'll send an usher to look after you meanwhile.'

'Yes, of course – we'll be all right.'

As soon as he had gone, Nicole turned her

attention to soothing Madame de Tramont's anxieties and comforting Paulette, who had dissolved in tears. 'Please – you must both pull yourselves together! This is a terrible blow to Philippe, we must be a help to him!'

'Wh-what can have h-happened?' sobbed Paulette. 'It's such a sh-shame!'

'These Paris mobs,' Clothilde said, wrapping her stole closer about her neck to hide the rather handsome pearls she was wearing. 'They love an excuse for violence.'

'We'll be all right. Look, they're all streaming out to reclaim their money.' The truth was, many of the audience had had complimentary tickets and were now on their way to see if they could make a profit by claiming they'd bought them.

An elderly man in the uniform of the theatre's footmen came to stand guard at their door. More, he had brought a bottle of brandy and glasses. A few sips steadied Paulette. Madame de Tramont shook her head and decided to display moral superiority. A long time went by.

'These things happen,' said the footman. 'If you'll excuse me, ladies, I think you're making too much of it. Some hitch – you know what it is in the theatre. It'll be all right tomorrow night.'

'But so suddenly – without prior warning?' Nicole said.

He shrugged burly shoulders and rumbled

in his throat about the government, something that she couldn't understand.

After half an hour Philippe returned, white and shaken. At first he seemed incapable of speech. 'Tell us, tell us, Philippe,' his mother begged.

Nicole, more practical, poured brandy and held it out.

He gulped some down. 'The play has been forbidden by the censor.'

Whatever they had expected, it wasn't this. 'By the censor?' Madame de Tramont echoed.

'Yes, exactly. By the censor.'

'Who is the censor?' Paulette whispered in her sister's ear.

Well might she ask. It was the proud claim of the Emperor-Consul that censorship no longer existed in France, and it was true to this extent – Louis-Napoleon had no direct powers to prevent anything being published or performed.

But an ingenious system of 'warnings' had been instituted. If a newspaper or journal 'offended', its owner received a warning. If he received three such warnings, publication of the periodical was discontinued on the grounds that it imperilled public safety.

Warnings were given by all sorts of officials, often out of a surplus of zeal but mostly after a direct hint from a cabinet minister.

In this year of 1853, by means of warnings and closures, Louis-Napoleon had reduced the number of political daily newspapers from nearly fifty to fourteen. Concerts at which political speeches or songs were given were few, unless it was known the songs and speeches would praise the government. The witty sketches that used to give zest to music-hall and *bal-musette* were watered down.

But none of that explained how Philippe's play came to be banned.

'How can a play about a Syrian princess of two thousand years ago be in any way political?' Nicole asked in wonder.

'They say much of the dialogue reflects badly on the marriage of Louis-Napoleon to Eugenie.'

'What?'

They all sat and stared at him. It was impossible to see what relevance the mishaps of the Syrian Berenice could have to do with the marriage of a red-haired Spanish countess.

'But that's ludicrous!' Clothilde cried.

'I agree. But the censor does not.'

'But surely Verilat argued—'

'Verilat says he spent two hours arguing with the local prefect, who told him in no uncertain terms that the orders came almost direct from the palace. It seems the Emperor-Consul is very vexed with my play.'

'But how did he ever come to read it?'

'I'm not sure that he has read it. He's been told of some of the things it contains, apparently. He seems to have taken exception to a theme that's repeated several times – that monarchs have responsibilities which they must remember even when in love.'

'But how does that pose any threat to Louis-Napoleon?'

'As far as I could gather, he thinks it's a reflection on the speed with which he chose and married Eugenie.'

It was true that France had been rather taken by surprise over the marriage. The Emperor had made offers for two other princesses but had been unsuccessful. The Countess de Montijo was a lady of Parisian society, well-known and well-thought-of and beautiful – but she was a great deal less important than a princess from a foreign royal house. What made it all the more extraordinary was that the engagement was announced on the 23rd January and the wedding took place on the 30th – scarcely the royal event that the Parisians had been looking forward to.

Philippe had no views at all about the Emperor's marriage. He took almost no interest in Louis-Napoleon but if he had been pressed, he'd have said he had to respect the man who had been chosen overwhelmingly by the people of France in a plebiscite. Philippe was a secret democrat, a fact which he took care to hide from his royalist mother. But democrat or royalist, his views weren't strong enough to lead him to make political statements in his plays.

'You must see the prefect yourself,' Clothilde declared. 'You must explain to him—'

'Mama, what is the use of that? The play has been banned, there can be no performance tonight, and the only way it can be given permission is if I re-write extensive passages.'

'Couldn't you do that, then?' inquired Paulette in all innocence.

'Re-write…?' Philippe looked at her. 'It would take me another year.'

'Oh.'

'Besides, if it were ever presented now, it would be the play that was banned by Louis-Napoleon. People would come to see it to detect the places where it had to be re-written.'

'Darling, don't think any more about that now,' Nicole begged. 'You're too close to it at the moment. Let's go home.'

Grimly Philippe allowed himself to be ushered out. A cab was waiting. They dropped Paulette at her hotel before going to Clothilde's apartment. There she began a lecture of instruction on whom to contact to have the decision reversed.

'I will see Monsieur Contineau tomorrow. I will tell him a great blunder has been made–'

'Oh, fine. Tell him the Emperor has made a mistake.'

'But it is so! Of course, one could expect nothing else from a member of that upstart family. The Napoleons never had any breeding or discrimination–'

'Madame, please don't let's talk about it any more tonight,' Nicole urged, seeing the thunder clouds building up on her husband's brow.

'But we must plan a campaign. The toadies of this fool of an emperor can't be allowed to insult a de Tramont–'

'Mama, will you for God's sake be quiet!' shouted Philippe.

She stared at him. He had never in his life spoken to her in that manner. 'Philippe!'

'Madame, please – let's all just try to be–'

'Nicole, I don't need instructions from you on how to handle my own son! I understand of course that this has been a great disappointment but we can make our protest tomorrow, and even if we cannot have the ban lifted, we can at least have an apology–'

'Damn it, I don't want an apology! I want a performance! Don't you understand that I don't care about the politics and the prestige – I wanted to see my play come to life...'

His voice died away. He went suddenly to the bedroom, returning with his cloak, hat and cane.

'Philippe, where are you going?' Nicole cried.

'Home. Home to Calmady to find some peace and quiet!'

'At this hour of night? It's past midnight–'

'All the better. I shall be alone.'

'But how can you travel–'

'I'm going on the railway.'

'Philippe – wait – I'm coming with you–'

'No, Nicole.'

'Please, darling. Let me come with you. I promise not to say a word. Just let me be with you.'

He stood in the vestibule, hand on the doorknob. For a moment she was afraid he would refuse. Then he shrugged and walked out.

Clothilde's maid, having overheard everything, came hurrying with Nicole's wrap. She grabbed it and ran out, calling over her shoulder to Clothilde: 'Please, madame, look after my sister, she doesn't know Paris at all.'

The concierge had already hailed a hansom when she got downstairs. Philippe climbed in without looking back for her. It was the concierge who helped her in. The journey to the station was accomplished in silence. There, an eager porter hurried to get tickets for Philippe and to conduct them to a first class compartment.

Nicole had never travelled by train. If she hadn't been so concerned for Philippe she might have been frightened by the snorting monster at the end of the platform, by the clouds of steam that made everything look mysterious and slightly menacing, by the muted lights, the shouts of porters placing morning papers on board.

All through the rail journey Philippe sat in a corner with his eyes directed towards the window. The blind had been down when they boarded but he had had the porter raise it. There was nothing to see outside for the first hour or so: the countryside was impenetrably dark.

Later, streaks of light appeared in the sky, clouds like long ostrich plumes could be seen against an oyster grey layer – rain clouds and mild weather, coming from the south west. Automatically Nicole noted it. Weather was so important in the champagne business.

Husband and wife sat side by side, unspeaking. Somewhere about four o'clock Nicole dared to put a hand over Philippe's. His fist clenched, but he didn't interlace his fingers with hers. He refused comfort or sympathy. She understood.

The train pulled in to Epernay. It was a town Nicole didn't know well. In other circumstances she would have been glad to stay an hour or two, to see the great houses of the wine merchants, great villas which lined a great street and were famous.

But Philippe walked straight out to the courtyard, to the post-chaise office.

'Where to, sir?'

'Calmady.'

'Post only as far as Chalons along the river route, m'sieu. Will your own carriage be waiting there?'

'No, it will not. I wish to go to Calmady in the chaise.'

'That will be twenty francs extra, m'sieu–'

'For God's sake bring the horses round and let's get on the way!'

'Yes, m'sieu, certainly, m'sieu.' The clerk gave Nicole a glance of sympathy, as if to say, 'Your husband's in a bad temper, eh?', but she turned away, taking Philippe's arm.

Within ten minutes the horses had been put in the shafts, the postilion had wakened himself up by putting his head under the pump, and they were off.

On the fast road they changed horses twice. At Chalons, the postilion made a great fuss of choosing good horses – for the difficult country road ahead, he wanted them to know. It was in hopes of a good tip at the end of the journey.

But Philippe scarcely noticed. He leaned out as they took the turning for Calmady, knocking on the side of the carriage with his cane to attract the man's attention. 'Can't you go any faster?'

'Ha! If you want to go fast you should get the railway to run a line out here for you, sir!'

It was a bumpy ride. Nicole had to hold fast to the leather and tapestry safety strap on her side of the carriage. But she scarcely noticed the jolting. She was watching Philippe, hoping for some word or smile now that they were nearly home.

As they rattled through the gateway on to the gravel of the drive, the estate was already alive and at work. Nicole saw heads raised from vine rows as they went past. A soft rain was falling.

The housekeeper saw them from the window of the drawingroom where she was supervising the re-hanging of the curtains, having had them cleaned according to orders during their absence. She ran down to the hall to throw open the door.

'Pay the postilion,' said Philippe, and stalked past her.

'Monsieur Philippe!' gasped she, astounded at his manner. He had never treated her impolitely in his life before.

He went upstairs to the study. He had thrown himself into a chair by the time

Nicole reached it. 'Darling, don't you think you ought to go to bed after a journey like–'

'Leave me alone.'

She shivered at his tone, and withdrew. The housekeeper was hovering in the passage. 'Is he ill, madame?'

'No, it's something else. Go down to the kitchen, have some fresh coffee made and some croissants – bring it up to me.'

'Nothing for m'sieu?'

'It is for him. But bring it to me. Don't go in with it yourself.'

'Oh … yes, madame.'

Nicole hurried to their bedroom. There her maid was waiting. She was helped out of her finery and into a wrapper. She washed, and had her hair brushed. At that point the tray was brought to her. She took it and went to the study, trailed by the housekeeper who was all but wringing her hands.

'Please go away. This is difficult enough without an audience.' Without waiting for her reply, Nicole opened the study door and went in.

Philippe was sitting in the chair by his writing table, head thrown back, eyes closed. But he wasn't asleep. He looked round as she came in.

'I don't want that,' he said.

'Please, sweetheart, you've had nothing since last night–'

'I don't want it.'

Nicole nodded. Then she said in a very low voice: 'You won't mind if I just stay here with you while I eat?'

'Please yourself.'

She sat by a little table loaded with books on which she balanced the tray. She poured coffee. Its strong, invigorating smell filled the room. She sipped, set down her cup, sipped again.

'Won't you have at least a cup of coffee, Philippe? It will refresh you.'

He hesitated. She could see he was dying of thirst and tempted by the aroma of the fresh coffee. She poured some, added sugar just as he liked it, and brought it to him.

There was a moment when she feared he was going to knock it out of her hand. But he took it, sighed, and drank it off almost as if it was a poison draught to end his life.

'Why don't you bathe and change into day clothes, Philippe? Then we could … go out for a stroll.'

Perhaps it was the right moment. He had been encased in the rigid high collar of his evening shirt for over twelve hours. He nodded. She pulled the bell for his valet and went out, saying with great casualness: 'See you downstairs in about half an hour.'

It was clear that everyone knew something had happened. Heads turned as they went out, conversations ceased abruptly as they approached.

Jean-Baptiste Labaud was standing in one of the yards supervising the movement of a cart with casks aboard. He turned to greet them. Philippe walked on without a word but Nicole paused.

'We didn't expect you back so soon, madam?'

'No. Well, things went badly in Paris. How are things here?'

'Going badly, madame,' he sighed. 'We're losing an awful lot of bottles in the second fermentation.'

'Oh, dear God... How much, Jean-Baptiste?'

He shrugged. 'We shan't know for a week or two but it looks as if it might amount to more than half.'

'More than half!'

'Well, then, madame... It's how things go. Last year we did well, lost almost nothing.'

'But we didn't have the demand for our champagne that we have now. If we lose so much, how will we fill the orders?'

'That's in the hands of God, madame.' As far as he was concerned, that was that. The processes of champagne-making were chancy. Man might do all he could to control them but nature, God, Fate – some other force took over at certain times. All one could do was live with it.

'It's this mild weather, I suppose.'

'The temperature has gone up over eight

degrees since you left for Paris – and still rising.'

'And you've done all you can to keep the cellars cool?'

'Of course.' The cellars were always cool – those who worked in them would have said they were downright cold. Yet the wine, sensitive as an opera-star, sensed the variations. And it protested at too much 'warmth' by fermenting too strongly, bursting the fragile glass of the bottles and pouring away in a rich, frothing stream into the gulleys in the floors.

Nicole moved towards the cellar steps, pulling closer to her neck the soft lawn shawl she was wearing in preparation for the chill that would strike as she descended. She had almost forgotten Philippe. He, still pre-occupied, was striking aimlessly at a frond of fern with his cane.

'Come and look at the wine, Philippe,' she called. 'There's a problem.'

He followed without demur. He had nothing else to do. No matter where he went, his thoughts were always back in Paris, picturing the moment when Verilat stepped in front of the curtain to destroy the one ambition of his life.

In the cellar the wine of last autumn was stacked in shining heaps of bottles to go through the second fermentation. Even as Nicole was coming down the steps she could hear the bang of a bottle exploding, the faint sizz of effervescing wine going free.

Men in oiled-silk aprons were moving about the stacks of bottles, placing basins of icy water at strategic points. Their clogs were wet with wasted wine. Fragments of dark brown glass lay everywhere.

Nicole picked up a basket-work protector for her face. Shards of glass travelled with the speed of a bullet and could do great harm to unprotected flesh. Many a champagne-worker had lost an eye as a result of accidents with the second fermentation.

Jean-Baptiste had come down behind them. 'From the way the wind's set,' he remarked, 'it looks like we'll have two more days of this.'

'How are other people getting on? Could we buy in enough champagne to blend a decent vintage?'

'So far, I hear there's been a lot of trouble. At Ambonnay they took dire measures and they've chilled the wine out of "working".'

'This is bad, Jean-Baptiste.' She turned the basket-work visor in her hands.

'You don't need to tell–'

His words were cut off by the sound of three or four explosions like pistol shots. A fountain of champagne went shooting out across the floor from a pile nearby. Philippe, his trouser legs soaked in the wine, gave a cry of fury.

'Everything is broken, everything's in a mess! Good God, is it a conspiracy? Go on, break – damn you, break!' He flailed at the pile of bottles with his cane. 'Break, why don't you break? Ruin us completely, break, break, curse you!'

Nicole rushed to catch his arm. The thought of losing even one bottle due to the crashing blows of that cane was anathema.

Just as she reached him, the heap of bottles on the edge of the aisle on her side exploded. Ten out of twelve bottles on the top row broke asunder.

'Madame!' shouted Jean-Baptiste, leaping to protect her.

Too late.

The flying glass had nowhere else to go but out towards the aisle. It embedded itself in Nicole's head and shoulders like knives.

She screamed in agony. The pain was unbearable. She felt the blood gushing out over her cheeks, over her neck, and lost consciousness.

Chapter Eight

Philippe de Tramont couldn't believe it was happening. He threw himself on his knees beside his wife, to gather her into his arms.

'No, Monsieur Philippe, don't!' cried Jean-Baptiste, grabbing his shoulder. 'Don't touch her–'

'But I must–'

'There's glass embedded – every movement drives it further in–'

'Oh, my God!' He drew back. Jean-Baptiste knelt beside him, gently gathering together the gauze shawl from Nicole's shoulders to drape it over her face.

'No!' cried Philippe in horror. 'She's not dead–!'

'It's to protect, sir, that's all. And to staunch the blood. Everybody – when I say lift, we pick her up.'

The other men had come rushing to help. The youngest portering boy had already gone scuttling up the cellar steps to run to the house, borrow a horse, and ride bareback for the doctor.

To Philippe's grief-crazed mind, it was like a funeral party slowly mounting the staircase – six men as if they were carrying a

173

coffin. But they knew what they were about. They had seen other accidents in the vaults, they knew how much care was needed.

At the door to the house they relinquished the body to Philippe and Jean-Baptiste. With infinite gentleness they carried her up to the bedroom, where they laid her on the canopied bed. Her maid, white-faced and shuddering at the bloodstained gauze, had already whipped off the tapestry cover.

Dr Jussot had spent all his adult life in Champagne. He had arrived as a young surgeon with his degree in medicine. Then the workers of the district had taught him what they had learned over the years, about the treatment of the injuries they could receive in the course of their labours.

The first thing was to irrigate the many cuts to ensure that all the glass was removed. This wasn't easy, as some of the fragments were like grains of sand. Indeed, many a man of the area had scars in which tiny grains were embedded in the skin. In time, the little fragments might work their way out but if not, they remained, in the weal of skin which could not soften and disappear.

Dr Jussot was used to dealing with the distracted relatives of injured men. Generally it was a wife, in despair that her man might die or be crippled and unable to earn the bread for himself and his family. It was the first time he had had to soothe and re-assure a rich young man that his pretty young wife would live.

'None of the glass reached any vital organ, thank God. She has many cuts in the scalp, shoulders, neck and face – we were lucky indeed that the great artery of the neck wasn't severed.'

'She'll be all right?' begged Philippe.

'Well, it will take time, of course. And you must understand that when she is conscious she'll be in great pain. So I leave with you an opiate, which must be administered every four hours, to give her plenty of rest so that she has the strength for the healing process.'

'All the cuts will heal? She'll have no scars?'

'Hm … I … er… We shall have to wait and see, Monsieur de Tramont.'

'Oh, God,' Philippe groaned.

Jean-Baptiste had waited in the hall until the surgeon finished his first examination. Satisfied that Nicole wasn't going to die, he'd gone back to his work. But later, after the long process of dressing the wounds had been done, he returned to inquire. He met Dr Jussot coming out of the front door.

'Well, then, doctor? What's your opinion?'

'She's young and strong – she'll survive, although the shock has been tremendous.'

'Yes, yes, I know that. I'm talking about that piece of glass that went in by her temple.'

'Ah. You saw that, did you, Labaud?'

'Is she going to lose her sight?'

Dr Jussot stroked his moustache. He knew Labaud of old. No use trying to put him off. One could give soothing-syrup to the young milord, who had probably never seen a wine-cellar accident in his life before, but Labaud was different.

'We'll hope for the best, Labaud. The gash is certainly deep, but the bone seems to be only slightly parted and as far as I can see protected the eye. No bone fragments went into it nor, one hopes, any shreds of glass. But we can only know that for certain when she recovers full consciousness and tell us whether she can see properly or not.'

'That young idiot,' snorted Labaud.

'Who? Madame? Oh, come, Labaud. She's been about in the cellars all her life–'

'I meant that husband of hers. Hitting the bottles with his cane! All right, he'd had a big disappointment the night before, but that's no reason for donkey nonsense in the cellars. You know how touchy the wine is–'

'Come, come, Labaud. You can't expect a man of Monsieur Philippe's station to understand about the wine. Hitting the bottles with his cane?' repeated Jussot, having just understood what Labaud said. 'Why on earth was he doing that?'

'That's a good question.' Jean-Baptiste frowned, his dark, sallow face fierce with resentment. 'It's all his fault!'

'Are you saying he caused the explosion in which she was hurt?'

'No, but he was striking at a pile with his stick and she came running to stop him. And the pile she was passing just went up...'

'Now, there – you see – it was an accident. He couldn't possibly have known that would happen.'

'He should have known better than to behave like that in the cellars. People's *lives* depend on good safety precautions in the cellars.'

'Yes, yes... I well remember hearing the famous Monsieur Dumas say, on a visit to the wine vaults at Rheims, that it was wise to have his famous iron mask when among the champagne bottles.'

'Well then...' Labaud was thinking ahead. 'Are you coming back today?'

'This evening. I'll drop by your house to let you know how she is, Labaud.' As he mounted his horse and rode off, the doctor was musing that Labaud seemed more concerned about the lady than was strictly proper in an employee. Ah, well... A pretty girl, Madame de Tramont.

Yes, pretty ... until now. Who could tell how she would look when the wounds healed?

Clothilde de Tramont received the news next day by special post messenger.

177

Horrified, she set out at once for Calmady. She was surprised at how much concern she felt. The poor child – so pretty and lively. But then, she shouldn't have concerned herself so closely with the wine trade. If she had been more lady-like, she wouldn't have been in the cellars in the first place.

When Clothilde was shown in to the bedroom, Nicole was asleep, under the influence of the laudanum drops left by Dr Jussot. Her mother-in-law crept close, moving quietly so as not to rouse her. She stood by the bed gazing down, pity and anxiety rising in her at the sight of the bandaged head and shoulders.

Then she gave a startled exclamation. 'Good God! What is that?'

'What, madame?' cried Lucie, Nicole's maid, who was acting nurse.

'That grey stuff – peeping out between the bandages!'

'That, madame? Why, it's cobweb.'

'Cobweb?'

'Why, yes, madame.' Lucie was a local girl, well accustomed to the traditions of the wine district. 'It helps the blood to clean itself.'

'Cobweb? Cobweb cleans the blood? Are you mad?'

Her raised voice caused Nicole to stir in her sleep. 'Shh, madame,' warned Lucie.

Clothilde glared at her. She would *not* be

shushed by a maidservant. 'At whose instructions was this disgusting stuff put on my daughter-in-law's wounds?'

'Dr Jussot's, of course, madame.'

'Preposterous!' cried Clothilde, and stormed out.

Philippe, waiting out on the landing, had heard her exclamations. He had half-opened the door to inquire the trouble, and was almost brushed backwards by her eruption from the room.

'Who is this Dr Jussot?' his mother demanded.

'The local doctor, Mama—'

'You have a local man dealing with your wife? What are you thinking of, Philippe? You will send at once for a proper doctor! I never heard the like – some village bungler dealing with the injuries of my daughter-in-law. Philippe, who knows what harm may already have been done? I am ashamed of you – this isn't the care I expect you to take of your wife!'

Philippe, sleepless for three days now and hollow-eyed with fatigue and grief, was in no state to argue. 'I'll see to it at once, Mama—'

'And meanwhile I will take proper steps to look after her. Girl!'

Lucie hurried out of the sickroom.

'Go at once, fetch me a bowl of warm water and some towels. I must get rid of that dirty mess that's been plastered on the poor girl's wounds.'

Lucie did as she was told. The house-keeper was the only person who dared to argue. 'Do you think you should, madame? Dr Jussot is very experienced–'

'Dr Jussot is obviously a fool and an ignoramus! Cobweb? Which has been hanging in dirty cellars–'

'Excuse me, madame, the cobweb is from the wine vaults – and they are very clean, you know–'

'I think I know best about such things,' Clothilde cut in in a tone that brooked no further argument.

Philippe had gone downstairs. To his valet he said, 'Order the curricle out, and fetch my driving coat–'

'You're going out, m'sieu?' Jacquot was surprised. Since the accident, his master had stayed within ten yards of the mistress, even if often it meant sitting outside the door of the sickroom.

'I'm going to Paris, to fetch a proper doctor.'

'I see, m'sieu. Shouldn't you wait until the morning? The light's going and there's rain coming–'

'Do as I tell you!' To tell the truth, Philippe was glad of the excuse to be doing something. Three days of guilt and self-reproach had worn him down to the point

180

where he could scarcely bear to draw breath.

He knew it was his fault that Nicole had been hurt. If he hadn't been acting the fool in the wine vaults, it could never have happened. True, that pile of bottles might still have exploded, but ten to one Nicole would have been nowhere near them. It was because she was rushing across to stop him that she had been in the line of the out-rushing glass.

Dr Jussot had been gentle and soothing, yet Philippe had a feeling he wasn't being told everything. And it was so awful, not being able to speak to Nicole. She was always under sedation. Of course, that was best, otherwise the pain would be unbearable. But just to have been able to exchange a word – to hear her say, 'I forgive you, Philippe...'

The curricle was ready at the front door within ten minutes. His mother, busy upstairs unwrapping the bandages on her unconscious daughter-in-law, heard the carriage drive off. 'What is that?' she said to Lucie.

'I don't know, madame.' Lucie went to the window. In the fading evening light she saw the curricle going down the drive at a fast pace. 'It's Monsieur Philippe, madame – driving off in his fast carriage.'

'Ah, I understand – he has presumably

181

decided to go to Rheims to send a telegraphic message for a doctor.' Clothilde nodded in satisfaction.

She had not given a thought to Philippe's exhaustion. Surprisingly, all her attention had been centred on Nicole. She had scarcely taken in the whiteness of her son's face, the trembling of his hands.

Philippe knew he was in no fit state to handle two lively thoroughbreds. He should have sent one of the servants with a letter to go by express postchaise. Yet it was such a boon to be doing something, to feel he was contributing something to Nicole's recovery. Even the coolness of the evening air was helpful: for three days he had never left the house.

He turned on to the country road as the rain, promising all day, began to fall; large, heavy drops, precursors of a thunderstorm. The clouds had been piling up for hours, the atmosphere had been heavy with impending thunder. He urged the horses forward, not wanting to have to stop and put up the hood. The rain began to lash into his face. He wiped it away with his sleeve, twisting the reins round one wrist to do so.

The horses, brought out from a quiet stall into this sudden downpour, were edgy and had to be held close in hand. But it was the road itself that caused the accident.

The dreadful surface had had no attention for the whole winter. Its ruts and stones averted the wheels from their proper direction. As the horses surged forward in answer to the touch of Philippe's whip, the offside wheel skipped and skimmed against a long rut of heavy clay that was beginning to disintegrate in the rain.

The wheel ceased to turn momentarily. The nearside wheel took all the strain, cracked, hit a stone, and buckled. The horses, feeling the sudden drag at the nearside, pulled harder to correct it. Philippe felt only the extra tug on the reins, drew in hard. The nearside horse reared, and the curricle – always an unsteady vehicle on its two slender wheels – went over.

Philippe felt himself go over in a great arc. It seemed to be happening slowly, as if he was flying. His hat went one way, he another. He hit the ground with his left shoulder, heard a bone snap.

All might yet have been well. But the curricle came down on top of him. The horses, still held by the reins he had twisted round his wrists, leaped and plunged to escape its falling weight on their haunches. They hauled forward. With them went the curricle and, entangled in its side spring, Philipe de Tramont.

There was one moment as he was dragged

along that he knew he was going to die. He said half-aloud: 'Nicole ... Nicole!'

After that came everlasting darkness.

Chapter Nine

Nicole vaguely understood that she was very ill, because once when she returned to consciousness she saw her mother sitting by the bedside, weeping quietly. She knew that her mother would have to be helped or carried up the long staircase to her bedroom, and no one would bother over a thing like that without good reason...

Another time, Paulette was there. She was attempting to brush those locks of hair that were to be seen among the bandages. Nicole tried to say her name. But all that came out was a vague sound, which Paulette took to be a protest. She gave up her brushing, but sat down, taking her sister's hand in both of hers.

'Oh, Nicci darling...'

Nicole tried to say: 'Where's Philippe?' but only a sigh emerged. She fell asleep again.

Dr Jussot was surprisingly pleased when Paulette reported this episode. 'It means she is improving, thank God. I began to be alarmed, you know. Eight days in a fever... It's very weakening.'

The events of the past eight days had been so strange that he could hardly understand whether he had been lucky or unlucky. He had arrived at the house for his daily visit on the Tuesday morning, to find that Madame de Tramont had come from Paris the previous afternoon. She had taken it upon herself to interfere with the dressings on the wounds, with the result that blood poisoning had set in overnight.

When he expressed alarm Madame had brushed it away. 'Naturally she has a slight temperature–'

'It's not slight. It's higher than it ever has been hitherto – and let me tell you, in case you didn't know it, madame, that in such cases the temperature is lower during the night. We shall see it climb during the day, I fear.'

'Nonsense,' she responded. She was sure he was a silly country bumpkin.

But he was proved right. By midday Nicole was in a bath of sweat. But by midday that didn't matter to Madame de Tramont, for her son's broken body was brought home at that hour.

He had been found in a tangle of wreckage by a passing waggoner around dawn. As bad luck would have it, the driver didn't know the de Tramont curricle nor its owner. He examined the young man, realised he was dead, and travelled on to the next village where he reported the death. Unfortunately he was travelling away from Calmady, not towards it.

By the time a team of men had reached the scene of the accident and lifted the body on to a decently covered flatbed cart, it was mid-morning. The mayor of Calmady was sent for, to accompany the cortege to the manor house. No one thought of sending a messenger ahead to warn the family. They knew Nicole was very ill but were unaware that Madame de Tramont had come from Paris during the previous day.

The shock to Clothilde was overwhelming. Before anyone could prevent her she turned back the canvas which covered her son. She gave a great cry and fell to the ground.

Dr Jussot was still in the house. He rushed to her assistance, had her carried up to her bedroom, administered hartshorn and arnica, told Lucie to apply cold compresses to her forehead, and when she came round, at once gave her a bromide.

Clothilde was in a state of shock and hysteria for two days. There was no doubt in Jussot's mind that those two days saved Nicole's life. Had her mother-in-law continued to interfere in her treatment, the fever would have raged on and the blood-poisoning would have killed her.

But those two days allowed Jussot to take the steps he knew must be taken. There was no 'remedy' for the illness: recovery depended on helping the patient to fight back. He had to bring her temperature down, try to cure the infection that had entered somehow when Madame took off the dressings, and cool the wound.

This he did with wet mosses made known to him by the country people over the years, and with cloths continually wrung out in icy water mixed with aqua fortis and sugar of lead. It was a treatment that needed continuous attention, and here the unassuming elder sister Paulette proved a tower of strength.

Paulette had been whisked back to Calmady from Paris by Madame de Tramont but it had been made plain to her that she must content herself with playing with the children and supervising the house. Madame was going to take over the care of Nicole. Paulette was allowed to visit for ten minutes on the day of her arrival, but it had been implied she must stay out of the way of the great doctor who was coming from Paris.

The great doctor never arrived. No more was said of that. And Paulette stayed in the sickroom from morning to night, her hands becoming raw with the continual wringing out of cloths in the water laced with ice from the ice-house.

Her sister was in a delirium very often. But then the temperature would dramatically fall, there would be moments of natural sleep. 'Good, good,' said Dr Jussot, rubbing his hands. 'She's winning the fight.'

It was on the following day that Nicole tried to speak. Jussot knew his fight was almost over. 'Tonight her temperature will go down as usual. But I believe tomorrow morning it will not go up again.'

'Do you really think so, doctor?'

'I've seen cases like this before. I think the fight is almost over.'

He was proved right. But then came the problem – what was to be told to the young widow?

'She mustn't know,' Paulette insisted. 'You don't understand, doctor – she'll give up trying to live if she hears Philippe is dead.'

'Then we must prevent her mother-in-law from seeing her for a day or two, because she'll blurt it out at once.'

Paulette nodded. She pitied Clothilde in her loss but she was growing impatient with the extravagance of grief that the older woman showed. It was she, Paulette, who had arranged the funeral – Clothilde had been quite unable to consider the question. That being so, Philippe had had a simple village burial, the workers of the estate filing behind the bier and strewing the grave with vine leaves as a last salute. The gentry who attended had shrugged: no black ostrich plumes, no black and silver harness on the horses... Well, poor Madame de Tramont,

189

she'd scarcely seemed to know where she was or what she was doing at the church.

Now Clothilde kept to her room. It was quite easy to keep her unaware of Nicole's improvement for a few days.

Eleven days after the death of her husband, Nicole de Tramont lay in bed supported by a mound of lace-trimmed pillows and said in a hoarse whisper: 'Why hasn't Philippe been to see me?'

'Nicci, darling, you've been so very ill…'

'I know that…' There was a long pause while she gathered strength for the next question. 'Why are you in black, Paulette?'

Paulette's hand flew to her mouth. It hadn't occurred to her that her sister would be so quick to notice her clothes. Everyone in the house was in black, of course – it would have been an affront to Madame de Tramont otherwise.

The two sisters looked at one another. Nicole lay on her pillows, her face almost as white as the fine linen. Tears began to trickle down Paulette's cheeks. Nicole watched their progress. Her mind, clogged as if by fog, was slowly working.

'Has … something happened … to Philippe?'

'Dearest, never mind about that now–'

'Tell me, Paulie.'

At the old childish nickname, Paulette broke into a great sob that wouldn't be

190

stifled. 'Oh, Nicole, Nicole,' she cried, and buried her head in the sheets that lay across her sister's lap.

Nicole slowly raised her hand and rested it on her sister's black-trimmed lace cap. After a long moment she said, 'Don't cry, Paulie. Tell me.'

'No, no...'

'Look at me, Paulie.'

Unwillingly Paulette raised her head.

'He's ... dead?'

Paulette took Nicole's hand and held it hard. 'He was killed in his curricle while he was going to fetch a special doctor, Nicci.'

'Ah...'

Silence flowed into the room. Paulette knelt by the bedside, holding her sister's hand, watching the white face, trying to guess what she was thinking. If she had cried out, fainted – that would have been easier to bear.

At long last Nicole said, 'I would like you to go, Paulette.'

'No, dear, you mustn't be alone–'

'I would like you to go. Just go... Outside the door...'

The habit of doing as she was told was strong in Paulette. She got to her feet and went out. She sat on the chair outside the door, the chair where Philippe had sat while he waited to be told whether his wife would recover from the accident for which he felt responsible.

For a time the silence was unbroken. Then Paulette heard weak, helpless sobs. She sat motionless. Her instinct was to rush in and take Nicole in her arms, but she had been told to go.

The surge of grief had given Nicole the energy to turn herself on her pillows. She buried her face in their soft surface to stifle the sound, and wept.

'Philippe … Philippe… My darling, my only darling, my love… Oh, Philippe, why were you taken and not me?'

The tears flowed long. Yet when they ceased, strangely, she fell at once into a deep, healing sleep from which she didn't rouse even when Paulette and Lucie changed the pillows under her head.

Later that day she was being fed bouillon from an invalid cup. She drew back her head and asked: 'How is Madame de Tramont?'

'She's … she's staying in her room, Nicci.'

'And the children – they're well?'

'Oh, fine, fine, Nicci – just fine.'

'Have you told Alys and Delphine…?'

The attempt at heartiness deserted Paulette. 'I tried, dear. But they're too young to understand.'

'Of course.' The meal was resumed. When the contents of the invalid cup were gone, Paulette wiped Nicole's mouth with the napkin then plumped up her pillows.

'How is Mama?' Nicole asked. 'She was here, wasn't she?'

'Yes, we brought her. We were afraid...'

'That I was going to die?'

'Never mind about that. Mama is rather poorly at the moment but she'll pick up – you know the warmer weather always helps.'

'Yes.' Nicole had as much to think about as she could cope with at present, in her hazy, weakened state. She drifted off to sleep again.

When she woke it was evening. Dr Jussot was by the beside. 'Ah, you're awake. How do you feel, madame?' He took her wrist, consulted his big pocket watch while he counted her pulse.

'I feel strange. Very light and ... not here.'

'That will pass. Now, since you have done so well today, I'm going to allow your daughters to come in for a peep at you. They've been very puzzled, not understanding why they can't see you.'

A great surge of longing overwhelmed Nicole. Tears slipped over the rims of her eyes.

'Now, now, if you're going to cry about it, we must put it off till another day.'

'No, no, doctor... Please...'

The children were brought in, in nightgowns and velvet slippers. They stood gravely by the bedside, afraid to move, for they had been warned they must be very

193

good. Delphine, too unsteady to stand upright by herself, clutched fiercely at Nanny's hand.

'Mama!' cried Alys in a sudden despairing shout, and rushed to throw herself against the carefully folded counterpane of the bed.

'There, there,' Nicole said, putting her hand on the child's curly head. 'Don't cry, Alys... Mama will be taking you for a walk again before very long.'

'But where have you *been?*' howled Alys. 'I wanted you!'

Delphine, infected by her sister's grief, began to cry in convulsive gasps. 'Mama ... Mama...!'

'You're being very bad,' scolded Nanny. 'You promised you would be good, Alys.'

'Be quiet,' Nicole said to her with un-expected authority. 'Now, children, please be quiet. I've something to tell you.'

She was summoning her strength to say that their father was dead. But when it came to the moment, she found she could not utter the words. Instead she said, 'You can come and see me tomorrow again. And because today is special ... you may have a marron glace divided between you before you go to bed.'

She lay back, exhausted. The little girls, comforted by her voice and the promise of sweets, were lifted up to kiss her.

When they had been ushered out, Jussot

said, 'You are tired now. You must settle down for the night.'

'Yes.' She submitted to having her pillows rearranged by Lucie and was closing her eyes when she remembered something important. 'One more thing, doctor.'

'Yes?'

'Will you ask my mother-in-law to visit me?'

Jussot pursed his lips. 'Ahh … Madame, I don't think you're strong enough for that.'

Nicole shook her head. 'It's Madame de Tramont I'm thinking of. I hear … she's shut herself up in her room…?'

'I'm afraid so. But that will pass.'

'The sooner the better… Ask her, doctor. Tell her I want to see her.'

'Very well.'

He was dubious about it, but carried out her request. Clothhilde stared at him from a gaunt face. 'No, I don't want to see her.'

'She asked especially madame. After all – it's nearly two weeks since you went near the sickroom.'

'I don't want to.'

'Very well. I'll tell her you refused.'

'No!'

'Well, what shall I say, madame?'

Clothilde didn't know how to answer him. She was sure she didn't want to venture out of her room, and especially not to visit Nicole in her bedroom, the room that had been the master bedroom of the house, the room of the husband and wife. It spoke to her of Philippe, as did his study with its untidy piles of books and papers.

'For the moment, I shall say nothing,' Jussot suggested. 'Young Madame de Tramont is asleep. Time enough to give her your decision in the morning.'

Next day Clothilde was still of the same mind. But by the following morning curiosity was beginning to grow. The housekeeper, who came every day for orders about household matters, reported that the young mistress was improving. She was sitting up today, had had some of the bandaging removed so that she looked more presentable. The children had been to see her again.

'And you? Have you seen her?'

'Of course, madame.'

'How does she look?'

'Pale, madame. Very thin. Many red scars where the glass went in. She says she doesn't see too well with one eye, but Dr Jussot says that is probably due to some tiny scar on the ... the ... some part of the eye. He says it will heal. We are so grateful to God she wasn't blinded.'

'Of course, we are grateful to God for that.' But we hate Him for taking away Philippe, Clothilde added inwardly.

All the rest of that day, she struggled

against the desire to see Nicole for herself. It was nothing to her what happened to her daughter-in-law. Nicole had only been important to her because Philippe loved her enough to marry her.

Yet some unsuspected affection must have taken root, for she began to worry a little about what her daughter-in-law's appearance would be like once the scars were all revealed. A pretty girl... Would she become displeasing to look at? If so, what a tragedy... It would have grieved Philippe to the heart.

It was a bright, sunny April evening when she sent word to the sickroom that she would like to visit the invalid if it was convenient. Paulette was reading to Nicole at that moment. She sprang up in terror. 'Madame is coming?'

'Good gracious, Paulie, don't take on so! She's only human, you know.'

'Are you sure?' Paulette inquired, only half joking.

She and Lucie flew about, making a tidy room even tidier. Wilted flowers were tweaked out of vases, a used water glass was spirited away.

Madame de Tramont came in with little of her usual imposing manner. She was dressed completely in black. She came to the bedside, leaned over, and kissed Nicole briefly on the forehead. Then she looked around for a chair which of course appeared as if by magic.

'How are you, child?' She studied her frankly as she spoke. She saw a fragile figure with her head artfully covered with a turban of gauze to hide shorn hair and bandages. Dressings were still attached to her shoulders and back by sticking plaster but these were largely concealed by a loose wrapper of lilac silk. On her face were many small cicatrices but these were already fading under the experienced attention of Jussot.

'I'm improving, madame. How are you?'

'I am as you see.'

'Yes.' Very sombre, very dramatic. 'Are you well in yourself?'

'Oh, my health is excellent.' Her tone implied, as if that matters.

'Have you seen the children? They've visited me every day since I took a turn for the better.'

Truth to tell, Clothilde had not. She had not asked to have them brought to her boudoir and until now had not thought of visiting them in the nursery. All at once that possibility became real. 'I'll go to see them tomorrow morning,' she said.

'I wish you would. My sister, you know, has been acting as substitute for me but she must go home soon. She had a letter yesterday from Auguste – I think it was full of reproaches for neglecting him so long. So she and Edmond will be leaving and the children will need someone to read to them and play with them.'

The idea of playing with her grandchildren had never occurred to Clothilde, and if Nicole were honest she didn't expect that. But her aim was to give her mother-in-law reasons for venturing out of the fastness of her room.

After that, the household returned to something more like normal. Paulette, weeping bitterly, took her leave two days later. Clothilde gradually began to move about the house and grounds as formerly.

Yet when she was sitting with Nicole one morning her real feelings burst out. 'I shall leave this place,' she said. 'I want to see it as little as possible! It all reminds me too much of…'

Nicole nodded. 'I understand. You have your apartment in Paris, of course–'

'Oh, that… That was so that I could pursue the matter of regaining the title. But what is the point of that now?' There was great bitterness in Clothilde's voice. Her life's work was now useless. Her only son had died, and there was no male heir. The title of Marquis de Tramont could never be revived.

'I think I may travel,' she went on. 'I believe it would do me good. But I suppose, before I go, I ought to give some thought to the future of the de Tramont business.'

'If you feel ready to discuss that, madame,' Nicole said, 'perhaps we should settle a few things.'

'Very well. I should like you to stay on here and bring up my son's two little girls. After all, it is the family home. But as to the wine-making, I have decided to sell out.'

'What?' gasped Nicole.

'My dear!' cried Clothilde. 'You have gone quite white! Have I startled you so much?'

'Sell Champagne Tramont?'

Clothilde nodded with vehemence. 'You know I have never really liked being in trade. It is unsuitable for the de Tramonts. As I have no interest in it, I have decided to sell.'

Nicole recovered her voice. 'Have you spoken to Monsieur Pourdume about this?'

'Naturally not. He had more delicacy than to approach me on such topics when I was in the first depths of my grief, and when he wrote to me in condolence he merely added that he was at my disposal to arrange any business matters in due course.'

Nicole was lying on a chaise longue in what had been Philippe's dressing-room. She was wearing a fine cotton peignoir with a ruffled collar. She drew it closer around her, as if she felt cold. She suddenly saw that she was about to engage in a great battle with her formidable mother-in-law.

'Madame, you can't sell Champagne Tramont.'

'I certainly can – and shall. I understand, of course, that you have interested yourself in the work. But as to money, you needn't fear – I shall make arrangements that part of the proceeds of the sale come to you–'

'Madame, you misunderstand me. I don't mean you can't sell because I would prefer you not to. I mean, you are not able to sell it.'

'I beg your pardon?'

'You can't sell Champagne Tramont. The firm cannot be changed or disposed of without my agreement.'

Clothilde's brow grew dark as thunder. In that moment she looked very like her son when he was in a bad temper, and Nicole's heart almost melted. Nevertheless, it was necessary to be on her guard against her own feelings. She was fighting for the business and the livelihood of all the people who took part in it.

'My dear child, I think you overestimate your importance. Of course you brought us the cellarage as your dowry, but that does not give you control–'

'I think you will find it does,' Nicole intervened gently. 'The settlement of the property was arranged so that it went directly to Philippe, as was only right since it was my dowry. At his death, it returns to me, as his widow.'

Clothilde de Tramont drew in a great breath. She had had a sudden revelation. Somehow she had taken it for granted that everything belonging to the de Tramont family had somehow returned to *her*, that at Philippe's death she as head of the family would be in control.

'What are you saying?' she gasped.

'I see you've never looked very closely at any of the papers shown to you by Monsieur Pourdume,' Nicole said, trying not to make it sound like a reproof. 'If you had, you would have realised that the cellars belonged to Philippe and not to the company. I asked for that especially, when our marriage settlement was being arranged.'

'But ... why?' Clothilde's mind was whirling. 'We agreed to the marriage so that the business could have the use of the chalkpits–'

'But I wanted them to go directly to Philippe.'

'It was a plot? You want to wrest control from me?'

'Oh, madame...' There was deep reproach in the words. In a broken voice Nicole went on, 'I wanted Philippe to be his own master. I wanted him to be able to say he was head of Champagne Tramont with truth. There was nothing underhand in it.'

There was a long silence while her

mother-in-law came to terms with it. Then she said, 'Does this mean *you* have a controlling interest in the firm?'

'I'm afraid so. Also, when we began to make substantial profits and as manager Philippe received a percentage, I urged him to invest it in various improvements, specially registered as his investment. I think you will find that Philippe owned more of the firm before he died than you originally inherited when the Marquis died.'

Clothilde got up. 'I can't discuss this. You have shocked me. I must have time to think about it.'

'Very well, madame. But take this one last thought – I don't want Champagne Tramont to go into different hands. It's something I began to build with Philippe, and for that reason I never want to part with it.'

'What do you mean? It seems you cannot be asked to part with it, but... There is something more personal in your words. Tell me what you mean.'

'I mean that the firm is mine and I intend to run it.'

'What?'

'I intend to go on making champagne, madame, here on the de Tramont estate.'

'Run the business? Yourself?'

'Yes.'

'A woman run a business? You must be mad!'

'Not at all, Madame. I know how to do it, and I intend to do it – with help from such people as Labaud and Compiain.'

'But … it's indecent! A young woman – a widow – engaging in business?'

'Yes, madame.'

'You can't do it!'

'I will do it,' Nicole said, sitting up from her reclining position and clenching her fists. 'I must do it!' Then, seeing Clothilde stare at her uncomprehendingly, she added, 'Don't you see? I have to do *something* with the rest of my life!'

The other woman moved uncertainly towards the door. There she turned to look back. She saw a girl, only twenty years old after all, thin and pale after a serious illness, widowed…

She saw embodied in her the instinct to live, to use life.

'Very well,' Clothilde said in a low voice. 'I understand and agree. We'll send for Pourdume to make the correct documents. But I shall never take part in the wine trade again. I leave it all to you, Nicole.'

'Thank you. That's all I ask, madame.'

'My dear child, you are taking on something too heavy for your young shoulders. Think again!'

'No, I know what I want to do.'

Shaking her head, Clothilde went out. She felt pity and compassion for her daughter-in-law, but she began to think she would never understand her.

Chapter Ten

Clothilde left Calmady a few days later. She felt scant regret: the village, with its grey houses and slate roofs, had always seemed dreary to her, even in the summer sun. The manor house had been a disappointment when she arrived as a young bride and though, with the money brought into the family by the increased profits, she had carried out some improvements, it was still far from the elegant chateau she had hoped for when she became the (aspiring) Marquise de Tramont.

How disappointing her life had been... Her husband dead too early, her daughter too, her son gone in a stupid accident... No wealthy marriage to shed lustre on the family, no glittering heiress to bear sons who could inherit the title... No, all that was gone for ever. There would never be a Marquis de Tramont now, for lack of a male heir.

Instead, a grasping little peasant girl was in possession of the estate and the wine firm. Well, since that was no doubt what she'd always wanted, let her enjoy it if she could!

Depression and bitterness were Clothilde's companions on her journey to London. There she hoped to revive friendships of her youth, to start again from an environment which had always been amiable.

But she found everything much changed. There wasn't the same romantic interest in the French emigrés. London society was intrigued by the new Emperor and his Empress – oh, especially by his Empress. Most of the questions to Clothilde were about the clothes of the Empress Eugenie, which was vexing, because Clothilde had taken care never to be at court. It would have been against her principles to curtsey to any monarch except a Bourbon.

When the first flush of interest about the new French Empress was over, Clothilde found to her amazement that she was being introduced as 'Madame de Tramont of the famous wine firm.' At first she protested. She was the widow of the Marquis de Tramont. But she found that no one cared about that. As a French aristocrat she was uninteresting. As part of a great champagne firm, she was much sought after.

'But, my dear Mary,' she protested to the friend with whom she was staying, 'I wish you would explain to your acquaintance that I have never taken any part in the wine-making. I know almost nothing of it.'

'But you know which are the fine vintages–'

'Indeed I do not. I left that kind of thing to my chief of cellar.'

'I find that strange,' said Mary Davenant with a frown. 'I have to take an interest in Edward's business. He insists upon it. And you know, the production of scientific instruments is not a very feminine topic. Wine at least is less forbidding than science.'

Clothilde could have said that there was a great deal of science involved in the making of wine, but refrained because if asked to describe the technical side of fermentation she would have been at a loss. Politeness forced her to pay attention to the dissertations of her host, Edward Davenant, when he held forth about the need to invent new apparatus for the burgeoning sciences. And politeness forced her to go along when he took his wife and children on an educational visit to a glassmaking firm.

Later, in a state of great excitement, she wrote about it to Nicole. 'The place was dirty, of course, but then factories always are, I believe. The owner had set aside a special area for the production of scientific glass, which has to be of a particular strength so as to hold the various substances. I believe the globes and flasks I saw were intended for the measurement of various gases, although how, I cannot tell.

'But the point, my dear daughter-in-law, is this. The glass being produced by Mr

Lotworth for Mr Davenant is of great strength. This was demonstrated to me when liquid was put into a strange container – I believe called a retort – and then a vapour was pumped through the liquid. The contents bubbled and seethed, and a gauge alongside registered the pressure. I cannot repeat to you what the figure was but I am almost certain it was as high as the pressure of our champagne.

'Nicole, it seems to me that the glass being made by Mr Lotworth would resist the fermentation process of our wine. Its strength has something to do with its ingredients and those I do not pretend to understand. But might it not be worth while to learn more about the glassmaking manufacture of England? Perhaps Mr Lotworth could supply bottles that would withstand the rigours of our wine-making.'

To say that Nicole was surprised by her mother-in-law's letter was an understatement. She had imagined Clothilde would never want to think or speak about wine again so long as she lived. But elsewhere in the long letter there were glimpses of the interest taken by the English in the house of Tramont. Always quick to sense the ins and outs of a situation, she understood that Clothilde enjoyed the reflected glory of the wine firm.

Certainly, the information about English

glassmaking was of prime importance. England had always been among the foremost in the manufacture of glass and the discovery of new processes. Threats and cajolery to the French glassmakers had had no effect – their glass was still too fragile for the wines of Champagne although they had strengthened it enough for the efficient bottling of still wines.

'What do you think, Jean-Baptiste?' Nicole asked her head cellarman, having read out to him the relevant pages of Madame de Tramont's letter.

'It astonishes me that she ever let herself be dragged to a factory,' Jean-Baptiste said with a sardonic grin. 'But, having got there, she seems to have taken a proper interest. And if the glass is strong enough for scientific purposes...'

'But it will be very expensive, Jean-Baptiste. And as for having bottles made in England, that's absurd. The cost of bringing them to Calmady would be enormous.'

'And no matter how strong, the breakage would be great. No, it's hardly possible.'

'If only one knew what the ingredients were,' mused Nicole. She rose from her chair and paced the office, formerly Philippe's but now her own.

It was November. Outside the weather was grim. Grey clouds pressed on the roof of the house, the trees were wreathed in mist. The assembling of the various categories of wine was in progress in the cellars, where the racking had ended. Soon would come the resting of the wine, when the intense cold of winter would take to the bottom of the vats the unwanted particles not removed by the racking. Yet enzymes in the yeasts, impervious to the bitter temperature, would begin the process of lowering the acidity of the still wine, the changing of the vintage that would make it unique to that year.

Soon would come the most difficult part of the art of making Champagne Tramont. She and Jean-Baptiste must choose which of the various wines were to make the blend of this year.

Sometimes in the lonely hours of the night, the thought of making these decisions would fill Nicole with dread. There was no way of formulating what would make a good champagne, no recipe to write down once and for always. The wines were living materials, changing even after they had been mixed. The taste of the champagne at this stage wasn't what the champagne-drinker experienced when he poured it from a bottle. The blender was looking ahead – two years, ten years. The wine he made today must be a fine wine, an even finer wine, after years had gone by.

Against the chill of the weather Nicole was wearing a gown of fine black merino and a cashmere shawl of black and white. Her lace cap, specially made for her by Paulette, had lappets of lawn and ruched ribbon which came down at the sides of her face. Her worst scars were at her temples and cheekbones; the layer of lawn and ribbon hid them. Above her lips still, there was a white line where a piece of glass had gone in. Another scar, growing faint, could be seen at the bridge of her nose. Dr Jussot had worked wonders with his old fashioned vineyard methods – better, perhaps, than any famous Paris surgeon whom Philippe might have brought.

Jean-Baptiste had come in just as he was when the summons came from the house. He was wearing working clothes – black serge trousers, loose blue smock, a black and white checkered kerchief round his neck to catch the sweat that dripped down when casks had to be manhandled. Although he was chief cellarman he liked to take part in the physical labour of the vaults just to show his staff that he himself could do everything he asked of them.

He waited for Nicole to resume the discussion. Madame was looking better, he thought. Still not herself – who could tell when that might come about? She was too thin, and from what he could learn from the household staff she only played with her food.

'I brought you a present, madame,' he said, taking a half-bottle from the capacious pocket of his blouson.

'What?' Nicole turned in surprise.

'Something for you to try. Dr Jussot tells me you're bored with our wine, although he wants you to drink it for the tonic properties.'

'Dr Jussot is a gossip,' she replied with a smiling shrug. 'Well, what is this, something from your own vines?'

'Oh, no, madame, I don't have time to bother with our vines except to make a simple house wine. No, this is from the Tramont cellars. It's a champagne.'

'But as you've just said, I'm bored with champagne. It's such a sweet wine–'

'Exactly, that's what I heard. You're tired of sweet wine. Well, try this with your supper, madame. It's a dry champagne.'

She raised her eyebrows. 'A dry champagne? That's a contradiction in terms.'

'So we have been brought up to believe. Yet if one thinks of it, the dosage of sugar can be kept to a minimum or even omitted–'

'But who would buy such a wine?' she interrupted, her mind flying at once to the practical point. 'The whole attraction of our wine here in Champagne is that it is sparkling, sweet–'

'A woman's wine, in fact.'

'Well, some people call it that. The wine of

213

the courtesan… But men buy it for their wives and sweethearts, and as we have seen, the Russians and the Swedes buy it for themselves, male and female…'

The half bottle was standing on the desk where Jean-Baptiste had put it. It was an 'undressed' bottle, no label, no coloured foil to make it pretty. The cork was held fast by a plain metal muzzle. She put a finger on the cork, tilted the bottle, and turned it on its axis. In the dreary light of the November day the wine in the dark brown glass had no sparkle or attraction.

Jean-Baptiste gave a grunt, half a laugh and half a protective sigh. 'It tastes better than it looks, I assure you, madame.'

'Jean-Baptiste…'

'Yes?'

She had been about to say, I wish you would not call me madame. All her life, until her marriage, Jean-Baptiste had called her Nicole or Nicci. Of course it was fitting that he should call her madame in front of other members of the estate, but in private…

Yet she refrained from uttering the words. It was a step towards something that she ought to be wary of.

'I will try your wine,' she said. 'This evening, with my dessert.'

'No, I beg… They tell me you only eat light dishes – fish or omelette…'

'And so?'

'Drink the wine with the main course, madame.'

'Really?' She gave the bottle another little turn with her finger. 'It's dry indeed, then! To be drunk with the meal? Whatever made you produce such a strange wine?'

He gave his characteristic shrug. 'Well then... Some years back... There was an English wine merchant, a Monsieur Burnes, he asked for champagne in its natural state – that's to say, un-sugared.'

'No one could supply him with such a thing!'

'Well, then, in fact, he got some, but...'

'Well?'

'It wasn't a success.'

'Remarkable,' said Nicole. 'You then set about producing a sample for yourself, so that you could understand how unsuccessful it was?'

'Ha, Nicole!' said Jean-Baptiste, surprised. 'No need to be sharp with me about it! I only made a little, and let me tell you... The longer it is kept, the better it tastes. This wine I bring you, it's five years old, and in my opinion it's ... it's ... well, it's nectar.'

For Jean-Baptiste to wax poetic, it must indeed be a delicious wine. Nicole was so intrigued by the situation that she failed to notice he had called her by her first name, almost as if some telepathic communication had taken place between them. 'I look forward to it, then,' she said. 'But I warn you, I don't expect to like it. And I certainly don't think you should waste time and materials on experiments with wine which has been proved uncommercial.'

'I don't think it's uncommercial,' Jean-Baptiste said in a stubborn tone. 'One day, you'll see… When taste has changed… This wine I've made, it's a grown-up drink! It's not for drinking with cream cakes, it's for drinking for itself…' He let the words die away. Madame was looking at him with some disapproval. 'Well then, try it for yourself. I'm not saying we should stop putting a dosage of sugar in the final bottle, all I'm saying is that there may be a place for a dry champagne one day.'

She inclined her head. 'And as to what Madame de Tramont says about the glass of England…?'

'It's worth inquiring into. We should send our London agent to take a look. Only…'

'What?'

'We don't want to commit ourselves. As you say, the costs of transporting English-made bottles to Calmady would be prohibitive.'

'What we want is to have the glassmakers of Argonne use the formula for this strong English glass.'

'Ah yes – but the formula is probably

guarded well. After all, why should this English maker give the secret to his competitors? And yet, you know, it's probably something simple – a little more iron oxide, a little less sand...'

Nicole had scant knowledge of the recipes for glass. She knew that the bottles for the champagne region had to be of a particularly strong make, and was resigned to the fact that they were of a rather dismal dark brown. She also knew, because it was part of local legend, that one of the big champagne houses had had a special batch of bottles made with glass which, in use, had released sulphuric acids, thus ruining an entire year's wine production.

She wondered, after she had dismissed Jean-Baptiste, whether it was worth while pursuing her mother-in-law's discovery. The risks in new glass were great. Yet to find really good, reliable bottle-glass would be such a blessing...

As she had promised, she had Jean-Baptiste's half-bottle iced and opened for her evening meal. At first it took her so much aback, it made her cough. Knowing that it was champagne in the glass, and expecting sweetness when she tasted it, she found her palate rejecting the brisk, piquant flavour.

Yet a moment later her brain was saying: You were bored with sweet champagne, here

217

is something to test your discrimination.

She held the glass to her nose to savour the bouquet. It was lively, almost teasing. Lingering in her mouth now, after that first sip, was a faint perfume – not flowers, not herbs – almost like fragrant leaves. She held the glass up to the light of the lamp from the dining-room ceiling. The colour was a pale tawny gold, absolutely clear except for the silvery bubbles rising to the surface where they made a frost on the yellow wine. She sipped again, carefully, holding the wine in her mouth to taste it through and through. It was mellow for all its vigour – a wine that aged yet stayed young. There was a velvety after-effect. Yet nothing was owed to any sugary sweetness – it was the wine itself, the juice of the grape perfectly handled so that it sparked in rich vivacity.

Now she understood why Jean-Baptiste had called it nectar. Even the sardonic, unimpressionable Jean-Baptiste needed special words to describe this drink. He had made it for himself, to test out a theory – but what he had produced was a masterpiece. She debated sending for him, to tell him how much she had enjoyed the champagne. But it was late, the day's work was over, he would be with his wife and children in his house in Calmady.

She drank the second glass of his wine with the fruit and cheese. It accompanied them perfectly. What was more, it made her light-headed, light-hearted. She rose from the table humming a little song to herself, the first time in months that she had felt carefree.

She read a bedtime story to Delphine and Alys who, as usual, refused to go to sleep until she had gone through this nightly routine. She found the words on the page slipping about a little. 'I'm drunk!' she thought.

Drunk with Jean-Baptiste's wine.

When she went to bed the weather had cleared. Pinpoint stars sparkled in the blue-black skies – a frost would follow. Good, that would break up the soil between the vine rows, which had been fertilised and then banked up to protect the sensitive graftings on the older stems. At this time of year a frost held for three days or so, and then would come a milder wind, the clouds would gather again and there would be rain or snow in December.

She had always been in the habit of sleeping with the shutters open so that she could see the sky. Tonight she watched the stars wheel overhead – Orion astride the blue-black canopy sprinkled with lesser stars.

She couldn't sleep. Her mind seemed full of a thousand things – the new wine that she had tasted, the information sent by her mother-in-law, Jean-Baptiste and his frown of concentration when she discussed it with him, the children's demands to be taken to watch the men set out on Sunday's boar-hunt, the preparation for the *cuvée* that must begin at once now that the year's wine was 'resting'…

At length, around midnight, she sat up and turned up the bedside lamp. She would read herself to sleep. The book, however, proved unhelpful. Her attention wandered continually to next day's work.

Should they use more of the Côte des Blancs in the blend this year? The red Pinot grapes had been particularly rich and strong in September: perhaps a bigger share of wine from white grapes would gentle the blend. But then Tramont Champagne was famous for its body and smoothness, not its lightness…

The difficulty of producing a consistent product, year in, year out, was one that few of the purchasers understood. It was hard enough when all you did was to harvest a grape crop and make a wine from those grapes and nothing else. But champagne, subtly blended from the produce of several vineyards, and with white grapes and red grapes to mingle, was a matter of the finest judgement.

Nicole didn't flatter herself that she knew all about it. But she had been taking part in the making of the wine since she was four years old when she first went with her mother to the vineyards at picking-time. She had heard the endless discussions, she had tasted the vintage as she grew older. By the time she was ten she knew a good still champagne when she sipped it. By the time she was thirteen she was helping in the work of bottling the wine on the de Tramont estate so, naturally, tasted the product at the party which always celebrated the end of bottling.

Since her marriage she had interested herself deeply in the actual blending. To her, that was the moment at which the name of the house was made or lost. It had immediately been clear to her that Jean-Baptiste was the most important factor. It was his genius, his instinct, his experience, which gave Tramont champagne its final glories. His was the decision: how much of the product to use to make vintage champagne, how much to allot to non-vintage, how much to put by for future years' blending.

She had been an apt pupil. Besides, as he told her, she had a natural ability. This was proved to her by the attention he paid to her comments. Jean-Baptiste wasn't the kind to suffer fools gladly – if he accepted her suggestions, it was because they were sound, not because she was the patronne.

She got up, pushed her feet into Morocco slippers, wrapped herself in her warm velvet dressing gown, and went to the window to look out. As she had thought, a frost had touched the countryside. Twigs glistened silver in the starlight, she could see the glint of thin ice on the puddles in the courtyard.

Across the court and along a paved alley stood the workrooms of the chief cellarman. Here Jean-Baptiste had an office where he kept the records of the vintages and the workaday accounts. It contained a desk and a hard chair, ledgers in rows, and a sofa on which he often spent the night at times of crisis such as bad weather in the vineyards or pressure at the bottling plant.

Beyond the office was the tasting room, with shelves for the samples of wine which he would use to make the blend, a long trestle table with an ample supply of glasses, and at the far end a small collection of scientific equipment – microscope, thermometers, gauges and measures.

It occurred to her to wonder whether there was an ample supply of Côte des Blancs among the samples. If not, she must have it brought in first thing in the morning. She decided to go now to make sure.

There was nothing unusual in her going out in the night to the cellars or the workrooms. Even when Philippe was alive she had often left him sleeping to spend some time on some project that interested her.

She draped her cashmere shawl around her head against the frosty air, picked up the keys from the bedside table, and tiptoed out. The great front door was always bolted at eleven, and the drawing back of the creaking bolts would have roused the servants. But there was always the little side door in the passage outside the owner's office.

The sharpness of the night made her draw in her breath with a gasp. She hastened across the wide courtyard to the paved path leading to the chief cellarman's kingdom, leaving footprints in the rime. Inside the office was warm, but the tasting room itself was cool, high-ceilinged and airy. She lit the lamp on its bracket above the equipment bench then from that lit a candle to hold it up to the sample shelves.

She might have known. Jean-Baptiste had ordered in at least a dozen samples of the wines from the Côte des Blancs. She knew from experience that there would be plenty more lying in dark brown bottles in the *cellier*, the ground level cellar where wines were kept which did not have to be left for long maturing.

On the laboratory bench there was a stoppered bottle and a page of notes. She held up the bottle to her candle to see if she could judge the state of the wine but the light was inadequate and the temporary container was of very thick glass. So she sat down and began to read Jean-Baptiste's notes.

The measures of the various ingredient wines were registered in the ruled columns. The alcohol content was calculated, the sugar content also. Various little arithmetical totals stood about on the page. At the foot Jean-Baptiste had written: 'As usual, first attempt – interesting but impossible!'

She smiled. She could almost hear him say it.

At that moment his voice came from behind her. 'Well then! I thought you were a burglar!'

She whirled about. 'Jean-Baptiste!'

He was in his good clothes and leather shoes. Clearly he had just come home from some gathering, perhaps in Epernay where there had been an annual dinner of vintners tonight.

'I didn't hear you come in?' she said.

'No indeed, since I thought you were a thief I came on tiptoe – and armed.' He showed her the mallet he had picked up from the tools hanging on the wall.

'Good gracious! But what would a thief find here, Jean-Baptiste?'

'Little enough, to be sure. But there are fools who imagine that if they break into the office of a chief cellarman they can find the recipe for making the champagne.'

She nodded towards the shelves. 'I see you've already prepared for what I thought might be a need – to counteract the strength of the Pinot.'

'Who knows? The Côte des Blancs seems to be rounder than usual too. It may be a problem to lighten the blend this year.'

'But you'll do it.'

'It's what I'm paid for.'

'Oh, Jean-Baptiste…' Somehow she was hurt. She didn't like to think their relationship was based only on money.

'What are you doing here, madame?' he inquired, disregarding the note of reproach. 'It's very cold–'

'Oh, you know I'm used to that. I just wanted to make sure everything was ready for tomorrow.'

'There was no need to come out in the middle of the night–'

'But I often do that, you know I do.'

There was concern in his regard of her. 'Surely Dr Jussot gave you something to help you to sleep?'

'Oh, that! I gave up taking that months ago. One can't go on, Jean-Baptiste, drugging oneself to sleep. And you know I've always been a light sleeper, always apt to get up and work on some task–'

He said abruptly, 'You should go back to

225

the house. Come, I'll see you to the door.'

'What's the matter with you?' she said, rather indignant. 'I can go back to the house when I want to – I don't need an escort.'

'Madame–'

'And do for goodness sake stop calling me madame when no one is by! You seem to forget we've known each other for years.'

'I forget nothing, Nicole,' he said after a momentary pause. 'And I am aware of everything – which you are not.'

'Aware? Of what? I don't understand you.'

'What would people say if they knew we were here together alone in the middle of the night?'

She stared, then frowned. 'That is none of their business! I'm surprised at you, Jean-Baptiste. You're not usually concerned about the opinion of others.'

He said slowly, 'And I'm surprised at *you*, Nicole. You're not usually so slow to take a hint.'

'What hint? What do you mean?'

For answer he shot out a hand, grasped her wrist, dragged her against his chest and kissed her with brief, unexpected fierceness. Then he let her go.

'Now,' he said. 'Do you understand your danger?'

She was totally shaken, totally unnerved. She put up one hand to her lips as if to test that they really had been assaulted by that unexpected kiss.

'Don't you understand that I want you, that I've always wanted you ever since you changed from a little skipping girlchild into a woman? And here you stand, unprotected and alone with me in my own domain – and I've drunk enough good champagne this evening, Nicole, to make me forget all my fine resolutions.'

He stood over her, tall, dark, threatening. Yet there was something full of entreaty in his eyes. She leaned against the table for support, because she felt strangely weak.

'Are you saying … are you daring to say…'

'That I love you – yes, that's what I'm saying.' He almost glared at her. 'Well then! What will you do now? Dismiss me?'

She made a sound of protest, half-shook her head, then said, with a little laugh: 'Don't be silly! Dismiss the best chief of cellar in the Champagne region?'

'Ah!' He nodded. His tone when he went on was bitter. 'If you knew how it irks me to be thought of only as … as … an indispensable tool! Don't you ever think of me as a man?'

She suddenly understood that she had, recently, often thought of him in just that way. The impulse this afternoon to ask him to use her first name… The sense of his importance when she lay wakeful later in the night…

She drew her velvet robe closer against her. 'I think we had better bring this conversation to an end, Jean-Baptiste. And we'll forget all about it. Tomorrow it will be as if it never happened.'

'Very well, madame. Just as you say.'

He stood aside to let her pass him, going through the doorway into his office. As she walked, the candle he had picked up to light her way flared in the breeze of her passing so that a tiny spot of hot wax fell on his hand. He jerked it in reaction, the candle-wick broke, the flame went out.

In momentary alarm Nicole seized his arm.

She came once more against that broad-cloth jacket. But this time it was by her own volition. She could feel his heart throbbing beneath the fabric of jacket and lawn shirt. His other arm came round her gently.

'Nicole,' he murmured.

She made no response, but neither did she try to get away. She felt him put a hand under her chin to raise her face for his kiss. Now was the moment. She must say, 'No, Jean-Baptiste, it's impossible.'

Yet all the loneliness of the past months was receding in the warmth of his embrace. The desperation of losing the man she loved, the solitude of her position in the de Tramont manor house – it was to those she must return if she said no to Jean-Baptiste.

And why should she? She had known him all her life, liked him and respected him. He loved her – he had said that in so many words. She was entitled to some human warmth, some little flame at which to warm her cold spirit now that Philippe was gone.

When he picked her up and carried her to the sofa in his office, she made no move to stop him. Instead she wound her arms around his neck and whispered, 'Do you really love me, Jean-Baptiste?'

His answer was not given in words.

Chapter Eleven

In the first delirium of the love affair Nicole had no other thought than joyous acceptance. To be loved again, to give love in return! – it was as if she had come alive again.

And she had no feeling of being unfaithful to her beloved Philippe. Jean-Baptiste was so utterly different, it was as if she had started all over again in some new country.

With Jean-Baptiste there was no reading of poetic dramas, no tears over fictitious heroes and heroines, no fine words and fanciful musings. Instead there was a pure physical passion, rapturous and fulfilling. His ability to rouse her was a source of amazement to her – he called out depths that she hadn't known existed within her.

When she lay in his arms, exhausted and filled with delight, he would laugh at her. 'Well then, now you don't have much time to wander about at night looking for something to occupy yourself with – eh, my little love?'

'Jean-Baptiste, if I hadn't come to your office that night...'

'It would have happened anyway,' he said.

He sighed. 'I've loved you so long, Nicci. I couldn't have gone on for ever without saying it aloud some time.'

'And I never knew…'

'Perhaps you did. Perhaps you sensed it. I've noticed, recently, that you've often been on the verge of saying something to me, and then held back.'

'Yes. I was going to ask you to call me by my first name. I thought there ought not to be a distance between us.'

'Distance!' He laughed in boisterous amusement, glancing down at her white breasts on which his arm was gently lying. 'But I'm never far from you, Nicci. I carry you with me wherever I go.'

'Jeannot!' She looked at him in surprise. 'Do you really feel like that?'

'You know I do.'

'No I don't. I know very little about you. You've always seemed…'

'What? Old? I'm only twelve years older than you–'

'Not that,' she said, giving a playful tug at a lock of his dark hair. 'No, but somehow … you've always seemed a little forbidding. It's because you know so much.'

'I only know a lot about wine.'

'You know a lot about making love, Jeannot.'

He didn't say, 'But you're so young, my darling, you haven't had time to learn.'

Instead he kissed her and enfolded her in his arms, until they came once more to the realms where only he could lead her.

When almost three weeks had gone by, she was brought to her senses by a simple remark from her elder child. 'Mama,' said Alys seriously, 'why are you always in such a hurry to finish reading to us?'

The truthful answer was, Because I want to run to my lover.

Instead she said, 'Oh, Mama's busy at the moment. You know there's important work to be done with the wine.'

'Yes, Mama, I know.' The three-year-old regarded her from under her little frilled nightcap. 'When will you read properly again?'

'Oh, darling!' Nicole hugged her. 'I'll read the story again now, properly.' She began again on Cinderella, but before she had read two paragraphs both children were asleep.

Nevertheless it brought her up sharp. She was neglecting them, rushing through household affairs, disregarding almost everything for the sheer joy of being with Jean-Baptiste in the dark hours of the night.

How long could she behave so thoughtlessly without laying herself open to discovery? And if the affair became known, think of the scandal!

Not only for herself, but for Jean-Baptiste. His wife would be hurt and indignant, the whole village would be up in arms and on her side. Nicole would bring a hornet's nest around her ears if she wasn't careful.

Besides... Did she really want to be so much in love with Jean-Baptiste? The chief place in her heart still belonged to Philippe and always would – and if she cared to take a lover from time to time no one would make too much of it so long as she was discreet.

But with Jean-Baptiste she was allowing herself to be overwhelmed by a delight in physical pleasure. It wasn't that she loved Jean-Baptiste himself, she feared – she loved what he brought her, the inestimable gift of passion fulfilled. When she was with him, when she felt his strength come into her and float her away to the realms of paradise, nothing else mattered.

But if she looked at life with sober, realistic vision she could see that many other things mattered.

So she mused, and convinced herself she ought to be wary. That wariness was swept away a few hours later when they made love, but it so happened that he couldn't come to meet her for the next few nights. One of his children was ill, his wife was up and awake often into the small hours, he couldn't get away unseen and besides it would be unfair to leave her at a time of anxiety.

Just so. Each of them had other responsibilities. Nicole made herself examine the

233

situation in a level-headed way and this was her decision: she must put a stop to the affair at once before it became too serious.

There was an escape route. She would go to England to look at this new glass Madame de Tramont had discovered.

When she told Jean-Baptiste of her decision, he understood at once without further explanation. 'Perhaps it's best,' he said. 'Short and sweet, eh? And no hard feelings on either side once it's over.'

She hadn't expected him to be quite so matter-of-fact about it. She hid her hurt feelings, however, and said in businesslike tones, 'I shall be gone about a month. I'm inviting Paulette to come for Christmas with Edmond and to stay on until the end of January, so the children will have someone to look to other than Nanny. As to the business side, now that we've decided on the blend, I know I can leave the fining and bottling to you.'

'Yes, I believe I can take care of all that.'

'It's best, Jean-Baptiste.'

'Of course.'

Clothilde de Tramont was surprised – and surprisingly pleased – to get the letter announcing her daughter-in-law's proposed visit to London. Clothilde herself was then on her travels in Scotland, that region made fashionable by the works of Sir Walter Scott. It might well be that the country was as romantic as the portrayal in *Redgauntlet* or *Rob Roy*, but the comforts were few, the weather was even more uncertain than the Champagne area, and the food was abysmal.

Moreover, in this poverty stricken country, few had heard much of Champagne Tramont, so she was no kind of a celebrity here. She was glad enough to hurry south on the admittedly efficient railway to meet her daughter-in-law in London.

'Well, my dear, it's very flattering that you took my information so seriously.'

'Madame, I'm extremely grateful that you gave such a thing your attention. I'm hoping you will introduce me to your friends the Davenants who will then take me to the glassworks.'

'Of course, of course, nothing simpler. But wasn't it extremely inconvenient to leave Calmady when the bottling was about to take place?'

Nicole gave a little shake of the head. 'I believe it is important for the head of a firm like Champagne Tramont to be able to delegate.'

'Delegate? To whom?'

'To Jean-Baptiste Labaud, of course.'

'But ... is he sufficiently educated to be left in charge, my dear? He is, after all, a peasant.'

Nicole looked at her. Clothilde coloured

faintly. And then, with a burst of laughter, she said, 'But of course, so are you! Nicole, I'd quite forgotten that! How strange. It used to seem so important.'

Nicole took her hand in its black lace mitten. 'Madame, we've been through a lot together, haven't we? There are things to be forgotten and things to remember–'

'Yes, chiefly that we are after all still mourning Philippe.'

It was Nicole's turn to colour up. Yet it was true – despite the passionate interlude with Jean-Baptiste, in her deepest heart she still grieved for her dear, gentle Philippe.

The visit to the glassmaker was easily arranged, Mr Davenant rather flattered that this young lady from abroad should be even interested. There were problems: her knowledge of English was scanty indeed, seemingly based on Shakespeare and other English poets. This being so, it was agreed that she should stay in the background, rely on Madame de Tramont to translate for her, and say very little.

It thus came about that Henry Woodpath had no idea he was showing his works to the head of the great champagne house of Tramont. Perhaps he would have been less forthcoming if he had known. But he had two foreign ladies, both in demure black, to entertain, so he put himself out to be interesting and informative.

When, prompted by Nicole, Clothilde inquired about the formula for his new glass, he was surprised but took it to be naivety – after all, what could women understand of such matters? Expansive, rather lordly in his dark brown worsted tailcoat and checked trousers, he waved his top-hat at the laboratory where his chemists kept check on the product.

'Let us go this way. Careful of these steps, ladies – *prinny guard, mesdames.*'

Nicole smiled at him in admiration. 'You spik excellent French, m'sieu,' she lied.

By now Woodpath was so enchanted that he would have sold her every secret in his works for sixpence. He had his chief chemist show her samples of glass and test them in clamps to breaking point. When at last they came to the special glass used to make test tubes for Mr Davenant, he had no hesitation in commanding the chemist to recite the formula.

'Carbonate of soda, 15%, Carbonate of lime 7%, Manganese 2%,' the chemist began. The list contained six ingredients. 'Plus 70% sand to make 100%, and of course to that you can add as much cullet as you wish.'

'What is "cullet"?' Nicole inquired of her mother-in-law, for the other names she had taken the trouble to look up in a dictionary before leaving France: she had learned the

English words for all the chemicals generally in use in glassmaking.

'*De la verre brizzy*, madame,' said Woodpath.

'Brizzy? Oh, broken glass. Ah yes, I understand.'

'You may think it strange that we add old glass to new,' Woodpath expatiated, 'but we find it gives toughness and though of course the exact chemical components of old glass are unknown, we find that there is little danger of harmful elements...' And so on, delighted to have an audience for his lecture.

When Nicole returned to France she visited Argonne, where the works that supplied her with bottles was situated. There she had an acrimonious conversation with the owner, who in the first place didn't wish to be told what to do by a woman and in the second certainly wasn't going to use any information from an English manufacturer.

'What, do you think we should fall in behind the English, then?'

'I think we should at least walk a few steps in their path, m'sieu, if it means making better bottles.'

'I greatly doubt it. What do the English know about putting wine in bottles?'

'Very little, perhaps, but they put gases in bottles when they do scientific experiments and champagne after all contains a gas –

carbonic acid.'

He frowned. He disapproved of women repeating, parrot fashion, some few facts they had learned.

'Then, to be more mundane, the English put beer in bottles.'

'Beer!' said the glassmaker, in tones that expressed what he thought of beer, and English beer at that.

'Despise it as much as you wish, m'sieu, but I want you to make some bottles according to this formula, and if you refuse, I can easily go elsewhere.'

'Ah, madame!' That was different. He didn't want to lose the custom of a prestigious house like Tramont. 'Very well,' he said, in a manner that implied, I'll humour your womanish whim.

He was greatly astonished when the glass proved to be fine and smooth and strong. He subjected it to every test, but it withstood almost every pressure. He was much more subdued when young Madame de Tramont came back to view the results.

'Of course, we don't know what effect it might have on the champagne,' he mused.

'No, and that is why we will have only a trial batch for this year. Tell me, m'sieu, is it possible to have a colour other than brown?'

'Other than brown?' He was surprised yet again at this strange little creature, so pretty and self-assured despite her widow's weeds.

239

'I suppose so. But wine bottles are always brown.'

'I think,' Nicole said, rising, 'I should like the new bottles you make for me from this glass to be green.'

'Green!'

'I think so. I considered blue, but blue is connected so strongly with poison phials. And dark red… No, green seems to me the best colour.'

'Green! Madame, why should you do such a bizarre thing? It will set you out as different from among the champagne makers.'

'Exactly. I want to be different. Thank you, Monsieur Parannet, I look forward to receiving this extra order of bottles when they are ready. And if they have no harmful effect on the wine, and answer well otherwise, you may look forward to larger orders.'

When she reached Rheims she sought out an artist whose work was well-known in the Champagne region. 'I should like to have new labels designed,' she told him. 'It is for a champagne bottle, but the bottle itself will be green, not brown.'

'Green!'

'Good gracious, why is everyone so surprised? Glass can be any colour, and so long as it is dark enough to protect the wine, why should it not be green?'

'No reason, I suppose, madame...' said Pierre Crecy uncertainly.

'Very well. I want a new label and cravate to go on a green bottle. The foil on the cork can be of any colour you choose but I feel the colour should be repeated somewhere in the two labels – that's to say, if the foil is golden, I should like gold in the labels, if the foil is purple I should like purple in the labels. I am aiming for a unified look, do you understand?'

'Yes, madame.'

'The main label should have the coat of arms of the de Tramonts, as hitherto. However...'

'Yes, madame?'

'I should like you to design the main label with a slightly different name.'

Crecy's hands, already sketching with charcoal on a big sheet of paper, paused. 'In what way, different? If you use the coat of arms you must use the name as always.'

'Of course. But until now the name has always been that of my father-in-law.'

'Yes?'

'I should now like the label to read: The Widow de Tramont.'

'What did you say?' cried Crecy, breaking the charcoal stick in his thick fingers.

'The Widow de Tramont.'

'But ... but...'

'Have you any objection to designing a

241

label with my name on it?'

'But such a thing has never been done! To use your own name? It's a break with tradition!'

'My father-in-law used his.'

'But he founded the firm, he owned it–'

'And now I own it, and have enlarged it, and increased the business, and plan to do other things one day. So I think it would be a good thing to have my name on the bottle.'

'But a widow? Will people like to associate wine with a widow?'

'We shall see,' Nicole said, rising from her chair and putting on her gloves. 'It is for a small batch of wine which I intend to put into different bottles. It is a time, I think, for change. Let us try this new label – if it is a failure, I will change back.'

He showed her out, shaking his head behind her back. Nicole, well aware of his disapproval, sighed inwardly. Why was it so heavy a task to have men accept her as a businesswoman? Why did they insist on treating her as some sort of idiot?

At the thought, her heart leaped towards the one man who treated her as a woman of importance in her own right.

Jean-Baptiste…

The moment she summoned him to her office on her homecoming, they went into each other's arms. The parting had been in vain as far as it had been intended to put an end to their love affair. If anything, it had only made her long for Jean-Baptiste the more – for his strength and sturdy good sense, his appreciation of her both as a lover and as a woman.

'Welcome home,' he said as he let her go.

She smiled. Home, indeed.

Chapter Twelve

During Nicole's absence the work of the champagne house had gone as usual, except for one matter – a visitor had arrived in hopes of conferring with her. His name was Franklin Uthers; his quest was to gain information on how to improve the sparkling wine he was producing in his Californian vineyard.

Finding Madame de Tramont away from home, he had put up at a hotel in Rheims to await her arrival. But she had scant time to give to him, for her mother was failing now quite seriously.

'It's lucky I was here,' her sister Paulette said to her. 'I've been to the farm every day for almost the whole month since Christmas. But though she rouses when I go in, she soon sinks back into a kind of sleep. I think it's the end, Nicole.'

The sisters took it in turns to sit with their mother in the old bedroom of the farmhouse they knew so well. Every comfort that Marie Berthois would accept had been installed, but the contrast between this and the manor house never failed to strike Nicole when she entered.

'Mama! Mama, it's Nicci.'

The faded eyes opened. The hand twisted by rheumatism was painfully lifted to take hers. 'Ah, Nicci, it's good of you to come, with so much as you have to do... Dearest, when I'm gone, let Lucille stay on in the farmhouse, eh? She deserves to – and it would be unseemly to turn her out without a home after she's been so patient with me.'

'Mama, don't talk like that. You and Lucille will spend many another year–'

'No, no, dear. I know that's not true, and I'm quite glad, really. You know, I've been in pain so long... It will be nice to have peace.'

Peace came to her early in February. The funeral had all the ceremony of black-plumed horses and mass in the parish church, as the villagers expected. When Nicole turned to business again she found, somewhat to her relief, that the American visitor had left.

'I don't know what we could have told him,' she said to Jean-Baptiste. 'So much of the making of good champagne is to do with the soil here and the temperatures...'

'He talked too much, listened too little,' Jean-Baptiste grunted.

Greatly to Nicole's surprise, her mother-in-law had set off from London when she realised Marie Berthois was unlikely to last out the month of February. She had wished to show respect to her daughter-in-law's family, somewhat belated but pleasing nevertheless.

'My dear, my deepest condolences,' Clothilde said in greeting. 'I remember that when I left last year I said I would never be back... But you know, family ties are strong all the same. And you are all my family now.'

The two women kissed, with much less formality than on former occasions. It gave Nicole a pang of regret that they had not been so friendly while Philippe was alive.

For the first week or two Clothilde busied herself about the house, musing aloud that they ought to have new curtains for the dining-room and perhaps they should have gas lighting installed? It had just been beginning to be popular in London when she had lived there as a girl but now the Gas Light and Coke Company were extending the facility to even the humblest homes – surely it was time for the manor of Tramont to have something more up to date than candles and oil lamps?

'I have been thinking of that, madame,' agreed Nicole, 'but for the cellars rather than for the house.'

'Nicole, what an expense!'

'No, I believe not – once the pipes are laid the expense isn't great. My chief worry is the raising of temperatures in the cellars – I notice that in Pourdume's office in Rheims, the room becomes quite hot when his gasolier is lit.'

Clothilde had nothing to say on that score. She was quite taken aback at how far advanced Nicole was in her thinking. She turned her attention to her grandchildren for a while, who were grateful to be taken out for walks and read to, now that Aunt Paulette had gone home again.

It occurred to Clothilde that, despite the grief of her mother's death, Nicole seemed strangely content. She went about her business with smiling briskness. Even though she was still clad in the formal black of mourning – for her mother now – she seemed to glow with some inner light that made even black crepe seem gentle.

Clothilde was a woman of the world. The answer to the mystery soon came to her. Her little widow of a daughter-in-law was in love. Well, so be it. She was too young to be a widow all her life. Who could it be? On whom would she bestow her hand?

A little quiet observation gave the answer: there was no young gentleman in their circle of acquaintance in whom Nicole de Tramont was showing the slightest interest.

Clothilde's mood changed from tolerant understanding to alarm. If there was no one in the neighbourhood with whom Nicole was having an honourable courtship, did that mean...?

Unthinkable! Yet having once thought it,

Clothilde couldn't forget it. She would have despised herself if she had spied on her daughter-in-law, but she soon somehow became aware that Nicole let herself out several nights in the week by the side door near the firm's office on the ground floor.

After a night of slight snow, Clothilde went out 'for a walk' before breakfast. Light footprints, made crisp by later frost, trod a path across the courtyard to the alley leading to the chief of cellar's office. Other footprints had by now almost obliterated them, for the firm's staff were early at work. Yet it was impossible for Clothilde not to know that Nicole had gone in the dead of night to Jean-Baptiste's office.

A few more days of watchfulness convinced her she was right. Nicole hurried to any meeting with her chief of cellar, spent more time than was strictly necessary in his company. A shrewd observer could note occasional smiles that passed between them, unnecessary contacts.

Clothilde couldn't contain herself the night she became absolutely certain. She went to Nicole's room, there to await her surreptitious return about three in the morning. Despite her resolve to stay awake and on guard, she was asleep when Nicole at last tiptoed mouselike into the bedroom.

'So!' Clothilde cried, starting awake, confused and flustered and all the more angry because of that. 'There you are!'

'Madame! What are you doing here?' Nicole was astounded at the sight of her mother-in-law in her great woollen dressing gown and nightcap of cambric.

'I'm waiting for you!' cried Madame de Tramont, collecting her wits. 'I'm waiting to tell you you should be ashamed of yourself!'

'Ssh,' warned Nicole. 'You'll wake the household–'

'Oh, they sleep soundly, I daresay, or they'd have heard you go out night after night to meet your lover! What are you thinking of, girl? A man like that!'

'A man like what?' said Nicole, stiffening.

'He's old enough to be your father–'

'Who are you speaking of?'

'Labaud, of course – who else? A common workman!'

'There's nothing common about Jean-Baptiste,' Nicole replied, 'and as to his being old enough to my father, that shows how little you've troubled to know him. He's only thirty-four.'

'Well, that's twelve years between you – and at any rate, that's not the point! Your behaviour is scandalous!'

Nicole took off the cloak in which she had wrapped herself against the bitter March night. She was revealed in a fine silk nightgown trimmed with layers of soft cream lace. Clothilde was shocked. The gown had been bought to please her lover, that she was sure of.

'Well, what have you to say for yourself?' she demanded.

'Nothing.' Nicole sat down on her dressing stool to take off her little slippers. 'I'm going to bed. I advise you to do the same.'

'To catch up on the sleep you lost while you were in that man's arms? Aren't you ashamed? Creeping out like an alleycat–'

'Madame,' said Nicole carefully, 'please go to bed. If you stay here you will say things we shall both regret.'

'I shan't budge until you give me your solemn promise that this affair ends now – tonight!'

'I haven't admitted there is any affair.'

'Oh, come, don't let's be absurd! You don't slip out of the house night after night in a Paris nightgown and embroidered slippers to inspect the vines! I want your solemn vow to put an end to it at once, and get rid of that man–'

'Get rid of Jeannot? Are you out of your mind?'

'He's to leave this estate within the week or–'

'Or what? What?' Nicole stood up suddenly, pulling herself to her full height. She was not very tall yet she was formidable, eyes sparkling with anger, young breasts

250

heaving under the soft silk. 'Nothing would make me send Jean-Baptiste away – not unless he had committed some terrible crime–'

'Sleeping with the mistress of the house – that may not be a crime but it's a sin! Have you no morals, girl? No finer feelings? Good God, if you had to take a lover, couldn't you find someone other than a common peasant?'

'You forget, madame,' said Nicole with a thin smile, 'that I am a common peasant, as you so delicately put it.'

'Yes, and that's what it is, isn't it? The need for someone earthy, gross–'

Nicole went to the door and opened it. 'Please go, madame.'

'Not until you tell me–'

'I tell you nothing. What I do is my own business. Get out of my room!'

'When I think that this was the room you shared with my own dear son–'

'Go, go! Before I take my fists to you! You stupid, interfering old woman – get out!'

Clothilde didn't flinch. She was tall, heavy, well-able to have defended herself against an attack by Nicole if it had really come. She came to the door, however. 'You refuse to promise this matter is over?'

'I refuse even to discuss it with you.'

'Very well. If you will not, then I shall take further steps.'

'You will do nothing. You will pack up and leave, first thing tomorrow morning.'

'I certainly will not! This is my house, though you seem to have forgotten it. I shall stay here until I have made you see sense–'

'I will ask my maid to pack your things and have the carriage got ready. If you don't go with your trunk when it leaves, you will have to wear the same gown for the rest of your stay, madame.'

Clothilde stared at her. There was a cold anger in her daughter-in-law's face such as she had never seen before. All at once she felt old and insecure. Nevertheless, she held on to some shreds of her dignity as she went out. 'I shall speak to you in the morning, when I hope you will be less undaughterly–'

'Undaughterly! My God, you intrude in my personal affairs, unasked, and tell me the man I love is brutish and common! You don't even know him! How dare you sit here on watch against me in my own room? If I'm undaughterly it's because you've taken up an attitude that forces me to fight you. Don't you *understand?*' Nicole cried, clasping her hands together and holding them out towards Clothilde. 'I need Jean-Baptiste! I need someone to love me – I need to give myself, to belong to someone–'

'You have your children – Philippe's children! You should give your love to them.'

'I do, you know I do! But ... surely you

252

understand? That's different. I ... I'm lonely, the nights are long now that Philippe is gone...'

Clothilde steeled herself against the tears that trembled in the other woman's voice. 'I find all that disgusting,' she said. 'You are a widow now. You must do without all that.'

'But I *can't!*'

'I order you to remember who you are now and what is expected of you. I shall never allow you to demean yourself by carrying on this affair with an employee.'

Nicole pulled herself back from the verge of a storm of tears. 'Goodnight, madame. Be ready to leave first thing in the morning.'

But though she meant it, she was unable to carry out the threat. When her elder daughter saw the valises being put out on the landing for taking to the hall, she inquired artlessly, 'Why's Grandmama going so soon? You said she was here on a long visit and she's only been here a *little* while.'

Looking down into the child's troubled eyes, Nicole's resolve cracked. She climbed the stairs wearily. She knocked as she had always done and waited for a reply before going into Clothilde's room. Her mother-in law was standing at the bureau, putting books into a leather satchel.

'Madame de Tramont.'

'Yes?' Clothilde said, turning to give her a frosty stare.

'I am sorry for threatening to turn you out of your own house. I ask you to remain.'

'What?' Clothilde said, faintly, in surprise. She had been ready for renewed battle.

'You are after all grandmother to my little girls. You are Philippe's mother. I can't turn you out. I apologise.'

'Oh... Then... Well, I accept your apology.'

'As to what we discussed—'

'Discussed!'

'I must insist that you hold your tongue on that point.'

'I shall not speak to you about it again, if that is what you wish.'

Nicole nodded in relief. 'Thank you. Now please come down and take breakfast as usual.'

Clothilde stuck rigidly to her promise. She didn't mention the love affair to her daughter-in-law again. But she was incapable of letting well alone. She felt the relationship to be shameful. It must be ended.

The following Sunday brought her the perfect opportunity. The younger child, Delphine, had a slight cough. Nicole decided not to go to church, but to stay at home and read to the little girl. Clothilde, as usual, went in the carriage but when the service was over directed the coachman to find Jean-Baptiste's house.

Yvonne Labaud was flustered when she opened the door to the great lady from the manor house. 'Oh … Madame de Tramont … oh … what an honour … I don't…'

'I wish to speak to your husband,' Clothilde said in her most lofty tone. 'Pray tell him I am here.'

'No need,' Jean-Baptiste said, appearing from the room that opened off the back of the little vestibule. 'Madame de Tramont, please come in.'

She swept in, her crinoline barely able to get through the doorway. Yvonne, clearly surprised in the midst of preparations for lunch, shrank back out of her way. Jean-Baptiste, unimpressed yet puzzled, showed her into what was clearly the best room, small but furnished with more comfort than Clothilde had expected. It even housed, for God's sake, a piano! She was surprised. She hadn't thought villagers went in for such refinements.

She stared at the piano. 'Someone in your family plays music?'

'My elder boy shows some talent. Please sit down, madame. Can I offer a glass of wine?'

'No thank you. I shall not be staying long.' She let a little pause ensue, first to impress the chief cellarman with the importance of what she was about to say, and secondly to ensure that Yvonne Labaud had gone back to her kitchen.

'Labaud, I've come to address you on a

very personal and serious score. The relationship between you and my daughter-in-law must end at once.'

Whatever Jean-Baptiste had expected, it wasn't this. A startled frown appeared between his black brows. He stared at his visitor.

'What relationship? The young Madame de Tramont is my employer.'

'Come, come, I know she's more than that. I faced her out the other night when she came creeping home from your office, as she's done many a time before. I told her then, she must stop lowering herself in this degrading fashion and dismiss you from the estate at once.'

'Oh?' said Jean-Baptiste. 'Really?' An angry smile curved his thin lips. 'From the fact that she has not said a word to me and that several days appear to have gone by, I gather Madame de Tramont is not paying much heed to your advice.'

'She is a young and silly girl,' Clothilde burst out. 'She is allowing emotion to rule her head! No good can come from a liaison of this sort – it's beneath her in every way and it must stop!'

'That is not for you to say, madame.'

'Indeed it is!' cried Clothilde in indignation. 'I am the guardian of the family name! It has always been my first consideration! Is the honour of the Tramonts to be polluted by–'

'Madame, lower your voice, please,' said Jean-Baptiste, going close to her and towering over her so that she drew back in alarm.

'What? What do you–'

'My wife will hear you. This house isn't on the scale of the manor. Have the decency to keep this matter between the two of us – though why you should think you have any right to interfere I don't know!'

'Very well, let us be discreet,' she agreed, realising that she had perhaps gone too far already for discretion. The coachman was outside with the de Tramont carriage – the whole village must by now be agog with the news that Madame de Tramont had called on the estate's chief of cellar.

'I must tell you that I refuse to allow you to dictate my actions,' Jean-Baptiste went on. 'You are nothing to me–'

'Nothing? I am head of the house of–'

'Madame, the head of the house of Tramont is Nicole. She restored its fortunes, she made it famous for its wine. I take orders only from Nicole where business is concerned. Where personal matters are involved, I am my own master.'

'I'll have you know that you are a mere nobody, and your very extraordinary reply to my demands only shows me how wrong it is for a lady to … to…'

'Go to bed with a man she pays wages to?' he ended for her. 'Yes, well, it has its problems. I'd like to be Nicole's equal in money and position – it would make things a lot easier. But it doesn't seem to matter to her so why should I let it bother me?'

'Oh, I understand you only too well!' Clothilde cried, quite forgetting her agreement to be discreet. 'You can gain great influence in Champagne Tramont while you share my daughter-in-law's bed–'

'Will you lower your voice?' growled Jean-Baptiste. He seized her by one wrist, dragging her towards the door. 'And go! – I don't need to listen to nonsense like that in my own house.'

'I shall go only when I have said what I have to say! Have you no shame? No decency? After the way my husband singled you out to make you his chief of cellar – after the way I confided in you when he died – is *this* your loyalty?'

'As you just pointed out, I'm a mere nobody. I have no particularly loyalty–'

'No, not to the Tramonts nor to your own wife!'

'That's enough, madame–'

The door opened. Yvonne Labaud came in. 'Please make less noise, Madame de Tramont. You're scaring my children.'

Clothilde gaped at her. She was totally devoid of breath at the emergence of

Labaud's wife looking so calm and controlled.

'You needn't think you can cause trouble, madame, by accusing my husband of being disloyal to me. Oh, I heard you – it's difficult not to hear you, you seem accustomed to giving orders at the top of your voice.'

'Madame Labaud–'

'Do you think I don't know all about Nicci and Jean-Baptiste? Do you think I'm deaf and blind?'

'Yvonne,' groaned Jean-Baptiste, sitting down on one of the hard horse-hair chairs of the sitting-room.

'I'm sorry, Jeannot. I never meant to let it be said between us, but now *she* comes here, causing a fuss–'

'A fuss?' gasped Clothilde at last. 'Is that all you call it? Your husband is being flagrantly unfaithful and when I rebuke him, you call it "a fuss"?'

'Why did you interfere?' Yvonne cried, tears trickling onto her plump cheeks. 'Everything was all right until you began to meddle!'

'Madame Lebaud, you astound me! Do you mean you accepted your husband's unfaithfulness?'

Yvonne took up a corner of her apron to dry her cheek impatiently. 'You have a very short memory, madame. When old Monsieur de Tramont took little Isabelle Guerdon to bed, I don't remember that you did anything about it. Nor when he made a fool of himself over Marie Sobitte in Epernay, the one who served in the cafe.'

Clothilde went white, and then red. Her gloved hand went up to her lips to hide their trembling.

'Us married women,' said Yvonne, her voice weary, 'we have to learn to be sensible over things like that. I've had less to complain of than some, and I'm thankful for that. But I always knew my Jeannot loved Nicci–'

'Yvonne!' protested Jean-Baptiste.

'It's true, you know it is. From the minute her figure filled out and she stopped being a little girl, she's been the apple of your eye. I don't blame her – she's a pretty little thing and clever, too – educated, quick on the uptake. I always knew I wasn't the right wife for you, Jeannot. You needed somebody with the spirit to match your own.'

'Madame Labaud,' interrupted Clothilde, rallying, 'surely you must agree with me that this unsuitable affair must end at once!'

'Well, you see, madame, there's where we differ. I don't think it's unsuitable. I think that, if everything was equal, Nicci and Jeannot would be a good match. She's as full of character as an egg is full of meat, but she needs a man to help her with that great big business firm – and my Jeannot's just the man, really – now isn't he? But it can't be, because first of all she's a lady now and he's just a worker, and besides, he's married to me.'

'Yvonne, I never heard you talk like this before, never in my life,' Jean-Baptiste said in dismay. 'What's got into you?'

'It's *her* fault,' Yvonne said, pointing a hand reddened with housework at Clothilde. 'Silly, self-opinionated old fool! She can't see what everybody else in Calmady sees – that by rights you ought to be master of the House of Tramont because you're the one that gave it its champagne–'

'Everybody else in Calmady?' Clothilde said, catching at the words. 'You mean it's well-known that my daughter-in-law and your husband are – are–'

'Of course it's known,' Yvonne said scornfully. 'Oh, you and your blinkered life! You go off to Paris and London and don't even know how the village lives! We know everything that goes on in the manor house almost as soon as it's happened–'

'And you sneer about it behind my back!'

'Sneer? No ... I don't know that we even talk about it much,' said Yvonne. 'And of course nobody's said a word to me about Nicci. But I know. I knew from the outset.'

'Then... Then I rely on you to bring your husband back into line,' said Clothilde. 'It's your moral duty! I insist you make Jean-Baptiste–'

Yvonne laughed, a laugh of genuine amusement. 'Look at him,' she said. 'D'you really think he's henpecked? I can't "make" Jeannot do anything. Nor can you, and if you knew the first thing about the man you've been employing for the past fourteen years, you'd know *that*.'

'I think you'd better leave, Madame de Tramont,' Jean-Baptiste said, taking her by the elbow and ushering her to the door. 'You've wreaked enough havoc for one day.'

'But... But... I must know what you intend to do–'

'How the hell do I know what I'm going to do?' he cried in a voice that made her tremble, it was so full of suppressed fury. 'You've brought my whole world down about my ears! Get out before I strangle you, you old busybody!'

She almost ran out to the carriage. The coachman, who had been standing close to the cottage entrance so as to hear as much as possible, scarcely had time to open the carriage door for her. She tumbled in. 'Take me home,' she begged, tears streaming down her pink cheeks, 'take me home!'

She didn't appear for Sunday lunch. The manor house kitchen was abuzz with the drama that had taken place in Calmady, but no one said a word or gave a hint to Nicole. She knew something was wrong but couldn't find out what – Madame de Tramont stayed in her room, claiming she had a headache, and certainly, from the tisanes and hartshorn being taken in by the maid, it seemed to be true.

Her first notion of what had happened came next morning. The butler announced that Monsieur Labaud was in the hall, asking to see her before the day's work started. She left her breakfast untasted to hurry out to him. 'What's wrong? Has the *cuvée*–'

'It's not about the wine, madame,' Jean-Baptiste said. He made a gesture inviting her to lead the way to her office. She did so, with a sinking of the heart. Something bad was about to happen, judging by Jean-Baptiste's face.

'Well?' she challenged, whirling about as soon as he had closed the door behind them.

'I've come to give you notice that I'm quitting your employment.'

Icy fingers clutched at her chest. A momentary blackness hovered. When she recovered only seconds later, Jean-Baptiste was guiding her to a chair.

'What – what–?'

For one blissful moment she thought it was some nightmare she had just had.

But then she looked into her lover's eyes, and knew she had not dreamed it.

Chapter Thirteen

When Jean-Baptiste began to explain, it was a confirmation of all Nicole's worst fears, and more.

'She went to your house! Oh, how could she–'

'She feels she has a responsibility as head of the family, my love. We may not see it that way, but her conviction that she's the guardian of the family honour is strong. So she blunders in where others might let well alone. And the result is, I must go.'

'No, I won't hear of it! Go, just because she has ordered you–?'

'No, no, it's not that, Nicci.' He sighed. 'It's more than that. I suppose I was always aware that Yvonne knew about us...'

'What?' Nicole cried in dismay.

'Oh, come now, Nicci – you know village life. Nothing can be a secret. If you thought Yvonne didn't know, you were fooling yourself. And now, of course, she's had to come out with it, to put the old lady in her place. The only things is ... I can't hurt her any more.'

They had always avoided discussing Jean-Baptiste's wife. Nicole knew her, of course, had known her quite well when she was a village girl herself. Yvonne was plump, fair-haired, and of average good looks. She went to church regularly, made all her own preserves, and never talked about anything except the growth of her few rows of vines and the progress of her children. In Nicole's eyes, she had always been 'middle-aged'.

She and Jean-Baptiste had been married for sixteen years. Nicole understood that it had been a marriage more or less arranged by the families, none the less happy for that. Of the three children Lucien, the eldest, appeared to have musical talent which was fostered – against doubts on Yvonne's side – by his father. Andrew was interested in the vines. The girl, Josephine, was a smaller version of her mother, earnestly nursing her wooden doll and discussing its symptoms of croup with the other little girls.

'If you leave Tramont, you hurt *me,* Jean-Baptiste,' Nicole said. 'Doesn't that matter to you?'

He didn't even trouble to answer that reproach. Instead he said: 'You see, I saw Yvonne quite differently yesterday. She stood up to the old lady–! I was amazed, I'd never seen her like that. And I realized something that hadn't really occurred to me before, my dear. Yvonne really loves me.'

'Oh, Jeannot–'

'You've got to understand. She's one of

those people who gets nothing out of life except what's given to her. She's a simple woman – she just accepts whatever happens, and lives with it. It seems that for the past months she's had to live with a lot of secret grief. I can't do that to her any more, Nicci.'

'But if she always knew, and did nothing–'

'What do you want? That I should meet her unhappy eyes every time I go home, and know she's wondering if I've been with you? Be always apologizing?' His face went grim. 'Perhaps it's arrogant, but I can't live like that. There could only be two choices – either I stay here and brazen it out no matter how it hurts Yvonne, or I go. So I've decided to go.'

'You've decided! Without even discussing it with me!' She took him by the arm and actually tried to shake him. 'How dare you do that!'

'There isn't anything to discuss. I've made up my mind. I wrote to Monsieur Uthers last night–'

'To whom? Uthers? Who is he – oh, the American!' Her hands flew to her cheeks. She felt cold and frightened. 'The American? You wrote to America?'

'No, to Paris. He's still there. He told me he wouldn't be sailing until April because he intended to visit other wine-makers.'

'You had his address in Paris? I don't understand!'

'He offered me a job on his winery in California, Nicci. Of course I refused – I didn't have the least interest in it then. But he insisted on giving me his card with the Paris hotel written on the back, in case I changed my mind. And I have.'

'You can't go to California, Jeannot!' She threw herself against him, arms around his body to hold him safe and hard. 'You can't go so far away! I won't let you! Don't, don't talk about a thing like that, Jeannot, please don't!'

'But I can't stay here, Nicci.' He held her gently, stroking her cheek.

'All right, I agree – you feel you must leave Tramont, and I give in over that. But you could get a job at any champagne house in the district by simply asking, Jeannot–'

'What would be the good of that? We should see each other, it would be inevitable. We should come across one another in Epernay or Rheims and we'd be in a hotel making love within half an hour.'

'Jeannot!' She was blushing at his bluntness. She hid her face against his chest. 'No, we'd be honourable–'

'Don't fool yourself, Nicci. You went to England, remember? To break it off between us. And the minute you came back we were in each other's arms the very first moment.'

She had no argument against that. She struggled with the tears that were welling up as she understood that he really meant it – he was leaving her, going to the other side of the world.

'Yvonne and I talked it all out yesterday,' he explained, his voice a little unsteady. 'She's forgiven me for my unfaithfulness – or at least, she's said we can put it behind us, because she's so ... so *good* she doesn't think there's anything to forgive. And though she's scared at the idea of leaving France, she feels it may be for the best because the little girl has what Yvonne calls growing pains – but you know it could be the first sign of the bone-twister, and this climate is hard... California is sunny, Monsieur Uthers says. Mild weather all the year round.'

'He would have told you the streets were paved with gold if he thought it would get you there!' Nicole said, straightening and trying to argue back. 'What on earth would you do there, Jean-Baptiste! You're a man of Champagne.'

'There are other wines besides champagne, you know.'

She gave a shaky laugh. 'That's almost heresy. When I hear you talk like that, I know you mean it.'

'That I mean to go? Yes, it's settled. I'll wait to hear from Monsieur Uthers, of course, but I know he'll take me. He said we should have a good house and I could have a share of the profits. He even said he knew of a good music teacher for Lucien.'

She was shaken to understand how much negotiation had clearly taken place, while she was totally unaware of it. She'd looked on Jean-Baptiste as a fixture, like the sun in the sky or the buildings of Rheims. Unable to bear it, she burst out, 'What shall I do without you?'

He took both her hands, yet kept a distance between them. 'Don't be too worried. I've thought of a replacement as chief cellarman. You must promote my assistant, Compiain's son–'

'I didn't mean that, Jeannot! You know I didn't–'

'But it's got to be thought of. I can't leave you with no one to direct the cellars. Arnaud is less communicative than a thistle and about as handsome, but he knows the wine. He's been due for a promotion for some time now. He might have gone elsewhere to get it, since there seemed no chance of my moving out. But now he'll stay, and be glad of it, and he'll make good champagne if you just keep complaining when he goes a little astray with the blending.'

'Jeannot, don't talk business! You're going away – leaving me – I can't bear it–'

'Yes you can. You've got other things to fill your life.'

'What? You mean all this?' She made a sweeping gesture that took in the office, and beyond it the estate with its cellars and the land with its rows of vines. 'They mean nothing compared with losing you–'

'Nicci, you got over it when Philippe died, and that was a worse thing than this separation.'

She started, a gesture of surprise and denial.

'Oh yes it was, Nicci. Don't let's lie to each other. Philippe was the man you really loved.'

'But I love *you*, Jeannot–'

'Yes, but not ... not the way I feel about you.' He gave a great sigh from his deep chest, easing the burden of putting his thoughts into words. 'I always loved you, Nicole. From the moment you stopped being a little girl, you were the only woman in the world as far as I was concerned. But there seemed no point in even thinking about it. You loved Philippe – it brimmed over from you like champagne from a narrow glass. I knew I was only second-best – well, that was all right. You see, in love, there's always someone who loves and someone who is the beloved. You were my beloved, my darling, and you always will be. But you'll turn to other things, just as I will, and life will go on, and we'll both survive...'

'Oh no! No, no no! I can't bear it, Jeannot!

Don't leave me! Don't – the loneliness will kill me!'

'Not you, my angel.' He took her in his arms and kissed her, deeply and with intensity. Only afterwards did she understand that it was a farewell kiss.

There was an unexplained delay in starting work on the Tramont estate that morning. Madame, usually out and about soon after eight, was nowhere to be seen. Even Labaud was late in going to the cellars.

Nicole had gone to her mother-in-law's boudoir. She knocked as always. 'Who is it?' asked Clothilde.

'It's Nicole.'

'Oh! I ... I can't see you. I have the headache.'

'Madame, please let me come in. I have spoken to Jean-Baptiste.'

A silence on the other side of the door seemed to last for infinity. Then Clothilde said faintly: 'Come in.'

She was sitting by her fire with a breakfast tray on a small table before her. The croissants were untasted, the coffee looked cold and uninviting. Clothilde herself seemed to sag in her comfortable little armchair.

It was rare for Madame de Tramont to be seen except at her best. This morning her hair hadn't yet been done, nor was there that faint trace of powder on her cheeks to

271

tone down her florid complexion.

She looked up at her daughter-in-law almost fearfully. 'What has Labaud said to you?'

'He's leaving.'

'Oh.' There was neither triumph nor pleasure in the faint exclamation.

'Madame, a while ago I told you to leave, and now I tell you again. But I don't say it in anger this time. I think we should find each other poor company for the rest of your proposed stay. So it's best that you go.'

'Very well,' said Clothilde. It was almost a relief to have the decision made. She'd been debating whether to pack and go, yet it seemed like retreat to do so. Retreat not from her daughter-in-law, but from Jean-Baptiste Labaud.

'I won't heap reproaches on you. You thought that what you did was right, I suppose. But I can tell you you have lost me the best and most dependable friend I ever had.'

'Friend!'

'Oh yes, Jean-Baptiste was my friend. He was other things too – the best chief of cellar in the whole Champagne region. Did you think of that, before you went rampaging into his house to make his life impossible here?'

'I ... I ... I was more concerned with morals.'

Nicole nodded. It was useless to go on with the conversation. They were worlds apart in their view of life. At the door she paused, turning back to look at the older woman. 'Madame, have you ever been in love?'

'What?' cried Clothilde in astonishment.

'Your marriage with Monsieur le Marquis was arranged?'

'Naturally. But we became devoted to each other.'

'Devoted... Did you love him? Did it make your very bones melt when he took you in his arms?'

Clothilde gaped at her in complete incomprehension.

'No, I see it was never like that for you. Ah, well... I'm sorry for you, madame.'

She opened the door and went out, leaving Madame de Tramont more unhappy than she could explain.

Chapter Fourteen

Though Nicole steeled herself for the ordeal of an estate party to say farewell to Jean-Baptiste and his family, she didn't see him again before he left for Paris to join Franklin Uthers for the voyage to America.

A despairing letter came from Paulette, the ink running here and there where her tears had spotted the paper. 'I beg you to come! Auguste has gone. I now find there are unsettled debts all over Rethel. Contracts for building work cannot be met. The workmen are besieging me for their wages. I don't know what to do! Help me, Nicci!'

It was impossible to deny such an appeal. Nicole told Monsieur Pourdume to make a handsome present of money to Jean-Baptiste when he attended the farewell party in her stead, and set off for Rethel. By train and post-chaise it took only one day.

The Ardennes was a district that Nicole found forbidding. She had always thought it a pity that Auguste's home was there, for she was sure her sister was intimidated by the darkly-wooded hills stretching up from the valleys of the Meuse and Aisne, so different from the chalky plain of Champagne.

When she stepped down at the tidy little stone villa, her sister flew out to fall on her neck in tears. 'Oh, Nicci! If you only knew how glad I am to see you! Oh, Nicci darling, sort out this terrible mess for me!'

Little Edmond, hanging on to his mother's skirt, burst into tears. Nicole detached herself from Paulette after giving her a hug and a kiss, picked up the wailing child, ordered the coachman to bring in her valise, and led the way indoors.

'Now,' she said, sitting her down on the sofa, 'tell me all about it.'

'I don't know how to explain it! I never knew he felt like that! He was so angry, Nicci–'

'But about what?' And then she took a good look at Paulette. 'You lost the child?' she asked gently.

Paulette had just started a baby when she came for Christmas, but had been strong and well. But it seemed the strains of nursing her mother and then the funeral, and the difficult journey home in the cold spring rains, had caused a miscarriage.

'August blamed me for it. He said I didn't take proper care, that I packed my bag and ran each time you crooked your little finger–'

'Paulie!'

'Oh, he said so many strange things! I suddenly understood that he hated you–'

'Hated me? But why? I never did him any harm.'

'You have money,' Paulette said, wiping her eyes and trying to be calm so as to explain. 'You are a success.'

'A success,' Nicole repeated with hidden bitterness.

'Yes, and now, you see, I realise that Auguste is a failure – it rankled, he compared himself with you and somehow he felt you had harmed us, I don't know how. He said I depended on you too much, and only married him to get myself out of the attics at Madame Treignac so as not to be an embarrassment to you–'

There was enough truth in that to make Nicole colour up. 'But he came courting you,' she said. 'We didn't seek him out–'

'No, oh no, there's no truth in any of it, really. I liked him, Nicci, I was sure I could love him. And he seemed to think a lot of me. But ... I don't know ... I think I got on his nerves. You know I can never stand up to anyone who raises their voice...'

'Oh, darling,' murmured Nicole, embracing her. 'My poor darling... So you were never really happy, and all the time I thought...'

'It got worse since last autumn. I realise now that he was in a terrible pickle over money. August is one of those men, you know – a perfectionist – never really finishes a job, always wants to do just one more thing to make it better. And of course he ran behind schedule on all his contracts and incurred extra expenses that his clients refused to pay for – quite right, I suppose, they stood by his estimate and refused to be responsible for his "improvements".'

'But where has he gone? When will he be back?'

Paulette threw her wet handkerchief over her face. 'Never!' she wept. 'Never! He packed up his belongings and put them in the little waggon and drove to Sedan. The waggon was found abandoned outside the railway station there. He seems to have taken a train into Belgium. He's gone, Nicci – he told me he was never coming back, that I was like a millstone round his n-neck...'

'Never mind, never mind,' soothed Nicole, rocking her like a child. 'Good riddance to bad rubbish if he was making you unhappy!'

'But ... Nicci ... a woman without a husband... Whatever shall I do!'

'Never mind,' repeated Nicole. 'I'll look after you. Don't fret, Paulie – you'll never want for anything so long as I have a sou to share with you.'

'Oh, Nicci, Nicci...'

So Paulette wept herself out, and Edmond huddled against his aunt for comfort, and at last it was bedtime and a night's sleep restored some strength to the forsaken wife.

In the morning Nicole ordered the little housemaid to prepare a good breakfast and made her sister eat; it seemed she hadn't sat down to a meal since Auguste walked out four days earlier. Then Nicole sent out for a stick of barley sugar for Edmond, told him to be a good boy while Mama and Aunt Nicci went out on business, and took Paulette to the town centre.

Rethel was not an insubstantial town. It had manufacturers and army barracks. Therefore it had a telegraph office. Nicole sent a telegraphic message to Pourdume in Rheims: Name a good lawyer in Rethel.

She then took Paulette to the building yard, where the men were lounging about in an anxious group.

'Well, messieurs, I hear you haven't been paid for two weeks.'

'That's right, madame, and we need the money!'

'Of course you do. If you'll come into the office I'll give you a percentage of what's owing–'

'A percentage!'

'I can't pay you in full. I haven't brought money enough with me. But I'm Madame de Tramont, of Tramont Champagne.'

A murmur went round: 'Ah, the rich sister…'

'You shall be paid, I guarantee it. I've been poor myself, I know how important your

278

wages are. But it will take me a day or two to get money transferred here. Meanwhile, what about the jobs that are in progress – is anyone doing anything about those?'

There was a shuffling of feet and a glancing about. Clearly nothing was being done.

'Which are the most important customers?'

'There's a new blockhouse at the barracks... Monsieur Plerignac's stables... I think they're in a hurry over that storage hut at the hospital...'

'Who is the foreman?'

A sturdy fellow stepped forward. 'Me, I'm foreman, Jacques Cadal.'

'Will you undertake to go to the most important customers today? And tell them the work shall be finished as soon as possible but that we shall accept lower payments as penalty for the delay. Try not to lose the work, Cadal – assure them you'll be back tomorrow or the next day at latest.'

'Why not today?' he inquired.

'Today? Well, if you *would* – but mind, I can only pay about one-third of what each of you is owed.'

'That's all right, madame,' said one of the men with a grin. 'We reckon the House of Tramont is good for a few francs.'

'The only problem is materials,' said Cadal. 'We need cement and sand, and though we've got timber we need to have it cut and the sawmills won't give us credit.'

'I hope to see to that shortly,' said Nicole. 'My lawyer in Rheims will recommend a man of business who can reassure everyone who's owed money.'

Sure enough, by lunchtime came Pourdume's reply. Nicole went with Paulette to see Monsieur Apadoux, who had already had a telegram from Pourdume to alert him. 'My dear lady,' he said in a most welcoming tone, 'I am delighted at the opportunity to serve the head of Champagne Tramont. Tell me what I can do for you.'

Nicole waited for Paulette to explain, but Paulette as usual was overwhelmed with nervousness and embarrassment. In few words Nicole sketched the situation: the owner of the firm gone, no way to contact him, work outstanding, money owed, the books in a mess, materials unavailable, the men anxious over their jobs.

'I want you to come to my brother-in-law's office and make a list of everyone who needs reassurance. I then want you to go, or send your senior clerk, to all those people. Tell them that I stand guarantor for all Monsieur Fournier's debts. In short, make sure everyone knows that my sister's finances will soon be in good order.'

'Er … Madame… This is a little difficult. The business does not belong to your sister,

I infer. It belongs to her husband.'

'Quite so.'

'And he, though missing, is still alive.'

'Yes.'

'If you pay out these large sums of money, there is no way you can ever enforce repayment from him.'

'I don't intend to try.'

'And you cannot dispose of the business to defray your expenses, since it is in his name.'

'I quite understand that. I don't intend to sell the business. I shall put in a manager and it will be run in the name of Auguste Fournier. If he ever comes back, he's welcome to it.'

Monsieur Apadoux looked at her over his glasses. There was a grimness in her tone when she said it that made him think it would be best for Auguste Fournier if he never reappeared. And indeed he never did, although he was heard of in Antwerp some years later, ashore from a merchant ship plying to Africa.

Little by little the tangle was teased out. Cadal was willing to take on the role of manager at increased wages but it was clear he would never do more than keep things rolling along. It would be at least two years before the business would be in profit again.

But Paulette was saved from disgrace and the little stone villa, bought with her dowry, was hers for ever. An income would come to her eventually from the building firm but meanwhile Nicole would support her.

'Yes, of course I shall, don't be silly, Paulie.'

'But you've done so much already–'

'But I'm the rich sister – didn't you hear the men say so?'

'Oh, Nicci!' Paulette cried, bursting into tears of gratitude.

Once again Nicole soothed and comforted her. But truth to tell she was becoming exhausted by the efforts she had to make. She felt strained and tired, and had no appetite. She was sure that most of it was due to grief over Jean-Baptiste and, in a way, was grateful to have so much to do, thus blotting out the fact that even now he was awaiting ship to take him to Los Angeles.

Then came a morning when she understood at last that her exhaustion and sickness didn't spring from grief.

She was expecting Jean-Baptiste's child.

Her first instinct was to rush to Paris, tell him the news, throw herself into his arms. 'Now you can't leave me, Jeannot! I need you! You must stay!'

Yet two minutes' thought showed her that was the worst thing she could do. What could come of it but more sorrow? It would hurt Yvonne Labaud. It would probably not change Jean-Baptiste's determination to emigrate. He was the kind of man who, once his mind was made up, seldom altered it. He would go to California with the knowledge he was leaving a child behind him whom he would never see.

Who could possibly benefit from letting the knowledge spread? The coming baby was her responsibility, hers alone. And God knew it would cause scandal enough when she, a widow of some two years standing, bore a child.

She said nothing of her news to her sister for a day or two, thinking things over. Then at last, a plan having evolved, she confided in Paulette.

'*Enceinte?*' cried Paulette. 'You? But... Nicci – how is that possible?'

Nicole almost laughed. Paulette's horror was so naive, so typical. 'It came about in the usual way, my dear. And I'm paying the usual price.'

'Nicci! How can you joke about it!'

'I'm not joking. I have a great price to pay. You see, I can't marry the father.'

'Not marry him? But you *must!*'

'He's married already, Paulie. It's out of the question to think of any help from him.'

'Then he's a scoundrel–'

'No, dear. Don't say things like that,' Nicole said, taking her sister's hand and pressing it hard. 'He's the best man that ever stepped, but I don't want him ever to know he left me with a baby. I've thought about it – night and day, almost since I found out for sure at the beginning of the week. I've decided. I'm going to have the baby in secret.'

'Oh, but dear … that's not possible.'

'Why not?'

'Well … at Tramont … and Calmady … I mean… How could it be possible?'

'I shan't be at the estate. I've decided, Paulie. I'm going to travel.'

'Travel…'

'Oh business. There's a lot I can do, in fact – I made one visit to London and I realise there is information I ought to have about our markets. So I shall travel – to London, to St Petersburg–'

'St Petersburg!'

'The Russians love Champagne Tramont. I shall go and find out how I can make them love it more. And Berlin – I shall go there. And then in due course, Paulie, I shall come back. We'll find a place, dear – a quiet yet busy place where no one will know me. And that's where I'll have the baby.'

'You can't do that, Nicci. All that travelling – being shaken about in a coach–'

'No, no. Travel abroad is different. I know that from my trip to England. Trains are very comfortable. On board ship it's like a little floating hotel. Of course, if the weather turned bad … but we won't think about that.'

Paulette, once having got over her first surprise, had raced ahead in her thoughts. 'But once the baby is born, what then? I don't understand, Nicci.'

Nicci sighed. 'I shall have to find a foster-mother.'

'Oh no! No, no! One hears such dreadful tales – of neglect and ill-treatment.'

'I'll choose someone suitable – I have someone in mind.'

'No!' cried Paulette, leaping up and standing erect and forbidding. 'I won't allow you to hand over your child to a stranger! My own sister! Never, never in this world! If you're determined to have the baby without anyone knowing, then *I* must be the one to take care of it.'

Nicole hid a smile. It was exactly what she'd been aiming at. When she said she had someone in mind, it was Paulette herself. 'Oh, I don't know... It's a lot to ask...'

'After all you've done for me? Nonsense. Besides, Nicci... In a way, it's like Providence. I lost my baby. It hurt me more than you can imagine. Now ... I shall have a baby to care for. Oh yes, Nicci, let me, do let me! I promise I'll love it as if it were my own!'

'I know you would, Paulie. But it's a long-term thing, you know–'

'Oh, I know that! But after all – what am I

supposed to do with the rest of my life now I'm left all on my own? I'll devote it to bringing up Edmond and your child. I swear I'll be a good mother to them both, Nicole. I swear it on our dead mother's grave!'

'Very well,' Nicole said, just in time, for Paulette was about to dissolve in tears again. 'I accept your wonderful offer. You've taken a great load off my mind. I can begin the planning of the whole thing with an easier conscience.'

Once Paulette's affairs were more or less in order, Nicole returned to Calmady. She spent about six weeks playing and talking with her two little girls and, in business hours, watching young Compiain settle in as chief of cellar. They were busy weeks, but there had been so much upheaval at the estate that no one questioned her decision to go on a long journey abroad.

In July she set off, leaving instructions and warnings about every aspect of the business during her absence. Compiain was surprised that she would miss the harvest, one of the most important moments in wine-making. She said: 'You will buy-in the same as last year, according to the records Jean-Baptiste left. As to our own grapes, your father will have taken the usual care of them and if anything has gone wrong it would be beyond my powers to save them. But I don't fear that. I feel I must make this trip now, because I believe it's time to make a new start. You saw the new design for labels, and the new bottles I plan to use – well, I want to see that the market is expecting all that.'

'Yes, madame.'

'I'll be back for the assemblage of the still wines in November, I hope. If it looks as if we've made any mistakes, they can be remedied to a great extent at that point by buying-in some of the other vintages. Then while the wine rests I can catch up on anything that I have missed. So you see it's all taken care of.'

'Yes, madame.' To tell the truth he was flattered that she should trust him to such an extent, and was determined nothing at all should go wrong.

So Nicole went on her travels. She wrote regularly to Paulette, who replied as regularly to fine hotels in Vienna, St Petersburg, Amsterdam, London.

In October they met in Spa in Belgium, where they took rooms in a quiet, respectable hotel. No one knew them there: they were two quiet ladies, one with a little three-year-old boy, the other expecting a child and taking the waters for a kidney complaint.

But in truth Nicole was well and healthy, though tired after much journeying. She rested and took a little exercise. Just before the birth she entered a spa nursing-home. Attention was excellent, the child, a boy, was born without difficulty.

He was registered as Robert Paul, after Nicole's grand-father and father. His last name was given as Fournier, Nicole using her sister's papers. There was no difficulty: the description on the papers of Paulette was just as apt for Nicole. The absence of the father was easily accounted for: he had had to stay in Rethel to look after his business while his wife, of a delicate constitution, took the waters at Spa.

When they left the town at the beginning of November, they were headed for Strasbourg. Paulette had agreed that it would be difficult to account for little Robert in Rethel and besides, she had never been happy there except for the first year of her marriage. 'Everything there is touched with sadness for me.'

Nicole had bought her sister a neat little house not far from Strasbourg's cathedral of rose-coloured stone. 'It will seem quite like old times to you,' she said, 'to hear cathedral bells. You'll think you're back in Rheims.'

'Come and see me again soon, Nicci. Come and see little Robert.'

'I will, you can be sure I will.'

She sat back in the carriage taking her to the railway station, tears brimming from her eyes. She was leaving Jean-Baptiste's son in the hands of another woman. No one would know how much it hurt her.

But as she had said to Paulette: There was a price to pay. She would be a long time paying it.

Chapter Fifteen

The champagne cork popped with a satisfactory small explosion. A little vapour came from the neck of the green bottle. The sparkling golden wine frothed out into the narrow glasses.

'Well, madame,' observed Richard Patterton, 'it looks perfect and–' he took the glass brought to him on a silver tray by the butler – 'it smells delicious.'

Madame de Tramont – the Widow Tramont – watched while he raised to his lips the wine that bore her name, and sipped.

'Ah!' he said, raising his eyes to heaven.

Or rather to the shell-pink ceiling of the salon which Nicole had had constructed at the back of the Villa Tramont. It had become necessary, as the fame of her wine grew, to have a large room in which she could entertain day-time visitors to the manor.

It took up what had once been a breakfast room and a lesser drawing-room. Outside the long windows there was a terrace, and beyond that a lawn on which the young people were playing croquet in the summer sunshine.

The gathering in the salon consisted of the elder members of the de Tramont family – Madame de Tramont senior, Aunt Paulette, and of course the head of the House of Tramont herself, La Veuve Tramont. To some muted protests from Clothilde, Nicole had dropped the 'de' of aristocracy. 'The wine is aristocratic, madame,' she had said jokingly to her mother-in-law, 'I am not.'

She had done it for simplicity. It was difficult enough when doing business with the English, who mostly refused to learn any language but their own. Many English visitors, imagining it to be her actual name, addressed her as 'Madame La Veuve' – which, while quite correct in French, wasn't what they intended.

The visitors consisted of wine-importers from abroad, a few connoisseurs, and some of her own landing agents. Her chief of cellar was also present, but Arnaud Compiain was never any use to her on social occasions. He would scarcely speak at all, and when he did it was only about the wine. Social badinage was quite outside his ken.

The occasion was the launch of the new fine dry wine. There had been a growing interest in less sweetness in the *cuvées* since poor Mr Burnes attempted to make it popular in 1850. Through the fifties and into the sixties, a few wine-makers produced what was thought of as an 'English *cuvée*' with much less sugar, and in the forefront was The Widow Tramont.

'You had great courage, madame,' said Patterton. 'Once it is done it cannot be undone – I wonder you had the fortitude to go on with the idea when it was so slow to become profitable.'

'I had good reason. A friend of mine first gave me a taste of a champagne *brut*. He told me then it was a wine with a great future and, as he was generally right, I heeded his words.'

'Indeed? May one ask who he was?'

'The man after whom I've named the new brand – Le Baptiste.'

'Good heavens! I thought it was after the gentleman for whose head Salome danced!'

'That's what most people will think – because, of course, we champagne makers have chosen Biblical names for our bottles – Jeroboam, Rehoboam, Methuselah…'

'I've often wanted to try champagne from the largest,' put in Sir Arthur Mateman. 'Nebuchadnezzar, by Gad!'

'In my opinion the wine never tastes as good from a large bottle,' Nicole said. 'I ought not to tell you that because of course it would be good to sell large numbers of the Nebuchadnezzar. But the finest sparkle is in the half-bottle, the bottle and the magnum.'

'Can't find much wrong with yours no matter what it comes in,' Sir Arthur said gallantly. He had kept close to her side since arriving. By Gad but she was an attractive woman! Even the black dress that had become her famous attire made her look prettier. Her fine clear skin was set off by the soft black ruffles of silk against her throat, her slender waist by the very fashionable looped-up skirt with its fringed apron-front.

She always wore a soft silk cap with black lace. It had become a sort of trademark. But as the years had gone by it was less a part of widow's weeds and more a fashion accessory. They were made especially for her by a smart Paris milliner who liked to bring out something new for her each time there was a special occasion.

Today she had provided a little wired cap of cream silk edged with ruched black Valenciennes, held up from her ears by little satin flowers of cream and palest mauve. To this Nicole had added a spray of cream roses pinned to her dress.

All the ladies were very fashionable. The elder Madame de Tramont wore deep violet silk trimmed in self-coloured braid and a matching hat smothered in violets. Madame Fournier was in beige corded grosgrain with brown and pink fringing, worn with a small bonnet of cream velvet.

Out on the lawn the young people wore less formal clothes. Alys was in a flounced dress of fine muslin, blue sprigged with tiny pink roses. Delphine had chosen a gown in which the bodice and skirt were of two different fabrics so that she appeared to be in a some sailor-like outfit of white and dark blue. The boys, of course, wore beige trousers of thick cotton and short dark jackets, suitable attire for country pursuits. Even so their cravats were carefully tied and they were hatted against the dangers of the June sun.

'A fine family,' remarked Patterton, watching them as they moved eagerly after the croquet balls. 'How pretty the girls are.'

'Demmed pretty,' agreed Sir Arthur. 'Let me see now – the girls are yours, eh, what? And the boys are Madame Fournier's.'

'Quite correct.'

'I dessay you hope for a match between a pair of 'em, eh? Need a man to carry on the business.'

Nicole gave him a cold glance which she managed to change to a smile only just in time. Patterton said, laughing, 'That's not a very suitable remark to make to The Widow Tramont, old boy.'

'Eh? What? Oh, see what you mean! Demmed silly of me. All the same, I s'pose it would be an advantage if you could marry off one of your girls to a relation. Keep it all in the family.'

'I don't approve of marriage between

cousins,' Nicole said, with more terseness than she intended.

Soon it was time for the morning visit to end. Nicole walked with them to their carriages. 'You can rely on a large order for the Baptiste vintage from our firm,' said Patterton before stepping in. 'And by the way … Lord Grassington particularly asked me to give you his respects.'

She smiled and nodded as she held out her hand in farewell. It was always pleasant to have messages by word of mouth from Gerrard, although he was a regular correspondent.

Nicole had a wide circle of friends and acquaintances. She was much courted, both by those who admired her for herself and those who had an eye on her business. She had said many times that she would never re-marry. The only man who had tempted her to change her mind was Gerrard.

As the rest of the world saw her, she was an attractive woman who could easily have found herself another husband, to help her run the business and the vineyard. It was whispered jokingly in her circle that it was because she wanted to keep the de Tramont name on her champagne that she shied away from marriage.

The truth was that, alas, Gerrard was already married. More than that, he was important in political circles.

They had known each other for quite a long time before they exchanged so much as a kiss. On her quite frequent visits to London Nicole had met the Earl of Grassington in connection with a campaign to change the tax laws on wine. Naturally it was to the advantage of wine producers and importers if the British Parliament could be persuaded to reduce the very heavy import duties, but it wasn't until 1861 that the campaigners succeeded.

The unofficial committee which had concerned itself with persuading the government consisted of some ten or fifteen members, some able to be present in London at all times and some, like Nicole, only occasional visitors. Those who were present on the happy day decided to have a dinner in celebration.

Naturally they drank champagne. To Nicole's consternation, it was the product of a rival house. 'We apologise,' Gerrard laughed. 'Unfortunately this establishment only stocks Moet!'

'After today's victory, I can submit to this lesser defeat,' said Nicole. She sipped. 'I will even admit that this is quite a good champagne.'

'Such magnanimity!' Gerrard kissed her hand in salutation.

She was the only woman present in a gathering with ten men. She was flattered and courted all evening, but fate had placed Gerrard by her side at the table. They had always liked each other, but in the warmth and gaiety of that occasion they seemed somehow to be drawn to each other.

It wasn't that he was handsome, or especially witty, or outstandingly talented. He had a good business head, a desire to do some good to his country by playing his part in the work of the House of Lords – but other than that he was relatively unremarkable. Some bond of understanding seemed to grow between them nevertheless, spun out of a shared interest in wine and the fact that they were lonely.

'Lonely?' Nicole said when he mentioned the word. 'How can that be? You are here in your homeland, surrounded by people you know...'

'Yes of course. I don't know what made me say it. It's more true of yourself – you are far from home, madame.'

'Yes indeed. And tonight, oddly enough, I feel it. I should so much like to have someone here from the House of Tramont, who would understand what a great thing we've accomplished.' She shook herself out of her momentary wistfulness. 'Come, sir! Explain how it can be that *you* feel lonely?'

His fresh-skinned face coloured up. He couldn't tell her that he was often lonely, even in his marriage. His wife was a good soul, but she had been chosen for him in his teens. She was a great huntswoman, took a keen interest in farming his lands – London she hated, so that when he came to Town for the Parliamentary sessions he was always solitary. So matters would remain until his only daughter was presented at court, after which it would be necessary to have at least one London season to find her a good husband.

But a gentleman never speaks critically of his wife so he turned the subject. However it became clear from his description of his life in London that he was almost always apart from Lady Grassington, and the rest was easy to gather by anyone with as keen an instinct as Nicole.

It was Gerrard who saw her to her lodgings shortly after midnight. She had rooms in a pleasant house in Mayfair. She invited him in to finish an interesting discussion they had begun in the hansom, concerning the possibility of growing good wine in the New World.

'No wine worthy of the name will ever be made anywhere else but Europe,' she insisted.

'Come now! The Chinese make wine. And it's always been made in the Middle East – it's mentioned in the Bible.'

'My dear Lord Grassington, you will remember that it's never mentioned as being any good!'

He laughed. 'You are an extraordinary woman,' he said. 'It's been a great pleasure to have so much of your company this evening.'

'Let us celebrate properly, milord. Let us open a bottle of my own champagne for a toast to our achievement.'

The sleepy manservant summoned from the basement brought up champagne from the cellar and ice from the icehouse in the garden. When he had gone, Gerrard expertly opened the bottle then poured the wine. He raised his glass. 'To our victory!'

'Our victory.' She sipped. Then she looked up, smiling. 'Now, milord, admit that this is better than the wine we had at supper.'

'Certainly. Anything would taste like nectar, drunk in such circumstances.'

She raised her eyebrows in query.

'I mean, drinking it here with you alone, at dead of night.' He emptied his glass and set it by. 'I must go, I suppose,' he said with a sigh. 'The poor hansom-driver is waiting.'

'Alas,' she said.

He picked up his hat and gloves, went to the door, then turned. 'Of course,' he said, 'I could always go down and tell him he's not needed.'

He waited. She could turn it off with a laugh, pretending it was merely gallantry, and that would be the end of it.

A silence fraught with suspense grew in the room. Suddenly he came back and took her hand. 'Don't send me away,' he begged.

She had an inward picture of her own room once he had gone – herself slowly undressing, trying to unwind after the excitement of the day, trying to relax enough to rest. She thought of many other such nights in lodgings in foreign cities, the long loneliness of her life since Jean-Baptiste went away.

'Stay,' she whispered, leaning her head against Gerrard's shoulder. 'Please stay.'

They had had a long and faithful love affair – made more precious by distance and the infrequency with which they could see each other. It had gone on now for nine years and, as Nicole often told herself consolingly, looked like going on for another fifty.

In a way, it suited her. She didn't think she would like to be married now, to have to defer to a husband, to have to share her business decisions. She had been head of Champagne Tramont for so long now that the habit of easy command was firm in her. Gerrard, too, was accustomed to power. They might have quarrelled if they had been man and wife. But as lovers, they were tolerant and considerate because their time together was so precious.

Thus deep in thought, Nicole came back

into the salon to give a glance at the clearing-up. Maids were hurrying about, removing glasses and little tables, putting empty bottles in rubbish baskets.

Clothilde was standing out on the terrace in the shade of the arbour vine, watching the youngsters at play. 'Sir Arthur Mateman was right,' she said. 'They are a handsome group. And though you pooh-poohed the idea, my dear, I believe there may be a romance burgeoning between two of them.'

'You think so?' Nicole said, coming out to join her. 'I don't see any sign of it.'

'But then, my dear, you're so busy while they're here.'

The two girls of course lived permanently at Tramont, under the care of a succession of governesses and special tutors. Paulette's boys came to join them at Christmas and for the summer, usually from June until the end of August, at which time the work on the estate speeded up so that Nicole had no time for visitors.

Although the summer was regarded as holiday time, there were still lessons. At the moment there was a German governess, attempting to teach them her language and some mathematics. Alys, now almost eighteen, continually rebelled, as did her cousin Edmond, though for different reasons. Alys felt it was unnecessary for a young lady to know anything about trigonometry: Edmond simply felt it was a rotten thing to be cooped up indoors with a dull old lady when the weather outside was fine.

Delphine never thought of rebelling. She was the steadying influence on her somewhat madcap elder sister. Besides, she felt it would be wrong to hurt poor Fraulein's feelings by skipping her lessons.

Only Robert, the youngest of the group, actually enjoyed his studies. He was a quiet boy, very tall for his age and very serious. Often by his conversation and attitude he could have been taken for the eldest of the quartet.

Nicole loved him with a quiet yet passionate love. To her, he was Jean-Baptiste all over again – less muscular as yet and with more brown than black in his hair, yet so like his father that she often wondered no one remarked on it.

It was strange how easily he had been accepted as Paulette's child. Years ago, when she left Tramont after her mother's funeral, Paulette was known to be expecting a baby. Then there had been the terrible upset of her husband abandoning her, all of which had been taken care of by The Widow Tramont. After that, for reasons that seemed good to everyone, Madame had gone travelling. When she came back she was very busy, but yet, like a good sister, found time to visit Paulette in Strasbourg.

When Paulette Fournier came again to make a long stay at the Villa Tramont, her two little boys were five and two. That was how it was – Madame and her two little boys, the first called after her husband's father, the second called after her own grandfather.

Edmond was, surprisingly, a blithe and buoyant child. It was almost as if his mother's nervousness and insecurity challenged him to be optimistic in the face of everything. Robert was cleverer and less talkative, but equally sure of himself in his quieter way.

They were, as the saying goes, a credit to their mother. Edmond was due to go to Paris to enrol in the university very soon. Robert as yet had had no plans made for him.

'There's no romance among any of them,' Paulette Fournier said with an emphatic shake of the head. 'I don't encourage that kind of thing.'

Clothilde shrugged. She hadn't the same strong feelings against marriages within the family as the other two women. To her, as an aristocrat, such things were commonplace. But if they had set their minds against it, that was that.

After a long family lunch, Clothilde retired to her room for a nap. The young people rushed out to go boating. Nicole had work to do, but to her surprise her sister came to interrupt her about an hour later.

'May I come in?' She entered timidly as she spoke: she was never at ease in the office, which Nicole had furnished with fine mahogany pieces and a rather frowning exhibition cabinet of antique glass.

'Of course. Can you sit quietly for a few minutes while I finish this? It's the bill of lading for the American shipment.'

Paulette took a chair, amusing herself by examining the old bottles in the cabinet. She couldn't see anything attractive about them but everyone said they were very valuable.

She looked at her sister's bent head. How clever Nicole was! Would she be clever enough to deal with the dilemma that seemed to be looming?

'Well, my love?' Nicole said at last, having summoned a clerk to take away the bill of lading. 'What can I do for you?'

'Nicole, you know what Old Madame was saying – about a romance between–'

'Oh, let's have none of that nonsense,' Nicole said, getting up with rather too much energy. 'I tell you – I see no signs of it–'

'But I do, Nicci.'

The two women regarded each other. They were so alike, and yet so different. Both had brown hair elegantly dressed, both had brown eyes in a clear-skinned complexion. But Paulette's mouth lacked the firmness of Nicole: the angle of her chin was never as determined as her sister's.

Nevertheless, at this moment she was showing a good deal of firmness.

'Very well, very well,' Nicole murmured, smoothing down the front of the looped skirt. 'Tell me about it.'

'Robert has a photograph of Delphine. He carries it in the inner pocket of his jacket in a little leather case.'

'A photograph? Where did he get that?'

'He cut it of the *Journal de la Marne* – it's the one you had taken when she received an award at the horseshow.'

'Well,' said Nicole, with an elaborate shrug, 'what of it? He admires his cousin – that's not uncommon.'

'She's not his cousin and that's what makes it uncommon! Come now, Nicci – stop trying to make nothing of it! I'm very worried.'

'But about what, for God's sake? The boy's scarcely fifteen–'

'I know his age, thank you,' Paulette replied with what, for her, was great tartness. She'd been about to add, After all, I *am* his mother – but she bit her tongue on the words. After a hesitation she went on: 'Robert has always been old for his age – you know that as well as I do–'

'But at fifteen boys get romantic notions – they idolise actresses and opera singers–'

'Oh, indeed? Then why has Robert chosen Delphine when he could have had a picture of Jenny Lind?'

Nicole went slowly to the exhibition cabinet to stare absently at the ancient bottles caught in the brightness glinting in at the side of the sunblinds. 'You cannot possibly think it's serious,' she said.

'I think it may well become serious.'

'But Delphine shows no signs of being attracted to him.'

'She prefers his company to Edmond,' said Paulette, who had watched with a terrible fascination as the relationship developed.

'But that's because they have more in common–'

'Nicole, I think we've made a big mistake in how we've handled this. If we had brought them up, all together, like a family of brothers and sisters, it could never have come about. But throwing them together at intervals for fairly long periods–'

'I often thought about having you here to live. I longed for it, Paulie... To see him every day, it would have been such a happiness to me...'

Paulette got up. She came to her sister's side, put an arm about her shoulders. They looked at their reflection in the glass doors of the cabinet. 'I'm sorry, Nicci. I know how you must feel.'

'I was afraid of giving it all away if he lived here,' Nicole said. She shrugged off Paulette's embrace and whirled to look at her. 'Well, what are we going to do? Are we going to take your fears seriously?'

'Better safe than sorry.'

'But surely... It's just a phase... He'll find someone else...'

'Robert doesn't change with every wind that blows, my dear.'

So like his father... Jean-Baptiste had been another who knew his own mind.

'Let me think about it,' Nicole said. 'The best thing is to get them apart instead of letting them play together all summer as usual. Let me work something out.'

'Do it soon, Nicole.'

'I promise.'

When Paulette had gone Nicole sat down to think. Separation... That was the key. But it had become such a tradition for the family to spend the summer together, a whole three months of picnics and outings and simple pleasures.

In the autumn Edmond would enter the Sorbonne; Robert would return to Strasbourg to finish his studies at the Lycée. He wanted to go on to the École Centrale des Arts et Manufactures with a view to becoming an architect. He had shown some interest in the building business of his supposed father, Auguste Fournier, even cajoling Paulette into taking him to Rethel to talk to the manager now in charge.

That in itself was typical. Edmond, three years his senior, had no idea what he wanted to do with his life. Robert already had plans.

The problem was that to get rid of the two boys would seem inhospitable. Some convincing explanation would have to be given. Nicole racked her brains, but nothing came.

Meanwhile, in the next few days, she watched the young people. And it was true: Robert had a special feeling for Delphine. He was fond of his elder cousin Alys, but when they paired off it was always Robert who sought Delphine as a partner.

What was worse, Nicole began to suspect that Delphine cared for Robert in a special way. Probably it was just a particularly warm friendship – Nicole couldn't believe that Delphine would actually fall in love with a boy of fifteen. And yet... Robert seldom seemed a boy of fifteen. He was taller than any of them, topping Edmond by almost a head. His voice had already turned to a pleasing light baritone. Acquaintances and visitors seldom addressed him as 'my boy' – it was generally 'young man'.

Nicole had other worries, never discussed with the family. An enemy was attacking the vineyards.

The name of this invader was Phylloxera, a small yellow aphis, so small that without a lens it was invisible to the naked eye. This little insect lived on the sap of the roots of vines, and in 1863 it had made its appearance in the vineyards of Provence.

It wasn't entirely unheralded. The disease caused by the phylloxera insect had been noted in the mid-fifties in the wild grapes of the Mississippi, but no one had paid any attention to that. Then it began to appear elsewhere in America, notably in the new vineyards of California.

Poor Jean-Baptiste, Nicole said to herself when she read that report. Was it for this that you gave up the Champagne vines?

This year the pest had been found in important vineyards of Europe – in those of Bordeaux and Portugal. 'Don't worry about it, madame,' said Leboileau, successor to old Compiain as manager of the vineyard of Tramont. 'It won't attack our vines – it's too cold for it here in the Marne. You can see that, by where it's gone so far – always in the south, always in the areas of long sunshine.'

Nicole read every report, every botanist's thesis. Those experts put forward no grounds to support Leboileau's claim – there was no mention that the little insect was killed off by low temperatures.

Certainly, so far, it had made its depredations in the warm areas only. But one day, one day... Who could tell?

It struck her as ironic that just when Champagne Tramont had reached pre-eminence, the whole of the wine trade was put in jeopardy by something as insignificant as an invisible plant louse.

This recurring anxiety was kept to herself. So too was the new anxiety brought to her by her sister. She must do something about that, and soon. But what?

The Gordian knot was cut by Fraulein Geber, the governess. She took to her bed yet again with eyes streaming and nose red. When Nicole went, duty bound, to visit her in her sickroom, she found the poor lady in tremendous discomfort and distress.

'Madame, I regret that I am once again incapacitated. This is three times since June has begun.'

'Don't let that worry you, Fraulein. It can't be helped. Is there anything I can do for you?'

'No, alas,' groaned the governess, moving her grey head about restlessly on her pillows. 'Madame, I have come to believe it is the climate here that causes the ailment. I never suffered from it at home in Bern. The air there is so clear...'

'The air here is clear enough,' Nicole rejoined. 'Somewhat damp at times, I agree–'

'How strange it is that all through the

winter I was perfectly well, never a cold or a sneeze. Yet the moment the summer comes, I catch this recurring cold.'

Fraulein Geber had come to them in September. True enough, she had been fit and well until the Champagne district broke into bloom at the end of May and the beginning of June. It was a mystery.

'I have come to the conclusion,' said Fraulein after sneezing a dozen times into her handkerchief, 'that I must return home. I deeply regret, madame – I have loved being in your employ and my two charges are charming. Nevertheless, I am of little use to them, *nicht wahr*, if I am laid low every week or so.'

'Oh, Fraulein, don't say that. I should hate to lose you–'

'I think it best, madame. To tell the truth, I am so miserable each time this plague strikes me, I long to be at home among the mountains. So forgive me if I give notice to leave as soon as possible. I realise I forfeit some salary if I–'

'Pray, Fraulein Geber, don't think of that!' Nicole's mind was racing. 'Tell me, you expect to be perfectly fit once you get to the Bernese Oberland again?'

'Oh, certainly. I'm sure it has to do with the climate.'

'You wouldn't object to having my girls with you in Switzerland?'

'Ha?' cried Fraulein in surprise.

'It seems to me – they are making very slow progress with their German conversation, sad to say. Wouldn't it be a good thing if they went with you for a month or two–? Naturally, I should have them put into a good hotel with you and you would continue to treat the summer months as a holiday period. In that way you could complete your year's contract with me, and then... Then I believe I shall send them to London, to improve their English!'

'What an excellent plan!' cried Fraulein Geber, for the moment regaining her voice and her enthusiasm for life. The prospect of losing one-quarter's salary had been dispiriting.

When the girls heard the plan they greeted it with differing emotions. 'Bern?' cried Alys. 'Mama, why on earth must we go to Bern? According to Fraulein, there's nothing there but mountains!'

'I think it will be interesting. There are some very fine buildings, I believe. It will interest Robert,' said Delphine.

'Robert is not going,' Nicole said. 'Neither is Edmond.'

'What? You mean you are sending us off without them?' Alys protested. 'Oh, Mama, that's not fair! We *always* spend the summer together.'

'My dear,' Paulette put in, 'I can't afford

to send my two boys off on a three-month trip to Switzerland.'

Delpine looked reproachfully at her mother. She was waiting for her to say: Money need be no object.

But strange to say, Mama made no move. And Aunt Paulette went on: 'In any case, I think it would be a good idea if I took my two to Paris. I should like to buy some new clothes for Edmond – one doesn't want him turning up at university looking like a country bumpkin.'

'Paris!' cried Edmond, eyes sparkling. 'Well, that's not so bad!'

'How about you, Robert? You don't want to go to Paris, do you?' coaxed Delphine. 'Come with us to Switzerland.'

'Certainly not!' his mother intervened. 'It's time in any case to make a change in our routines. We can't go on for ever spending the summer in each other's pockets.'

'I don't see why not! We've always enjoyed it up to now! Mama, tell Aunt Paulette she's to let the boys come with us to Bern.'

'Hey, not so fast!' objected Edmond. 'I would *much* rather go to Paris.'

'But Paris will be so hot and dusty in summer–'

'But a lot less dull than Bern!'

'All right then, you go to Paris. Robert comes with us. Mama won't mind paying for one extra. You'd rather come to Bern, wouldn't you, Robert.'

'Much rather,' he agreed, looking anxiously at his mother for permission.

She shook her head. 'No, dear, we impose far too much on your aunt already. She's given us hospitality every summer for a dozen years or so. It's time to make a change–'

'But why? Why, when we've always loved it just the way it was?' cried Delphine. 'Mama, tell Aunt Paulie that it doesn't matter about "imposing"–'

'Delphine, dear, the time comes when everything has to change. I want you to go to Bern and speak good German. Then I want you to go to London for a year to learn English–'

'London!' cried Alys. 'Oh, Mama!' She rushed at her, to throw her arms around her and kiss her thoroughly. 'Oh, London! How wonderful! Shall we see the Queen? And the handsome young Prince of Wales?'

Even Delphine's objections were overcome by this news. Nicole, observing her, was relieved. Fond though she might be of her cousin Robert, she was fonder still of the idea of a year in one of the world's great capitals.

Chapter Sixteen

Alys de Tramont was very annoyed when at last the disdainful English footman had closed the room door behind him.

'This isn't at all what I expected!' she cried, taking off her travelling bonnet to throw it in exasperation on the walnut dressing table. 'Mama has cheated us!'

'Oh, Alys, come now–'

'What do you mean, come now! You know we both expected to be staying with Lady Grassington–'

'*You* expected it. I don't know that I did. After all, Mama hasn't met Lady Grassington above twice, and her friendship with milord is for business only.'

'But when we wrote to her – I always took for granted that we would be in a house in Mayfair–'

'Did you actually say so? If you had, I'm sure Mama would have put you right at once.'

'Oh Delphine,' cried her sister, sitting down on the end of the bed and beating the blue satin quilt with her fists, 'why must you be so *reasonable* about it?'

'Because I don't see much to get in a great

state about.' Delphine made a little gesture that took in their comfortable surroundings. 'What's wrong with this?'

It was a pretty room, not large but neatly arranged. It had a big double bed with deep blue hangings, covers, and valances that came down to meet a Turkey carpet. There was an elegant wash-stand of Italian marble, a dressing-table of the latest design, and a little desk for work on any of the studies undertaken by the pupils of Mrs Mac-Ardle's School for Young Ladies.

'I'll tell you what's wrong with it,' protested Alys. 'It's in Kensington! *Kensington!* I didn't come to England to be tucked away in a village ten miles from Buckingham Palace–'

'I'm sure it's not as far as that, Alys. It's only about four–'

'Four, five, a million! It's outside the possibilities of an afternoon stroll, at any rate! What chance of meeting the Prince by accident, of having him raise his hat to us, as he did to Mademoiselle Fibranc?'

'Dear sister,' Delphine said, untying her bonnet strings and laying the bonnet carefully on the bed, 'I must tell you that I am unconcerned whether or not the Prince of Wales raises his hat to us. As far as I could tell as the carriage brought us in, this seems a pleasant spot. There are gardens and a good street with shops. No doubt there are ballrooms and concert halls. It may not be London proper, but it certainly offers more possibilities than Bern.'

Alys began to laugh. Their sojourn in Bern had been a mixed pleasure. The town proved rather more sophisticated than they'd expected, with plenty of agreeable young gentlemen with whom they went boating on the Aare or on carriage rides to the Botanical Gardens, under the watchful eye of Fraulein Geber. There had also been frequent occasions when, Fraulein having gone to spend an evening with her parents, the two girls slipped out to visit a cafe and join in the singing and dancing to a Bernese peasant orchestra.

On the other hand, they had been taken to museums to admire very dull paintings, attended lectures on the history of Switzerland, and made to do mathematics, geology, and to sketch in the mountains. All the while, they were strictly forbidden to speak French – German only was permitted. Since Alys wouldn't apply herself, Delphine had had to do most of the talking, and very boring it became. Fraulein Geber was Protestant, and talked mostly about the Protestant religion.

'Mama, you've no idea how monotonous it became,' Alys had reported when they were met by their mother in Paris. 'I think she wanted to convert us.'

'And did she succeed?'

'Of course not. I never really listened.'

'Then what are you complaining of?' Nicole laughed. 'Ah, you didn't have a bad time, I can see that. You both look very well. And I assure that Mrs MacArdle is a good Catholic so you will have no such problems in England.'

'And who is Mrs MacArdle?'

'The directrice of the school to which you are going.'

This was the first they had heard of it. Alys argued all the way from Paris to Boulogne, and was still arguing when Nicole bade them goodbye on board the steam packet.

But it had done no good. Here they were and here they would stay, under the governance of Mrs MacArdle, a gentle-woman from County Clare.

'It will be quite enjoyable,' Delphine smoothed. 'At least we don't have a govern-ess any more, watching our every move. And the other girls may be fun. Besides...' Delphine went to the window and looked out. 'I see a hackney stand not far off. Alys my darling, we can hire a hackney any time we are free, to take us to the town.'

'Do you think so?' groaned Alys. 'I wager Mrs MacArdle won't let us go anywhere unchaperoned.'

But life wasn't as grim as that. Mrs MacArdle's regime was based on 'Trust and

Honour'. It was written up in Gothic lettering in gold on a purple shield which hung over the mantel in the dining-room.

'You'll find she's quite reasonable,' the de Tramonts were told by Louise Quezerel, another French pupil of some months' standing. 'If you show an interest in the songs of Thomas Moore and his friend Lord Byron, she will approve of you, and with her approval comes her trust.'

'But in what way are we "trusted"? Can we go out alone?'

'Oh yes. But only for limited periods, of course. Sundays are the worst – we have to go to church twice on Sunday and carry our rosaries in our hands when we go out.'

'Dear heaven,' said Alys. 'Another religious crank!'

'No, no – I think it is more a demonstration to the public of the moral climate of her "establishment". But only learn a few songs by Thomas Moore and sing them at our soirées, and she will love you like a daughter.'

The girls handed over the letters of introduction they had brought from Calmady. Mrs MacArdle wrote inviting the various people to call. Lord Grassington came, bringing his wife, who stalked about the school looking for dust on picture frames and behind ornaments. 'Not bad, not bad,' she remarked. 'You can mention to

Madame de Tramont, when you next have business with her, that the place is by no means deficient in its standards.'

Gerrard Arkley, Earl of Grassington, smiled fondly at his lady. She was a good sort, always had been. He had no reason to regret his marriage to her, for she had given him a son and a daughter, was the best rider to hounds in Cumbria, and stood no nonsense from anybody.

But he had never loved her. He had found diversion in the usual places as a young man, had had a mistress or two among the pretty married women of his circle. He never had any difficulty attracting affection – tall, with the pale complexion and bright blue eyes that often go with red hair, he wasn't unattractive, though far from being exactly handsome. But it was his open, outgoing kindliness that drew people to him.

When Gerrard Arkley first met Madame de Tramont, he felt as if a thunderbolt had hit him. He had never believed in love at first sight, and certainly not for men in their forties – yet it seized him like the talons of a hawk and thereafter never let him go. Now that he was nearing fifty, his heart still leapt like a boy's if he had news of a projected meeting with Nicole. Just to be with her for an hour or two was delight. To be able to spend a night with her was bliss itself.

Her two daughters were known to him already: he had met them on visits to Tramont. But it was almost a year since he had seen them. He was surprised at the difference in them. They had ceased to be children – they were young ladies now. Alys must be … what …? eighteen by now. And even the younger one, always the quieter and the less excitable of the two – she too, little Delphine, seemed almost a woman now he saw her again.

'Invite 'em to spend an evening, Emma. Or better still – let's take 'em to a theatre and a theatre supper.'

'Oh, d'you think so, Gerry?'

'Why not? It must be pretty dull for them, out here in the sticks. And look here – Milly's birthday party – why don't you tell Milly to send them an invitation?'

So, although not fully in the swim of the London winter season, the two girls were asked out and about. 'This is more like it!' said Alys under her breath to her sister as they were handed out of their carriage at the Grassingtons' mansion in Belgravia. 'This is what I thought we came to London for!'

Lady Grassington had gone out of her way to provide a throng of pleasant young people for her daughter's twentieth birthday party. It wasn't done for the sake of the French visitors, but for Milly who, now entering her twenties, was still not engaged.

She had been 'out' for two seasons, and was growing anxious that she'd be reduced to accepting a match made for her by her parents.

'It's so vexing,' she sighed to the two French girls. 'I nearly got Harold DeBarclay in the spring, but Laura Spofforth hooked him from under my nose.'

'I am so sorry,' Delphine said politely. 'Did you care for him particularly?'

'Not *particularly*,' Milly confessed, wrinkling her rather broad nose, 'but he was the best of the bunch last March. And then we went down to the country for the summer, and I thought Matthew Primm was going to offer, but he hurt his back poling a punt and had to be taken home lying flat in a waggonnette.'

'How very sad,' said Alys, stifling a laugh. She glanced about urgently for the young man whose name appeared on her carnet for the next dance. She was longing to escape from this stocky, uninteresting girl.

Help came in the form of Gavin Hope-town, a personable young man in a very elegant set of evening clothes. Moving across the salon to find the partner he had been promised to for the polka, he caught Alys's wildly signalling glance. Impelled by more than sympathy – for she was an extremely pretty dark-haired stranger in a fetching crinoline gown of soft rose pink –

he deflected his path.

'Our dance, I believe?' he remarked, offering her his arm.

Alys consulted her card. 'Monsieur Dennis?'

'Not in the least,' said he, capturing her hand as it hovered over his sleeve, 'but you want to escape and I am at your service.' He led her through the arch to the second drawing-room, where the floor had been cleared for party dancing.

'M'sieu!' Alys gasped, not having followed all he said. Her English deserted her. She went on in French, 'If you aren't Monsieur Dennis, who are you?'

'Ah, you're one of the French girls I've heard so much about,' said he, in excellent French. 'My name's Hopetown – I'm employed by Monsieur Richard Patterton, known to you, I imagine?'

'Ah!' She was relieved. It was very bad, to go off to dance with someone other than the promised partner, but perhaps it was excusable if the new partner was a friend of a friend. 'You are in the wine business?'

'Only in the lesser ranks,' he said with a rueful smile. 'And just to make sure you understand my situation, I was only invited tonight to make up the numbers.'

'Oh, how sad. Nevertheless, I thank you for rescuing me. I was hearing all about Miss Arkley's failures in the marriage market.'

'Poor girl,' he said in a voice of friendly amusement. 'If she'd only not *advertise* her tumbles... It puts the fellows off tremendously.'

'You know her well?'

'I've met her often. You see, Lady G needs me to pad out her parties – the suitable young men steer clear.' The music began so he took one of her hands in his and with the other held her at arm's length. 'Tell me how you like London,' he said as they jogged off to the spritely tune.

'I believe it will be very enjoyable,' she said.

'Oh, is that because you've just met me?'

'Ah, come – you can hardly expect me to say yes to that! You rescued me, and I am grateful, but my enjoyment of London doesn't depend on you, m'sieu.'

During the weeks that followed, that statement became largely untrue. Gavin Hopetown became very important in Alys's scheme of things. At first it was all quite open and above board – he called at the school, was inspected by Mrs MacArdle and approved of because he was vouched for by an acquaintance of Madame de Tramont. He was of a respectable Scottish family, had received an excellent education, had travelled much in France and, though engaged in 'trade', it was the wine trade, which everyone understood to be especially elegant. He escorted both girls to one or two concerts and lectures. Mrs MacArdle was untroubled.

To the contrary, Delphine became more and more anxious as Christmas approached, bringing their mother on a short visit. 'If she catches one hint of how often you see Gavin, she'll–'

'She'll what? Fetch us home? I don't think she'll do that, Delphine. Now I come to think of it, I believe she wanted us out of the house for some reason. That decision to send us to Bern with Fraulein was very odd–'

'Now don't talk nonsense,' Delphine interrupted. 'Just because you have a guilty conscience, that's no reason to claim that Mama has been underhand–'

'My conscience is quite clear! Gavin and I have done nothing wrong–'

'Are you saying he hasn't even held your hand? Really, Alys, you know as well as I do that you're behaving badly. Otherwise why have you never mentioned Gavin in any of your letters to Mama. Why do you slip out to meet him in secret–'

'Delphine!'

'Good gracious, Allie, you can't really imagine I don't hear you when you creep out of bed at night and slip through the french windows to the gate at the back–'

'You've been spying on me!'

'Nothing of the kind. What worries me is that one of the others may hear you and raise an alarm that a burglar has got in–'

Alys collapsed in a fit of giggles. 'Oh, wouldn't that be awful? Caught red-handed with mud on my slippers–'

'Or worse than mud! I do think that meeting in a mews with horses going munch-munch at their oats is terribly unromantic!'

'Oh, Delphie, darling!' They fell into each other's arms and on to the side of the bed, laughing until the tears came. But when they had sobered Delphine gave a frown and a sigh.

'We may laugh, Allie, but you've got to make up your mind. Either you tell Mama about this young man and get permission to see him openly–'

'She'd never consent. He's so unsuitable. Do you know, Delphie – he has scarcely any money except what he makes as an agent in the wine trade?'

'Mama might not think too badly of him. You know, although she speaks little about it, she was poor herself as a girl.'

'Ye-es... But that doesn't prevent her from wanting us to make grand marriages. And you know Grandmama wants at least one of us to get a title.'

Delphie gave a snort. 'Mama won't be too much influenced by Grandmama. They get on well enough but I always feel Mama doesn't like Old Madame to interfere too much. If she met Gavin, and liked him, I think she might allow the friendship to go on.'

'So long as it remained only a friendship.'

'Well, it's only a little more than that, isn't it? A flirtation after all.'

'I don't know,' Alys said, with unexpected tears brimming under her dark lashes. 'I thought so at first but... When I think of Mama telling me to end it, I somehow ... I couldn't bear that, Delphie.'

'Alys!' Delphine leaned away to study her sister's face. She caught the glint of tears. 'Alys, you *can't* be growing serious about him.'

'No. No, of course not. Only ... the thought of being forbidden to see him is... Well, let's not tempt Providence. Promise me you'll not mention him to Mama.'

'Of course I won't, Allie. All the same...'

'All the same what?'

'You're playing with fire.'

'Oh, you don't know him! He's so nice and good... It's just a *shame* he hasn't a title or a fortune!'

'You're not thinking of him as a suitor? Mama would have a fit! She doesn't want you to marry an Englishman, Allie! Now look here – promise me, *promise* me, you won't for one moment think of anything more serious than a few moonlight kisses and notes left for you in secret places. Allie! Promise!'

'All right,' sighed Alys, 'I promise.' Yet she knew even then that she was unlikely to be able to abide by it.

Nicole was pleased with them when she arrived for a short stay in December. They looked well, seemed contented, and could certainly speak English a lot better than she could herself.

London was pleasant with pre-Christmas gaiety. Candle-lit fir trees, made popular by the late Prince Consort, decked the vestibules of the larger shops, and coloured globes in some of the gasoliers lent a touch of fantasy to the less dignified emporiums.

Owing gratitude to Lady Grassington for kindnesses to her daughters, Nicole paid a morning call upon her with Alys and Delphine.

'My dear Madame de Tramont, I would have done more for them,' her ladyship said with a shrug, 'but you know, as they're at finishing school, they cannot be regarded as "out".'

'I prefer it so,' Nicole said. 'They will have their first season next year in Paris, when they will be introduced to the young men whose families are in touch with me.'

'In touch?' Alys said, a sparkle of indignation coming into her brown eyes. 'Mama, you haven't begun negotiations–'

'Come, come, my dear, we don't want to discuss family matters at the moment–'

'Ah, madame, I do sympathise,' Lady Grassington sighed. She gave a glance towards her own daughter, who was sitting with a piece of embroidery into which she was inserting clumsy stitches. 'You know, in the end it's easier to take things into one's own hands...'

'That's terribly oldfashioned!' cried Alys. 'These days it's considered wrong to–'

'By whom?' Nicole said lightly. 'By high-spirited daughters who don't know what's good for them. Now tell me, milady, what do you think of this great new canal in Egypt? Shall you ever travel through it, do you think?'

Lady Grassington followed her visitor's lead in changing the subject, said a few complimentary things about the French engineers of the Suez Canal, and the visit ended after the usual quarter of an hour. Late that afternoon a vanman in the livery of the firm of Champagne Tramont delivered a case of the finest champagne, together with a charming card thanking her ladyship for all her kindness. Honour was thus satisfied on both sides.

'Mama, what did you mean?' demanded Alys in the carriage taking them back to Kensington. *'Have* you started match-making?'

'Allie dear, it's inelegant to use that term and improper of you to inquire. In due course you will meet several young men in Paris. That's enough for you to know.' Nicole turned with a smile to Delphine. 'You too, my dear. Of course you have always known that the business is to be left to you equally when I am gone–'

'Oh, Mama, don't be gloomy!' Delphine protested. 'It's Christmas! And don't talk about husbands!'

'The word has never passed my lips,' Nicole pointed out, laughing a little. 'All the same, it's as well for you to have it in mind. When you return home next year I hope everything will be in good train, but of course these things take time, inquiries have to be made, lawyers have to be consulted – and lawyers are seldom in a hurry.'

A slight difficulty with the traffic at Hyde Park Corner caused a break in conversation. When the driver had at last controlled the horses and made his way through Knightsbridge, Nicole spoke of plans for the rest of her stay.

As they dined with her at her hotel that night, Alys went back to the subject. 'Mama, I know you say it's improper for me to inquire, but … let's speak about marriage. After all, you know, there's no hurry. I'm still only eighteen–'

'Yes, quite true, but one can't do nothing.

Look what has happened to poor Milly Arkley. But you must leave it all to me, dear – such things need careful thought.'

'But Mama, after all it concerns me – I mean us, both of us, Delphie and me. Listen, Mama, I hope you're not too set on us liking a gentleman with a title – after all, that's not important–'

'Quite, I agree with you. Of course it would please Grandmama–'

'But it's more important that we should *like* the man. You agree there?'

'Certainly,' Nicole said in some surprise. 'I should never dream of forcing you into anything that you didn't want – my dear, you haven't been imagining I would do that?'

'No, no, of course not.' Alys looked in appeal to Delphine. But Delphine was quiet, as usual – quieter, perhaps, than usual. Perhaps she too was thinking seriously for the first time about the business of marriage.

'Suppose, Mama … suppose that in Paris we were to meet someone – suppose we liked someone, but he wasn't on your list of possible suitors?'

'Well then, my love, I should look at him carefully and consult Pourdume and find out if he had an income that gave me confidence in his ability to support you properly. You see, Alys dear,' Nicole said with a muted sigh, 'it happens that you are the daughters of a very rich woman. And one wants to be sure that anyone who dangles after you isn't out for the money only. There are a lot of fortune-hunters in wait for girls like you, unfortunately.'

'Of course, that's true, but suppose there was a gentleman we included in our circle in Paris, but who perhaps–'

'That's all quite hypothetical, dear, and I don't think you should worry your head about it.'

'But Mama – after all, it's our lives we're talking about! What if one of us fell in love with a man who had no money?'

Nicole frowned. 'Alys… What makes you bring up such an idea?'

'Well … I…' Alys longed for the courage to say, 'I've met such a man, and I'm in love with him!' But she found she couldn't utter the words under the surprised gaze of her mother. 'I just wondered,' she ended weakly.

'Then I'll give you an answer. I should of course not want any daughter of mine to be unhappy over a man. But I should also hope that a young man with no money would have enough sense of honour to take himself off out of the way if he thought there was any danger of that sort. I'd have a poor opinion of him otherwise – and some doubts of his sincerity.'

Having thus disposed of some little romantic notions that were only natural in girls of that age, Nicole concentrated on giving her daughters as much fun as possible for the rest of her stay. She left for Dover three days after Christmas, wishing to be at home for a New Year Ball in Rheims in aid of a charity for which she was patroness.

Both Alys and Delphine had enjoyed her visit. Yet it had meant almost no opportunity to meet Gavin. Alys ran to her first rendezvous with him, swept along on winged feet, understanding at last that he was far too important to give up just to suit Mama's plans.

'Have you missed me, Gavin?' she asked.

'Not in the least. I was sent on business to Southampton and had hardly any time to think about you at all.'

'Oh, if that's true–!'

'No, my angel – I was absolutely miserable!' he confessed. 'It was wet and cold in Southampton and my hotel was dismal. But even if it had been a palace I'd have been unhappy there.'

She looked up into his solemn face, and at that moment knew that he really, genuinely loved her as she loved him. 'Gavin...?'

'Alys!'

It was their first kiss, tremulous and hesitant. Their lips scarcely brushed. Yet a moment later they were wrapped in each other's arms, murmuring endearments and exchanging caresses in growing passion.

'No!' he gasped at last, pushing her away. 'No, Alys – we must be honourable.'

'Gavin, I trust you–'

'But I don't trust myself! Don't you see… You're so adorable, and I long for you so much – but we mustn't, we really mustn't. I'd hate myself if I caused you the slightest unhappiness.'

'But I'm always happy when I'm with you, Gavin. Nothing else matters.'

For the moment he abandoned argument. They spent that meeting holding each other fast against the dreary cold of a winter afternoon in Kensington Gardens.

But when he saw her again Gavin was adamant. 'We mustn't allow ourselves to get carried away,' he said, his strict Scottish upbringing stiffening his resolve. 'I love you, Alys, and I want you to belong to me, but I've thought about it and thought about it and there's only one way – I must write to your mother and ask for your hand in marriage.'

'No, don't!' she cried in panic. 'Don't, you'll spoil everything!'

'But it's the only honourable step–'

'She'll whisk us home, I tell you! We talked about it over Christmas – she's already started the marriage-broking, there's already a list of suitable young men–'

'Alys! You'd never accept any of them?'

'Of course not! But you see – she said she wouldn't trust a young man who had no money – she'll think you're after my fortune.'

He went fiery red. 'If *you* think that–'

'Don't be silly! Oh, darling, I know you would never think of such a thing... But of course Mama...'

'If I were to go there,' he proposed. 'If I asked to see her? It's true I've almost no money, but my family's a good one, the Hopetowns come from a long line of Border earls...'

She shook her head. 'It wouldn't be any use. She'd forbid us to see each other.'

'Oh no – I couldn't bear that–'

Each time they met they went back over the same ground. They had certain things that they held on to as absolute truths – they were in love, they wanted to be married, Alys's mother would refuse her consent.

In the end they solved their problem. Delphine woke one morning in March to find a note pinned to the pillow next to her in the prettily-hung double bed.

'Gavin and I have gone to Scotland to be married. Parental permission is not required there. I know this will grieve you and Mama but there seems no other way. Yr. loving sister Alys.'

Chapter Seventeen

Mrs MacArdle was having weak hysterics. Lord Grassington, summoned by her as the only male with any authority to deal with this problem, was writing a hasty note while a messenger waited to take it to Richard Patterton at Lindom and Company.

Delphine was sitting on a hard chair in Mrs MacArdle's office, apart from the drama now. Her role had been played: she had brought the note to Mrs MacArdle as soon as she had dragged on a dressing-gown. Now, clad in a morning gown and with her hair in a simple cap, she awaited her doom.

'We must get a message to your mother by the next packet available,' his lordship said, with a brief glance of sympathy. 'Don't look so stricken, Delphine – we may yet be in time to prevent the marriage.'

She didn't think so. The runaways would have taken a night train to Scotland and there, knowing the laws and customs of his own country, Gavin would have found them a place to wait in security until the marriage could take place. Lord Grassington had told her it took three weeks. That sounded a long time. But if they could remain out of sight in some unexpected spot until the time was up, nothing could prevent the ceremony.

'Your poor Mama!' wept Mrs MacArdle. 'What will she say? She told me she had a splendid marriage arranged for Alys... Oh, oh! Such a thing has never happened before during the entire time I've had girls under my care! Oh, my reputation is damaged for ever!'

'You are not to blame, Mrs MacArdle. I'm afraid the young people used a great deal of guile.' He sighed. 'As to Hopetown, I'm ashamed of him. He's been a guest many a time at our house...'

In his capable hands, inquiries were pursued and letters sent. It seemed indeed that the young couple had taken the mail train to the north but at what station they had alighted no one could tell. Grassington instructed a private investigator to trace them, but without success. Nicole arrived three days later, accepted the actual note from Delphine's trembling hands, and looked grim.

'She writes of him to you as "Gavin". You knew this young man?'

'I have met him – at Lady Grassington's.'

'You knew of their plan?'

'Of course not!'

'Don't say "Of course not!" as if it were impossible! I would have said no daughter of mine could ever deceive me so, but I am proved wrong.'

'You must understand that Alys–'

'I understand that she has been secretly meeting with a young man of whom she knew I wouldn't approve. You were aware of these meetings?'

'Yes.'

'Why didn't you put a stop to them? Or tell Mrs MacArdle?'

'Mama, you wouldn't have had me act as telltale ?'

'Oh, by no means! Let us at all costs preserve your sense of schoolgirl honour!' Nicole said with a bitterness Delphine had never heard in her before. 'The result is, your sister has thrown herself away on a good-for-nothing–'

'Mama, I assure you, he is a perfectly good, respectable young man–'

'Really? Then why did they not come to me and ask for my consent? No, we shall find that there is something you aren't aware of. He probably owes thousands in gambling debts or tailor's bills, or else he's already committed to some other poor young lady who will now bring suit against him for breach of promise.'

'No, no, my dear Nicole,' Grassington said when he heard her fears. 'All my inquiries reveal him as a decent enough young fellow. He comes from a respectable family in the Borders–'

'Respectable!'

'Indeed, yes – they own some acres of barren moorland and a property or two in Edinburgh–'

'Edinburgh! Then that's where they've gone!'

'No, it seems not – my investigator hasn't been able to find them there. I think you must resign yourself to it, Nicole. This wedding is going to take place.'

'And there is nothing I can do to prevent it?'

'Under Scottish law, nothing.'

Gerrard was unwilling to interfere too much. He had done what he could to prevent the marriage but, having failed, was of the opinion that it was best to accept it. But he hesitated to put that thought to Nicole.

He knew, of course, that Nicole herself was of peasant origin – she never made any secret of the fact. Exactly how she had come to marry into the French aristocracy she had never explained but he couldn't help thinking it strange that she was so utterly set against this young Scotsman who had carried off her daughter.

'My dear,' he ventured, 'couldn't you find it in your heart to accept the match? If Alys loves him–'

'Love!' she cried. 'You don't understand! She's fallen head over heels for the first clever scoundrel who came along! She's led a sheltered life – oh, I blame myself, I should have made sure she mingled with all kinds of men but...'

'I can't really accept that Hopetown is a scoundrel–'

'He should have come to me and asked for her hand!'

'But you would have refused, Nicole.'

Yes, she would have refused. She herself was conscious of the irony. She had come from a background much poorer than Gavin Hopetown's yet had made a love-match with a much richer man. Why shouldn't she believe that her daughter's husband was as honourable as she herself had been?

The answer had nothing to do with logic or sense. She was hurt – that was all. She was wounded to the heart that Alys had deceived her. Alys, the firstborn, the child who had been Philippe's little princess, who was to have made a glittering marriage to prove to the world that the House of Tramont was paramount... And *there* was another wound, to her pride. She had given her life to the House of Tramont. If Alys spurned it and all it could have brought her, it meant Nicole had wasted her life.

It was a thought she couldn't bear.

She ordered Delphine to pack. 'We are going home.'

'But, Mama – aren't you going to wait until Alys and Gavin come back from Scotland?'

Her mother gave her a glance so cold that Delphine almost shivered. 'I shall never meet them. I shall never accept them. Now, summon your maid, have your trunks packed. We are setting off for Dover tonight.'

It was a miserable crossing. Spring storms tossed the little steamer about. They had to spend a day in Boulogne recuperating. When they at last reached the Villa Tramont it was to find both Grandmama and Aunt Paulette there, full of anxiety for news.

'Nothing,' Nicole said. 'We've been unable to trace them.'

'What a disaster!' cried Clothilde. 'Old Monsieur Pourdume has had to withdraw from all negotiations with the families who were interested in a match, and even young Monsieur Pourdume is shocked.'

'Poor little Alys,' mourned the softer-hearted Paulette. 'I only pray she isn't making a terrible mistake.' She was thinking of her own disastrous marriage.

'Mistake? Of course it's a mistake! We are all made to look fools because a little miss wanted her own way over a very unsuitable match!'

'Grandmama, how can you be so sure it's unsuitable?' Delphine put in, provoked

341

beyond good manners. 'I have met the young man. He is very agreeable, well educated, and I think goodhearted–'

'And penniless,' Nicole interrupted.

'Why is that so bad? From what I hear from the villagers, you yourself were not at all rich when you and my father got married!'

'That was different,' said Clothilde, indignant at the suggestion. 'Your dear mama and my beloved son came to me openly and asked permission. I agree that I was unwilling at the time, and only gave in over a proposition of business – but there was nothing underhanded about the marriage, no running away to have a secret ceremony.'

Lord Grassington arrived early in April, bringing a letter addressed to Delphine at her former address in London. Inside was enclosed another, for her mother. The letter to Delphine begged her to give the enclosure to Nicole 'at a favourable moment'.

Since it seemed a favourable moment might never arrive, Delphine handed it over at once. The plea to Nicole was short and rather dignified. 'Gavin and I were married in a Catholic church this morning and received a certificate of marriage according to the Scottish law. He joins with me in begging your forgiveness for the distress we have caused and asks to be received by you as soon as possible. Our address is as above for the moment but he has accepted a position with a winegrower in Portugal therefore pray send your reply quickly so that we may call upon you en route. If any unforeseen delay occurs, direct your letter as below.' The address of a wine estate near Portugal followed and the closing phrase, 'Your loving and supplicant daughter, Alys Hopetown.'

Nicole had taken this to her office to read, with only Gerrard for company. 'I shall have the married annulled!' cried she. 'I won't allow–'

'No, my dear, don't cry out like that,' Gerrard said, taking her hand. 'There's nothing to be done. The marriage is valid, both in clerical and civil law. You have nothing to claim against it except your disapproval – and I think the Vatican would need more than that. Besides, an annulment would only have effect if Alys agreed to give up Gavin. From what I can gather, she has no such intention.'

'She is a very wicked, disobedient child! How could it come about that I raised a daughter with so little regard for her family?'

Gerrard essayed a joke. 'I wish someone would come along and run off with our Milly.'

But Nicole refused to be amused. She also

refused to reply to the letter. Delphine wrote in secret, to say that she wouldn't recommend a visit to Tramont at present. 'In time something may be done, but Mama is very shocked and hurt. Let some time go by.' She ended with her good wishes, which were sincere. Despite the turmoil that Alys's wedding had caused, she genuinely believed it would succeed.

There was an embargo on discussion of the subject after Alys's letter. Even Clothilde, generally rather blind to the feelings of others, respected her daughter-in-law's distress.

Nicole was more hurt by the affair than she allowed to show. She had always been a kind and loving mother, not indulgent perhaps and not always present when her children wanted her – but she'd always thought they understood the pressure of business under which she existed.

Alys's behaviour struck her to the heart. She couldn't understand why her daughter had not come to her and asked for permission. She was honest enough to admit to herself that she might have refused – but then if Alys had been strong-minded enough to resist all the marriage offers that Pourdume was pursuing, in time Nicole would have had to look again at Gavin Hopetown.

She was no judge of her own manner

when, at Christmas, Alys ventured to talk about marrying for love. She scarcely recalled the discussion now. If she did, she thought she had dismissed the topic with a little joke.

Now her elder daughter was gone – lost to her, married to a nobody who had been forced to accept a minor post with a minor vineyardist. Gone forever were the hopes of a brilliant alliance with the young politician who had wanted to marry into the Tramont money. It was no use thinking of offering him Delphine instead – Delphine would never be happy in political circles, whereas Alys would eagerly have accepted the chance to be a leading hostess and patroness of talent.

But worse than that was the sense of failure, both as a mother and as the head of the family. All her attention had been centred on avoiding one catastrophe, the possible growth of affection between Delphine and Robert. Because of that she'd thrown Alys into the arms of a totally unsuitable husband, a stranger, a schemer and opportunist.

Well, if he thought he would get any of Alys's fortune while his mother-in-law lived, he was mistaken. She had at once cut off Alys's considerable allowance and cancelled the settlements she'd intended to make on her daughter's twenty-first birthday. Although French law forbade her to cut her out of her will entirely, she would get the absolute minimum. And control of the House of Tramont would go to Delphine and Delphine's husband, who would be a man she would choose with the utmost care.

Besides this family distress there were other problems nagging at Nicole. The weather was very unfavourable to the vines that year. The spring had been long and cold, the blossoms had been late developing. Now a wet summer seemed to be setting in, with temperatures scarcely rising above the spring averages. The outlook for the grape crop looked poor.

Then there were political problems. France was going through one of its periodic terms of uncertainty. The provincial population played little part in the changes now going on, yet even in Rheims and Epernay there was a feeling of uncertainty in the air. The politicians in the great cities and the people of Paris, always volatile, seemed to be on the verge of some great action.

In general France was happy enough with the Emperor Louis Napoleon. He had taken the country into the Crimean War, but that was a long way off and although men had died rather from diseases of the gut than from glorious feats of arms, in the end there had been a victory. Later France had taken control of various parts of the world – Indo-China, Algiers... Trade was doing well, Paris was a centre of high fashion thanks to the patronage of the Empress Eugenie.

And yet... And yet there was a feeling of insecurity. Between France and the new Germany being formed by King William of Prussia and his chief Minister Count Bismarck, there was rivalry. Prussian power was such that, at a conference in Biarritz some five years earlier, Napoleon had weakly agreed to Prussian rule over greater Germany.

Those Frenchman interested enough to follow international affairs had naturally taken it for granted that Bismarck would be content after that. But the following year the Prussian army had had a wonderful victory over the Austrians at Sadowa, a real old-fashioned triumph which had made the whole world look with sudden respect towards King William.

True, France had got something out of the ensuing peace settlement. Venezia in Northern Italy had been ceded to Napoleon. Somehow it seemed rather like the jackal sneaking in after the lions have made the kill, and French national pride (felt mainly among the military) wasn't appeased when Napoleon nobly handed the province over to the Italians.

To make matters worse, the French venture into Mexico in support of an Emperor imposed on that country, Maximilian, had ended in disaster. Maximilian was shot by Mexican patriots, a piece of news that considerably damped the festivities of the Paris Exhibition. Maximilian's widow came back to Paris to beg for help, got nothing, and made everyone feel horribly guilty by losing her reason.

Last year France had been too interested in her own affairs to do much abroad. Napoleon had granted a parliament to the nation. 'Ha!' Clothilde had snorted when it was announced. 'No good can come of handing over decisions to a rabble of men in a talking-shop! Kings should *rule!* And even though this fool Napoleon is a usurper, he should at least keep a firm hand on the reins.'

Nicole steered a course that kept her clear of politics, though her support was often canvassed. 'No, m'sieu,' she would say to a delegate sent to persuade her to speak one way or the other, 'my aim for the nation is that I should make good wine.' And who drinks it to celebrate a victory is no concern of mine, so long as he pays, was her inner conclusion.

Nevertheless, the sense of some storm about to break was strong. Napoleon was old and ill and had lost his grip on his government. Clothilde often spoke in whispers of a proposed coup to bring back the Bourbons. Scandals were being discovered everywhere – even the great Baron Haussman, who had given Paris the new boulevards that made her the envy of Europe, was forced to resign owing to accusations that he had fiddled the books.

A cousin of the Emperor, Prince Pierre Bonaparte, shot a young Republican journalist for insolence and the resulting sensation rocked Paris. Radicals and revolutionaries pointed to it as yet one more act of arrogance by 'royalty'. They were known to be at work in the cities, making speeches at working-men's clubs. The First Workers' International was organising street demonstrations of a kind that hadn't been seen since Napoleon was elected First Consul.

And yet, when Napoleon called a plebiscite, he received an overwhelming vote of support. Why then should Nicole and many like her, with friends among politicians and bankers, be so uneasy?

Her anxieties made her poor company. Delphine, over-sensitive, felt her mother's coolness was a punishment for bad behaviour.

'Take me with you to Strasbourg?' she begged Aunt Paulette when she began to pack for her homeward journey.

'No, that's impossible!' Paulette was taken aback. The last thing needed was to throw Delphine into Robert's company.

'I'm sorry,' Delphine said, hurt by the immediate rejection. 'I didn't mean to be a nuisance. It's just that I seem so much in Mama's black books at the moment.'

'Darling, I'd take you if I could,' Paulette said, inventing wildly, 'but the fact is I've got workmen coming as soon as I get back – I'm having a conservatory built, and the house will be covered in dust until they finish.'

There was no escape that way, it seemed. It was Grandmama who came to her rescue. Seeing Delphine looking very cast down as the carriage took Aunt Paulette away to Rheims for the train, Clothilde had pity on her.

'My child, I know you feel yourself to be in disgrace. How would you like to come with me to Paris until things have settled down a little?'

She jumped at the offer. Grandmama was rather a dull old thing, and all her friends were of the same kind – elderly ladies and gentlemen, fond of cards and afternoon snoozes. Yet her apartment was on one of the beautiful new boulevards. There was an active and elderly maid, always willing to accompany the mademoiselle on a shopping expedition. Even though the weather was bad, Paris in May was a happier prospect than staying at Tramont while Mama was still in an angry mood.

Nicole was quite glad to see them go. In their absence she could throw herself into the ongoing work of the wine firm, finding some little consolation for the loss of her daughter. She wouldn't need to be conversational at meal times, nor listen with patience to her mother-in-law's view on politics.

There was one thing she didn't know, however, which would have made her forbid the visit at once. In the obsessive talk that had gone on about Alys and her marriage, little of the usual family chit-chat had been exchanged between Nicole and Paulette.

Paulette was planning to send Robert to Paris to receive some special tutorials from a private teacher, in order to ensure his success in his entrance examination for the École Centrale on which his heart was set.

If Nicole had known that, nothing would have induced her to let her younger daughter set out with Grandmama.

When Robert arrived, naturally he went at once to pay his respects to his relations in the Boulevard Malsherbes. And equally naturally, Delphine's grandmother made him welcome. He was quite a favourite with her – quiet, respectful, serious, suitable to introduce to her elderly friends and to hand round little petits fours and creamy hot chocolate.

Besides, he was good company for the girl. Poor child, she had put herself very much in the wrong by allowing Alys to form that terrible misalliance.

She watched from her sitting-room window as they set off for a stroll to the Tuileries Gardens in fleeting sunshine. These two, she mused, they seemed fond of one another. Young yet to be thinking of marriage, but if they came one day to the notion of making a match, it wouldn't be a bad thing. Of course the boy had no money worth speaking of, and Nicole would probably prefer a suitor of somewhat higher standing...

Yet marriages of love didn't always turn out badly. Look at Nicole and Philippe. She had been very much against it, but it had worked well – while it lasted. As to Nicole's escapade with Jean-Baptiste, Clothilde knew very well that it could never have happened if Philippe had lived. No, Nicole had been bound to Philippe by pure affection and perhaps that wasn't a bad basis for a marriage.

These being her thoughts, she had no idea of preventing the two young people from seeing each other. And see each other they did.

Robert had lessons every morning, and a certain amount of private study which he had to do in the early evening. But once he had acquitted himself on those scores, his tutor had no hesitation in giving him complete freedom. In Monsieur Daudon's view, Robert Fournier was a young man who needed taking out of himself. Paris was just the place for him – a few nice little flirtations with the pretty millinery girls, a few thick heads from a night's drinking, and young Robert would be a man of the world.

Robert had a better use for his free time. Each afternoon he set off immediately after lunch for the Boulevard Malsherbes, or for any other rendezvous he and Delphine might have arranged.

Sometimes they joined a group of young acquaintances. More often they preferred to be by themselves. They walked together on the banks of the Seine, watching the painters or the anglers. They took rides on the omnibus. They went to concerts and recitals. They listened to the military bands in the parks – that summer there seemed to be innumerable band concerts of military music.

Delphine wrote home each week, duty bound. But she was still under the somewhat mistaken impression that she was in disgrace and she would have despised herself if she'd tried to curry favour with long, loving letters. So she tended to write only briefly: 'We attended Mass with Madame de Hogue. I believe Grandmama has tickets for Le

Bourgeois Gentilhomme on Tuesday. The weather has been better, so on Sunday we all went on a boat trip.'

If Nicole read 'we all' as being Madame de Tramont and some of her friends, that was mischance: Delphine was not concealing her meetings with Robert because she had no idea there was any need to conceal them. She took it for granted Aunt Paulette would have told Mama that Robert was in Paris.

They were in, of all places, the cemetery of Père Lachaise when they looked at each other and realised they were in love. They had gone to hear a reading of poetry at the grave of a lesser genius of French literature. The reader was a well-known actor, with a voice like an orchestra of violins. Unfortunately, the breeze kept flapping into his face the paper on which the verses were written out.

Delphine was overcome by a fit of the giggles. She covered her lips with her gloved hand, but when the sheet of paper not only flapped but took flight, she was unable to stay. She hurried off behind a nearby, imposing tomb.

Robert joined her as she was wiping her eyes with a lace-trimmed handkerchief. 'Oh, dear, I oughtn't to laugh,' she said. 'This isn't a place for getting the giggles!'

'It's quite romantic in a sad sort of way,' Robert pointed out. 'And some of the

354

sculpture is really very fine.'

'Let's go and look at it. It will be less likely to make me laugh than Monsieur Guivere.'

He offered his arm, she took it. When they came to an unevenness in the path caused by the roots of a thick ivy, he guided her across it with a hand to her waist. She had a tiny waist, made all the tinier by the design of her soft gown of dark blue muslin.

He had always thought her prettier than her sister. Alys was about half a head taller and was darker of hair and eye. Delphine's hair was a colour Alys had once dubbed lightly-burnt-caramel, and today she wore it in 'shepherdess' ringlets to echo the faintly pastoral look of her gown. She carried a matching parasol decked with a little bouquet of multi-coloured flowers at the handle.

Robert looked down at her with delight. When he could have let her go, the uneven paving safely negotiated, he drew her closer.

They reached a gate. 'Shall we go back to the poetry? Or shall we make our escape?'

'Where to, Robert?' she asked, looking up at him with her mild, dark-amber eyes.

He had intended to say, 'To a cafe for a cool drink.' But they stood gazing at each other. And he said, 'I do love you so very much, Delphine.'

'Do you, Robert?' She smiled, putting a hand up to touch his cheek. 'I'm so glad.'

'I missed you horribly last year!'

'Never mind, we have the whole of this summer to compensate.'

'I have to leave Paris soon,' he said, with a deep sigh. 'I'm expected home by the end of June.'

'Well, by then your mother's conservatory will be finished. Perhaps I can come and stay with you.'

'Conservatory?'

'She's having a conservatory built.'

'It's the first I've heard of it. Well, I'll write to her and ask to bring you with me when I leave Paris. You won't mind leaving town?'

'Oh, Paris empties in July anyway. But even if there were to be fireworks and pageants, I'd want to go with you.'

This was encouragement enough for him to pull her close for a soft kiss on the mouth. If she didn't intend anything as serious as that she ought now to draw away.

But instead she stayed where she was, and when he kissed her again she dropped the parasol, threw her arms round his neck, and returned his kiss.

'Delphine!'

'I missed you too, Robert. I didn't realise how much until this minute!'

'You love me, darling?'

'I'm afraid I do! What a blow it will be to Mama's match-making plans again.'

They laughed, never imagining there could

be any problem. When he took her home, he stayed until Madame de Tramont's card party was over. Then he asked if he might have a serious conversation with her in private.

'Of course, dear boy, only don't be too long over it because I have to change for dinner.'

'Madame, I want to tell you that Delphine and I have discovered that we're in love and wish to become engaged.'

'My dear child!'

'I hope you approve? It changes the situation between us, of course, and you are her chaperone.'

'I have nothing against it at all.' Clothilde said with smug self-congratulation. She had foreseen this, had she not? Ah, she had insight into the workings of the human heart... 'But I would advise you, Robert, to let Delphine's mother know at once. She was greatly upset by Alys's deceitfulness – it would be a mistake to let any hint of that kind of behaviour occur.'

'Do you think she'll have objections?' he asked, nervous at the thought of displeasing Aunt Nicole.

'I can't see anything serious arising. Of course she had plans for Delphine, but after all... Well, my advice is to go at once to lay the matter before her and get her official permission for the engagement. Don't let her hear of it from some Parisian gossip.'

'I'll go tomorrow,' Robert said. 'I think that's best.'

'You are right, my boy.'

Delphine quite agreed, but had one improvement to add. 'I want to come with you, Robert.'

'Oh, I don't think that's quite–'

'I know you're supposed to ask for my hand in proper form, but I'd like to be there. Mama has had a bad shock already this year – I think I know how to handle her and make her see that this isn't something to be upset about.'

With her grandmother's agreement, Delphine packed and set off with Robert for the Villa Tramont. Full of optimistic certainty, they arrived while Nicole was out of the house on a day-long visit to the vineyards, where everything was going very badly this year.

The first trimming of leaves was in progress, a process which gave opportunity to handle the foliage and gauge its vigour. This rainy season had given rise to an outbreak of rougeot, an infrequent disease which showed itself by little greeny-red sores on the young leaves. Nicole had gone out to see how many rows had been affected and to decide what further steps, other than the fungicide always applied in May, could be taken.

She came home tired, wet, muddy and disheartened. The grapes were not going to do well this year. There was wine in store, of course, ready for such an eventuality – yet it meant a decreased output just when demand was growing greater all over Europe, particularly in Germany.

The butler took her hat and raincoat from her in the hall. 'Madame, your daughter has arrived.'

'Alys?' she said, her heart suddenly giving a great thud in her breast. Alys had come home!

'No, madame, I meant Mademoiselle Delphine.'

She recovered almost at once. Then she felt a stab of irritation. Why had Delphine chosen to come home today of all days, and without any warning?

Now what's happened, she muttered to herself as she crossed the hall and threw open the drawing-room door. I suppose she's done something to annoy Old Madame...

But one glance at the two people standing there hand in hand told her why Delphine had returned. She stopped in the doorway, feeling all her blood flowing away from her heart in an icy tide.

'Mama,' said Delphine, stepping forward, 'Robert and I have something very important to tell you.'

Chapter Eighteen

Nicole broke into speech – anything, anything to prevent the utterance of the words that could not be recalled.

'This is very inconvenient! If you'd written to say you were coming, I'd have put you off.'

Her daughter, lips parted for her important news, stared at her.

'This is the worst summer in living memory. The grapes will perish if it goes on. I really wish you hadn't come, Delphine.'

'Mama–'

'I don't mind your staying overnight, of course, but I wish you'd go back to Paris tomorrow. You wouldn't enjoy Tramont in this rain, anyway.'

'Mama, you haven't even said welcome home!' Delphine protested, laughing a little at the absurdity of it.

She'd imagined the scene a hundred times on their way here. She would explain their mission, Mama would be surprised then pleased, and give them her blessing after embracing them both.

The reality, with its prosaic talk of weather and business, was a strange contrast. She could see Robert smiling to himself.

'We'll go tomorrow, certainly, if we're in your way, Aunt Nicci. In any case we have to go to Strasbourg to give the news to my mother.'

By all the laws of commonsense his aunt ought now to have said, 'What news?' But Nicole said rather sharply, 'I thought you were in Strasbourg.'

'No, I've been in Paris, taking a special course of study–'

'In Paris. I see.'

'Mama, Robert and I spent much of our time together during the last few weeks and we–'

'It seems a pity to me that your mother wastes money on sending you for special studies and instead you spend the time enjoying yourself!'

'Mama!' cried Delphine, astonished.

'Well, since you're here, you had better tell Madame Grelliot that there will be two more for dinner. I must change out of these wet clothes – I'm soaked through.'

She walked out, leaving her daughter and Robert wordless in surprise at her bad manners.

Up in her room, she sank down on the chair by her dressing-table. Her maid came in at once to help her out of the rain-soaked skirt and little mud-caked boots. 'Go away! I'll see to it myself!'

My word, thought the girl, scuttling out as fast as she could, madame's in a terrible bad temper!

But the interview couldn't be put off for ever. Nicole sat for a long time, head bent, pulses throbbing with apprehension, yet in the end the answer was always the same: it's got to be dealt with. When she had had a hot bath and changed, she went downstairs again. The butler had placed wine ready for a pre-dinner drink. As her mother entered Delphine took it upon herself to pour some sherry, offering it to her.

'This is to toast a great piece of news, Mama. Robert and I have come for your permission to become engaged.'

Now it was out. Nothing could prevent the conversation they must now have. Still Nicole shied away from it. 'You know I detest sherry,' she said, gesturing the glass away from her.

Delphine drew back, flushing in distress. Robert went to her, took the glass from her hand and put it by, then turned to face his aunt. 'Aunt Nicole, didn't you hear what Delphine said? We're in love. We want to get married.'

'Married?' Nicole burst out. 'Absolute nonsense! You're still children—'

'I understand there's a difficulty about our ages,' Robert said, completely in command of the situation while Delphine stood in utter consternation. 'I've still got my education to complete – I quite see that. But of course we don't expect to get married at once. We just want to be engaged–'

'So that any prospective suitors would know they shouldn't waste time on me,' Delphine said, trying to lighten the atmosphere now that she'd got her voice back.

'I want you to stop talking rubbish!' Nicole said, her tone very hard. 'You're nothing but a pair of babies–'

'We're old enough to know what we're saying, Mama–'

'Your cousin is your junior–'

'By only two years! And by the time he's finished his studies and we get married, I'll be twenty-two and he'll be twenty – that's no difference at all–'

'Delphine, you are under age and so is Robert. I refuse my consent to any idea of marriage between you.'

'But – but why?'

'One daughter has made a fool of herself. I refuse to allow another to do the same.'

'So that's it! I'm being punished for Alys's bad behaviour–'

'It's never been part of my plan that there should be a marriage between my family and your aunt's. I have other plans for you, Delphine.'

'But you said – you said yourself, when

Alys asked you – you would never make us marry someone we didn't like!'

'Of course. That still holds good. But by the time the match is made, perhaps as much as a year will have gone by. You'll have had time to get over this silly infatuation–'

'It isn't an infatuation, madame,' Robert said. 'I've loved Delphine for years.'

'Then you've been wasting your time, for I've no intention of letting this go any further. I absolutely forbid any further consideration of it. You and Delphine had better not see each other again for the foreseeable future–'

'Mama, you can't really be saying this!' Delphine cried, suddenly reaching out towards her as if to clutch her by the shoulders.

Nicole drew back. She knew if Delphine threw herself on her neck in tears, she would melt. 'I know what I'm saying. I'm telling you that you've behaved very badly, allowing yourself to get entangled in a silly romance when you know I have several young men in prospect for you.'

'But you've always said, you had to be sure a man wanted me and not my money. You *know* Robert isn't after my money–'

'That's not by any means as certain to me as it is to you,' Nicole said, seizing the pretext. 'All he's likely to inherit is a share in a very mediocre business–'

'Madame,' Robert said, white with anger and towering over her from his superior height, 'I must ask you to withdraw those words.'

He was so like Jean-Baptiste in that moment that Nicole's pretended anger collapsed. She turned away, tears blinding her.

'Mama, you're being so unlike yourself. I know we've surprised you,' pleaded Delphine, 'but that's no reason to treat Robert like a criminal—'

'I treat him as he deserves,' Nicole said over her shoulder, though her heart was breaking with the pain of hurting him. 'He has betrayed my trust in him. He must know very well that I never thought of him as a prospective husband for you.'

'But we've fallen in love, Mama—'

'Love? Love? A few weeks seeing each other without my permission—'

'But Grandmama had no objections! She gave us her blessing. It's at her suggestion that we've come to you at once.'

'Your grandmother is a silly old woman. She should know better than to let an adolescent girl—'

'But you yourself were married at my age!' cried Delphine. 'How can you keep on talking about my being so young, when you—'

'I had no great fortune to be thought of! I

had no family responsibilities to consider!'

'So it comes to this, madame,' Robert said. 'You wish to marry Delphine to some rich stranger–'

'My plans for my daughter are no concern of yours, young man. All you need to know is that you play no part in them!'

'Madame, your manner to me makes it impossible for me to stay here any longer. I can't imagine what I've ever done to deserve treatment like this–'

'Oh yes, Mama, how can you? This is Robert! I always thought that, of the two, you preferred Robert to Edmond.'

'I have no preference. They are two young men I owe a certain family obligation to, that is all.'

'Mama!'

'Then you've been a consummate actress for years, Madame de Tramont,' Robert rejoined in a tone of ice. 'I always thought you were genuinely fond of us. If you'll excuse me, I'll leave now. Delphine, please let's have a word in private.'

'Delphine, I forbid you.'

Delphine stood uncertain in the centre of the room, her hand in Robert's as he was about to lead her out. Nicole went to the bell and pulled the cord. The butler came in much too quickly, making it clear he had been in the hall eavesdropping.

'Gaspard, order the carriage for Monsieur

Fournier and tell Coachman to take him wherever he wishes to go. While he waits for it, please keep him company in the hall.'

Robert's eyes blazed. As the butler came towards him, understanding that his mistress wished the guest escorted out of the room, he held up his hand. 'If you touch me I'll knock you down.' He looked with contempt at Nicole. 'I'm going, you don't have to have me thrown out. Good evening to you, madame.'

'Robert!'

'It's all right, Delphie, this isn't the end of it. She can't rule our lives like this.'

When the door had closed behind him, Delphine whirled on Nicole like a fury. 'I'll never forgive you for this! How could you be so cruel? Robert has never said or done anything in his life to deserve such treatment.'

'Be quiet! I have a few words to say to you, young lady! You have behaved very badly, and the more so because after Alys's example you should have known better! I am very angry with you–'

'And I am angry with you! I think your behaviour has been unspeakable! I'll never forgive you, never!'

A flood of tears, held in check while there was a fight to share with Robert, suddenly overwhelmed her. She sank down on the floor, hands hiding her face, head bowed over her spreading silk skirts. 'Oh, Mama, Mama! How could you, how could you!'

Nicole knelt beside her. 'There, there, my dear,' she soothed, in a voice that was breaking. 'Don't cry. It's over now. It's all over. You'll forget it all in time. Everything passes, the hurt gets less.'

'But why? Why? I don't understand it!'

Nicole gathered her up to hold her close. They rocked together in a moment of shared grief. Then Delphine realised whose arms were holding her. She pulled free, sprang up, faced her mother like a wildcat. 'I hate you!' she cried. 'I hate you, hate you!'

She ran out of the room. She reached the hall just as Gaspard was opening the door to usher Robert out to the carriage. She ran to Robert's arms. He caught her, Gaspard in a fluster opened the carriage door. Robert put Delphine in, sprang in after her. 'Drive away!' he called to the coachman. 'Quickly, man, drive!'

The carriage gave a lurch forward with the door still open. It closed as the vehicle moved forward through the wide puddles beyond the porte cochere. Nicole reached the house door to see it pass under the arch.

'Stop!' she cried. 'Stop!'

Her voice was lost in the rattle of the wheels and the clatter of hooves. The carriage careered off. She ran after it, the wild wind throwing rain into her face as she passed the shelter of the porte cochere and came out to the open driveway. The distance between them widened, yet still she ran, her black gown plastered to her breasts by the downpour.

They came out to her with a cloak and an umbrella, to find her standing helpless in the open under the black clouds of the late June evening. Rain poured down, moulding her fine lace cap to her head and gathering in great drops upon her earrings. Whether her face was wet with raindrops or tears, the servants couldn't determine.

Chapter Nineteen

The journey to Strasbourg via Metz on the mail train took about eleven hours. Delphine and Robert slept fitfully, startled into wakefulness each time the mailbags were loaded and unloaded. Then they would murmur comfort to each other.

'My mother will help us, darling. She'll be on our side.'

'But do you think she can do anything?'

'She and Aunt Nicole have always been very close – I'm sure *that* at least is true. Mother will speak up for us, Delphie.'

They reached Strasbourg just before seven. If the hackney-man thought it odd to see a gentleman escort a lady to his cab, he in a frock-coat against the unseasonable cold rain and the lady sheltered in his surtout, he made no mention of it.

Paulette's house near the Porte de Pierre hadn't yet roused itself for the day. As a girl Paulette had been used to early rising but, in middle age, she found herself unwilling to leave her comfortable bed – the more so as it still rained each morning.

Her housemaid, Adele, was cleaning out the stove ashes when she heard the key in the lock. She hurried to the vestibule, hiding her dirty hands under her apron. 'Monsieur Robert!'

'Ssh… Is my mother up yet?'

'Not yet, m'sieu. I was going to finish the stove first and then make the coffee.' Adele was staring with interest at Mademoiselle Delphine, who was leaning on his arm and looking exhausted.

'We'll go upstairs to rest, Adele. Mademoiselle Delphine will have Edmond's room – is the bed made up?'

'Why, no, sir … I…'

'It doesn't matter,' Delphine murmured. 'If I can just lie down on it for a while – and have some hot water…'

'Certainly, certainly, mademoiselle. Pray come this way.' She led the way upstairs, opening Edmond's room-door with some hesitation, for although it was clean, it was much cluttered with the stuff of Edmond's hobbies.

Delphine went in, to sit down on the nearest chair. She looked completely spent. 'Shall I bring you some coffee, mademoiselle? You look as if you could do with it.'

'Later, Adele, later. First I need a jug of hot water and … and… Could I borrow a dress from you?'

'A dress? My God, mademoiselle … nothing I own is fit for you to wear!'

'Anything, Adele, so long as it's clean and

fresh. I feel so … dreary in these damp and muddy things.'

'Certainly, mademoiselle,' said Adele, mentally running through her scant wardrobe. The gown she'd had given her by a previous employer and never worn? Dove grey poplin and green trimming … and little matching slippers she'd never been able to get her feet into.

Having seen Delphine looked after, Robert summoned Adele outside. 'Don't tell my mother we're here, Adele.'

'Oh, it's a surprise?'

'Yes, a surprise.' He suppressed a sigh. 'What time will she come downstairs?'

Adele glanced out of the landing window streaming with rain. 'Today … perhaps not until nine-thirty or ten. She likes to read in bed for a bit.'

'Very well. At nine-thirty, have coffee and croissants for myself and Mademoiselle. Perhaps Mother will like to share a second cup with us.'

When Paulette came downstairs at mid-morning, the scent of freshly made coffee alerted her to something unusual. A little perplexed, she put her head round the kitchen door. 'Adele, I didn't ask for more coffee.'

'It's for Monsieur Robert and–'

'Robert's here?' Paulette flew to the little dining-room.

In the sombre light of the rain-laden sky, her son and Delphine were sitting at the table with the remains of a late breakfast before them. They were both freshly dressed; Delphine had even done her hair quite expertly so that the effects of a whole day's travelling yesterday were not too evident.

Yet there was something unspeakably weary about them. Paulette hurried in, her heart suddenly in her throat.

'Robert, my dear! I didn't expect you?'

'It's a sudden decision, Mother. Won't you welcome Delphine?'

'Of course, dear.' Paulette took both her hands as she stood up, kissed her with affection. 'You look very pale, Delphine – are you unwell?'

'Only tired, Aunt Paulie. Oh, it's so lovely to be here, where someone wants us!' Delphine broke out, her voice quavering with unhappiness, fatigue, and relief.

'Wants you? Of course I...' Paulette hesitated, looked from one to the other. 'What has happened?'

'Sit down, Mother. Have some coffee.'

'Coffee? I don't want coffee–'

'Sit down, dearest. Delphine and I want to tell you something, something that will surprise you.'

She sat down gingerly on the chair her son was holding for her. She clasped her hands in her lap, tightly, below the level of the table so that he couldn't see. 'What is it, Robert?'

'Mother, Delphine and I are engaged to be married.'

'No!' She jumped up, jarring the table so that black coffee flew over the snowy cloth. 'No, that's impossible!'

The two young people stared at her. Slowly, tears gathered in Delphine's eyes and began to brim over. 'Oh, Aunt Paulie,' she said in a broken voice, 'I thought that you at least would be on our side.'

'What do you mean, impossible?' Robert said, standing across the breakfast table and watching his mother with astonished eyes. 'There's nothing impossible about it. We're in love and we've become engaged.'

'No! No, you mustn't, Robert!'

'But why not? What do you mean?'

'I... I...'

'Surely it can't be so totally unexpected. You must have guessed I loved Delphine—'

'Robert, you mustn't talk like this. It's simply not possible.'

'But *why?*' he demanded. He had raised his voice to her, a thing that had never happened before in her life.

'Robert... Robert... Don't be angry...'

'I'm not angry, Mother.' He came to her quickly, put his arm around her and made her sit down again. 'Come now, I'm sorry. I didn't mean to shout like that. But explain to me – why is it impossible for Delphie and I to plan to get married?'

'Well, you see… It's like this…' A moment she'd been dreading for months had actually arrived, and still she was unprepared, still she was floundering. 'Your Aunt Nicci–'

'My aunt made her opinion quite clear,' Robert said, terse and tight. 'We saw her yesterday.'

'You saw her? Oh then … you see … she told you…?'

'She told us she had plans for Delphine in which I could play no part. But you'll talk her round, Mother.'

'No. No, no, you mustn't ask it of me. I can't. It would be wrong.'

'Wrong? To help two people in love?'

'Please, Aunt Paulie,' Delphine put in, with all the affection and trust of seventeen years behind the words. Aunt Paulie was always kind and helpful.

'No, dear, I can't. You don't understand.'

'What don't I understand? I know Mama wants me to make an important marriage but she can be talked out of it.'

'No. You can't ask me to interfere.'

'But why not?'

'Well,' lied Paulette, 'I don't dare forfeit her goodwill. You know, Robert, we owe a lot to your Aunt Nicci. If she hadn't helped me, I could never have afforded to have you and Edmond so well educated–'

'Make out a bill!' cried Robert, in a fury. 'Set down every item she ever paid for, and if it takes me the rest of my life, I'll pay it back! My God! Are you saying we have to give in to her because she's richer than we are?'

'No, it's not that,' said his mother, beginning to cry. 'It's not that, Robert.'

'Don't cry, Mother. I'm sorry I blazed out at you. Don't, dear.'

She shook her head, leaning over the table and hiding her face with one hand while she sought for her handkerchief with the other. Across her head Delphine looked at Robert. Gone was the hope of support from Aunt Paulette.

'Dearest Aunt Paulie,' she said, reaching across to touch her on the arm, 'we don't mean to upset you. But this is a time when we need your help. I understand that my mother is a strong character, but please – *please* talk to her for our sake.'

'No,' said Paulette. 'I won't, because … because … you see, I agree with her.'

A long, stricken silence met this confession. When she had finished mopping her eyes and looked at them, she found they were totally astounded. At last her son summoned his voice.

'You agree that Delphie and I shouldn't think of marriage?'

'Yes.'

'But why? What's the reason?'

'I … I don't think cousins should marry.'

Suddenly Robert looked frightened. 'Is it … is there something in the family? Have I inherited some defect?' There was much gossip these days of a hereditary disease handed on by the children of Queen Victoria of England to their children. It came into his head that he might suffer from some such malady.

'No no! Oh, no! The healthiest child! Except for mumps and measles… No, no, darling, you're as fit as a fiddle.'

Delphine began to laugh almost hysterically. 'So he is strong and well, and so am I. And we love each other, and we're not promised to anyone else, and we want to be engaged. And yet we mustn't. I don't understand it.'

'No. Nor do I. Mother, you can't really be saying we have to give up all our hopes because of some notion of yours about kinship.'

Paulette let the tears come again. It was a defence: while she was sobbing she couldn't speak, and so long as she couldn't speak she could avoid replying to her son's arguments.

Her son… Oh, if only he were, in reality! How strongly she would have spoken up for him even against Nicole! Yet she could do nothing for him now, in perhaps the most important moment of his life.

Outside in the street the world of Strasbourg was going about its business. But now, added to the normal sounds of traffic, there came the rattle of carriage wheels. The carriage drew up outside.

Delphine leaped to the window. 'It's Mama!' she cried, looking out.

'Nicci?' There was thankfulness in Paulette's cry, although neither of the others noticed it in the confusion of the moment.

Adele had hurried to the street door. Nicole came in, her travelling cloak spattered with rain, her bonnet soaked. She gave them impatiently to Adele as her sister came running out to embrace her.

'Oh, Nicci!' Paulette whispered in her ear. 'What are we going to do?'

Nicole, hugging her, sighed. Then she went ahead of her into the dining-room.

Delphine, she saw, was in some dowdy gown of grey and green, very badly trimmed and a good deal too loose for her. It made her look small, and very tired. Robert on the other hand seemed strong and capable, standing to confront her as she came in.

'Good morning, madame. How did you know we would be here?'

She shrugged. 'That was easy. You asked the coachman to take you to Rheims station, and there of course they know you and remembered that you had booked to

Strasbourg. Where else would you be but at home?'

'And now that you're here, what do you want?'

'I've come to take Delphine back to Tramont.'

Delphine shook her head from side to side. She didn't speak.

'Yes, my dear, you must come home with me and forget all this nonsense.'

Robert smote the breakfast table with his fist. 'Has the world gone mad?' he said. 'Why is it nonsense? Why are you both so much against it? All we want is to be engaged for the next three years–'

'Robert, I told you yesterday that I forbid it.' She looked about her. It was clear they had found no comfort with Paulette – not that she had expected they would. 'Your mother agrees with me, doesn't she? So you see, you must give it up.'

'No. Never.' It wasn't said with bravado. It was a simple statement of fact.

'Yes, you must. I am against long engagements in any case. And within a year or so, Delphine will be married to–'

'No, Mama,' Delphine said, as calm as Robert. 'I shall not. I shall refuse everyone you bring. And if I have to go on saying no until I'm twenty-one, I shall do so. Then, when I've reached my majority, I shall marry Robert.'

Robert nodded. 'We'll wait. We intended to wait to get married in any case. So it's simply a wait without being engaged. The result will be the same.'

'Oh,' cried Paulette, putting both hands up to her face with her handkerchief as a mask, 'what are we to do? What are we to do?'

Nicole looked from Robert to Delphine and from Delphine to Robert. All she saw was diamond-hard resolution. She saw, too, the father in Robert and something of herself in Delphine. Courage, determination... Patience, too. What they said was true. They would wait until they were of age and then get married.

But she couldn't allow that to happen.

'Have I made it clear, madame?' Robert said. 'I intend to marry my cousin.'

'But she is not your cousin, Robert.'

'What? Not my–?'

'Delphine is your sister.'

For a long moment the only sound in the room was the sobbing of Paulette.

'That's impossible,' Robert said in a low voice.

'No, it's true.'

'My sister?'

'Half-sister. You have the same mother.'

'What? The same mother?' His hand went up, as if to defend himself from what she was saying. 'You mean that ... that *you*...

That Mother...' He turned in dismay to Paulette. 'You're not my mother?'

'Of course I am!' sobbed Paulette. 'At least – I mean – I've been your mother ever since you were born! Oh, Robert, I love you just as much as if you really were my son!'

He moved as if to touch her, but drew back his hand. Then he almost ran out of the room. They heard his footsteps on the stairs. An upstairs door slammed.

'Well,' Nicole said in exhaustion, 'it's done.'

'Delphie!' shrieked her aunt, seeing the girl sway on her chair. 'Oh, my poor little darling.' She ran to the door. 'Adele, Adele, bring the smelling salts!'

After some moments the mists cleared for Delphine. Someone was patting her wrists with eau de cologne, someone else was giving her sips of brandy. She lifted her head up and looked about. Her mother was kneeling beside her with a brandy glass in her hand.

'Mama...'

'You're all right, darling. You've had a bad shock.'

'I thought you... Oh!' The memory rushed back. She pushed away the glass, tried to get up.

'Stay where you are, dear. You're not yourself yet.'

'Let go of me, Aunt Paulie. Let me go! I

must… I want…'

'Keep still. Everything is all right.'

'All right?' cried Delphine. In her voice was all the misery of the knowledge that had just been forced on her.

Nothing in her life would ever be all right again.

Chapter Twenty

Delphine was persuaded to go and lie down on the chaise longue in the sitting-room, first taking a little sodium bromide in hopes she might sleep. Nicole and Paulette went back to the dining-room, where Adele had provided fresh coffee and fresh bread for Nicole, who was almost as exhausted as her daughter.

'What are we to do now, sister?' asked Paulette.

'I think they'll need little persuasion to separate now. I'll take Delphine home, and of course Robert will go to Paris to enter l'École des Arts, so they needn't see each other for months and months.'

'Ye-es... But what are we to tell Edmond?'

'Need we tell him anything?'

'But then... Old Madame ... she seems to have encouraged them.'

'I'll tell her it came to nothing. Paulie, I've dreaded this ever since you first drew my attention to the possibility, and one of the lesser miseries was how to live with Old Madame if she found out...'

Paulette poured more coffee for her sister and heaped sugar into it. As Nicole was protesting she said, 'No, take it, it will do you good. I've never seen you look so worn down since Philippe died.'

It was true. Her face was gaunt; the scars, usually well hidden, stood out in redness on her white skin. Her dark brown eyes seemed to have grown larger; they were without their usual sparkle.

They sat a long time, sipping coffee and warming themselves at the fire which Adele had lit, even though it was almost the end of June. By and by sounds of movement from the sitting-room warned them that Delphine was rousing.

'And Robert? What about Robert?'

'He's still upstairs. Lend me a cloak for Delphine, dear – I'll get her off home as soon as she's had a bite to eat – some soup, perhaps.'

They busied themselves with housewifely detail. It kept them from thinking about what had happened. By and by Nicole went into the sitting-room. Delphine was sitting up on the chaise longue, the too-big slippers of apple-green leather dangling from her feet. She met her mother's anxious eyes.

'I'm all right. I'm not going to faint again, you needn't worry.'

'I'd like you to have something to eat. And then if you feel well enough we'll be going.'

'Oh no,' Delphine said, her voice very hard. 'It's not quite as easy as that. There are questions to be answered.'

Her aunt came in carrying a cloak. 'I think this will do–'

'What angers me is the hypocrisy!' exclaimed Delphine. 'All these years you've told me how much you adored Papa, and all the time you were unfaithful to him while he was alive.'

'Delphine!'

'Well, it's true, isn't it?'

'How can you say such a thing to your mother?' Paulette cried, coming further into the room to stand over her niece in protest. 'Your father was dead a long time before all this–' a gesture indicated the situation '–happened.'

'So... Is that any better? Robert is the result of some passing affair–'

'That's not true!' Nicole interrupted. 'You know nothing of it! Robert's father was a wonderful man–'

'Excellent,' said a voice from the doorway. 'Please go on. Do please tell me about my father.'

Nicole wheeled. Robert had come downstairs while they talked; unobserved he had been standing listening. He looked quite composed, though white and strained.

'Go on,' he invited. 'I should like to hear. It's something new for me, you see. All my life so far I've been ashamed of being the son of a man who deserted us when I was a baby. Now I find I have to be ashamed of being a bastard.'

'Oh,' moaned Paulette, 'oh, Robert... Please don't be so angry!'

'Don't you think I've good reason? All my life, you've lied to me!'

'But it was for your own good, dear–'

'What good has it done? Here we are, in a maze of lies and miseries–'

'Very well, let us explain it all to you,' Nicole said, crisp and controlled. 'You need never have known anything of this if you hadn't developed an attachment to Delphine. It was our intention to keep the secret for ever. You were Paulette's son–'

'I still am! Do you expect me to stop loving her just because you say she's not my real mother?'

'Robert, don't be absurd. I don't ask anything of the sort. I love your mother too, you know. I wouldn't ever do anything to hurt her. And I would never have hurt you, either, if it could have been avoided. But a marriage between you and Delphine is out of the question.'

Her daughter spoke for the first time since Robert intervened. 'That has been made only too clear,' she said.

Her glance met Robert's. They gave each other a long look – a look of farewell. Seeing it, Nicole felt her heart yearn to say, It's all nonsense – you belong to each other, you have my blessing.

'I should like to know the name of my real father, madame,' Robert said.

'What would be the good of that?'

'I have the right, surely? I want to ask him why he has never made himself known to me all these years.'

'He doesn't even know of your existence, Robert,' Nicole said wearily. 'It was best to keep it from him.'

'Oh, indeed? You take a great deal on yourself! You keep it from me, now I learn you kept it from him – surely if you were a widow at the time you could have married him? Or didn't you love him enough for that?'

'Robert!' cried Paulette in protest. 'You don't know what you're saying!'

'No, no, dear, it's all right – he's hurt, he needs to lash out at someone.' Nicole went to her sister and put her in a chair. She leaned down to whisper. 'Best to let him have it out.'

When she turned back to him, she'd made up her mind exactly how much she would reveal. 'Your father and I couldn't marry – he had a wife and children. His wife had been greatly grieved by learning of our affair. We parted. It seemed best to keep them both in ignorance of your existence.'

'I want to see him. I want to see what kind of man he is.'

'That's impossible.'

'Why?'

'He's ... not anywhere that you could reach.'

'He's dead, you mean?' he said, trying to catch her meaning.

'No, he left France.'

'Oh, come! Another lie?'

'Robert, I forbid you to speak like that to Aunt Nicole!'

'Be quiet, Mother. Well? He left France – to go where? Switzerland? Belgium?'

'What would you do if I told you?'

'I should write to him. It seems to me he deserves to be told.'

'So that you could make him unhappy too?' Nicole shook her head. 'My dear child–'

'Ah yes! You mean that literally, of course?'

To her own surprise, Nicole felt tears start behind her eyes. 'Robert... You *are* my child... And his, too... I know you find it hard to believe, but I loved him, just as you love Delphine... I loved him, I love you, I don't want you to hurt each other. Dear child, I beg you to *accept* what has happened. Nothing can change it, nothing. If I had known, perhaps... If I'd known what the future held... But no gift of prophecy descended on me. I had the love of a man who meant the world to me – I couldn't refuse it, I needed him so...'

Her voice trailed into silence.

No one spoke. Then Paulette struggled to her feet, as if exhausted by the emotions of the scene. She held out the cloak to her niece. 'Put it on, go home with your mother, child. Go away and try to forget–'

'Forget!'

Paulette sighed. 'You won't believe me, but it will pass. Sorrow grows less. You're young, you have your whole life before you–'

'Oh, what use is it to be so trite about it! All I can see is that I have a whole life before me without Robert!'

'And your poor mother has had a whole life without either of the men she loved! Aren't you ashamed, to be so weak and complaining? Are you saying you have less strength of will than she has?'

Delphine was still in too much pain to care what her mother might have suffered. She took the cloak from her aunt, put it about her shoulders, and walked stiffly to the door.

'Are we leaving, madame?' she asked Nicole.

Nicole joined her. They went to the street door. Outside a watery sun had broken through the clouds to give promise of a bright afternoon at last. Paulette stood on the threshold to bid them farewell. She kissed first her niece, then her sister. 'We shan't see each other for a while, I suppose, Nicci,' she said in a low voice.

'It seems unlikely.'

'Try to get over it, dear.'

'Oh, *I* shall get over it. It's Delphie I'm worried about.'

'And Robert...'

Nicole shook her head. There was nothing to be said. No one could help either of the two lovers. They had to help themselves, in whatever way they could.

Outside Strasbourg's theatre they took a hackney from the waiting line. They were driven to the station, and were at home in the Villa Tramont in time for a late supper.

Theirs was a silent journey. Delphine was walled up in resentment against her mother. As for Nicole, she knew that trivialities would be unsuitable and that to discuss the scenes of yesterday and today would only embitter Delphine the more.

At Tramont their return was a matter of interest that soon died down. It was known, through the usual household gossip, that Monsieur Robert had asked for the hand of Mademoiselle Delphine, had been refused, and had carried her off with him to Strasbourg. Now Madame had brought home her daughter and there was no talk at all of a wedding. Moreover, Mademoiselle looked sad and dispirited.

Some said they thought Madame had

been hard on her to refuse the match, some said you couldn't expect the head of a firm like Champagne Tramont to accept a son-in-law with so little by way of a fortune of his own. It was a matter of discussion for a few days.

But then came the usual estate party for the end of bottling last year's vintage. Caught up in their own merriment and with flirtations and marriages of their own to further, the Tramont workers gave up discussing the affairs of the great house.

Moreover, something happened in the larger world to draw attention away from local matters. The newspapers were full of the affront to France whereby Prince Leopold of Hohenzollern had agreed to be a candidate to inherit the throne of Spain. All the political journalists cried out that Spain was a *French* interest, that the Emperor Napoleon must be consulted about who should succeed, that the German royal family had offered an intentional insult to him, and so on, with much patriotic fervour.

If the truth were told, the country people of France were largely indifferent about who sat on the throne of Spain. But it was a good news story, full of twists and turns of diplomacy with telegrams whizzing to and fro, and of course featured those two well-known sparring partners, France and

Germany. It was a thing said in the cafes when men had had a drink or two: One day we'll have to take those damn Prussians down a peg or two.

This was the opportunity. To the great glee of the newspapers, King William of Prussia made Prince Leopold withdraw his candidature for the throne.

Exactly what happened next was never quite clear to the rest of Europe. It appeared that the French Foreign Office, not content with the withdrawal, demanded from King William a guarantee that he would never allow himself or any of his family to be considered for the Spanish monarchy. What was said at the interview between the King and the French ambassador, Benedetti, was of course a diplomatic secret. Revelations came from a telegram sent by the King afterwards to his Chancellor, Bismarck, in Ems.

But it later seemed certain that the Chancellor somehow manipulated the news. What he allowed to be published wasn't quite the same as the information sent to him by his king. The Ems Telegram became a source of acrimony. Newspapers whipped up public opinion in both France and Germany.

On the 20th July, Nicole de Tramont went out as usual to supervise the transfer of the newly bottled wine to the cellars. The postman came riding up in his little dog-cart. 'Madame, madame!' he called as he reined in his pony. 'Have you heard the news?'

He was greatly excited, his red face shining with enthusiasm and his moustache a-bristle with importance at what he had to convey.

'No, what is it, Alphonse?' She took from him the leather satchel containing the mail for Champagne Tramont.

'We are at war with Germany! It was declared yesterday!'

Workers gathered round excitedly to hear the rest. Nicole opened the newspaper that had come with the letters. The headlines confirmed what Alphonse was now spluttering out. The Emperor had been greatly moved when his government recommended the declaration: the Empress Eugenie had clapped her hands in glee. The nation would rally to the colours. Prussia would be taught a lesson that had been long needed.

'Well,' said the estate workers, 'it's all right, as long as it's a short war with lots of victories.' Victories meant celebrations, and celebrations usually meant champagne.

It was the talking point for the next week or so. The newspapers cried: 'To the Rhine! To the Rhine!' Ambitions long held were to be brought to fruition: France would move her northern frontier to the great river which seemed to form the natural boundary between the two countries. Others, more warlike, called: 'To Berlin!'

It was confidently expected that the French army would be in Berlin before autumn had ended. No one seemed to notice that, though the government had declared war on the 19th, by the 30th no troops had as yet marched over the northern frontier into Germany. In fact an acute observer might have noticed that the troops were not marching much anywhere, except in towns and cities where a military parade would rouse patriotic approval. The truth was that the army of France wasn't ready to go to war, despite what its government might say.

Delphine took no interest at all. For her it was a matter of no importance whether there was war or peace. She walked about the estate, always alone, wrapped in her thoughts. She avoided sitting down to a meal with her mother but, if it couldn't be avoided, spoke hardly a word.

Nicole had their family doctor examine her. 'Nothing greatly wrong, madame,' Monsieur Chrepat said. 'A little anaemia perhaps, but that's common enough in young ladies. Some depression – I hear rumours of an unhappy love affair?'

Nicole nodded and shrugged.

'Ah well, I leave you this tonic for her. She

394

should eat plenty of steak with red wine. Perhaps a change of scenery might do her good.'

Nicole felt she dared not send Delphine away from home again. Each time she did, some disaster happened. 'Perhaps I will take her to the seaside for a week or two...'

'Excellent, excellent, madame,' agreed the doctor, and was taken off to sample the recently bottled champagne, a great favour since there was so little of it.

Nicole seriously intended to take her daughter to the coast. But then came a telegram from Paulette: Please come at once, am in great trouble.

Nicole packed overnight things and set out immediately. Her heart was knocking in her breast: she knew it must be something to do with Robert. She said not a word to Delphine on leaving, except, 'I have business to do, be good while I'm away.'

At Strasbourg station Paulette, fore-warned, was awaiting her. She ran to her as she stepped down from the train.

'I'm utterly dazed, Nicci. I felt *you* would know what to do.'

'But what?' urged Nicole, grasping her shoulder and giving it a little shake. 'What's happened? Is it Robert?'

Paulette nodded.

'What has he done? Tell me!'

'He's volunteered for the army, Nicole.'

Chapter Twenty-one

The little that Paulette knew was quickly told. The maid had come to her on Tuesday morning to say that Monsieur Robert's bed hadn't been slept in. Enquiries among Robert's friends yielded nothing, although he had once or twice stayed over night at the home of a young man called Rebecq.

Paulette, rendered efficient by the emergency, went to the hospital and then to the police. Nothing was known. On Wednesday she went once more to his friends, hoping for some clue. Rebecq confessed, shamefaced, that Robert had told him he intended to join up.

The recruiting office for Strasbourg was in the Mairie. Paulette had gone there. A kindly sergeant had patted her hand and told her her son would be quite all right: 'He's in the hands of the Grande Armée,' he said. When she insisted that her son was only seventeen and had not asked parental consent to join the army, his only reply was a shrug.

'Of course, if I hadn't been crying like a waterfall I'd have made a better impression,' Paulette said, well aware of her own defects.

'He just thought I was a silly woman. So that's why I telegraphed you – *you'll* be able to deal with him.'

Together they went to the recruiting office. The same bemedalled sergeant smiled a greeting to Paulette as she came in. 'Well, madame, I see you're more cheerful today! Have you reconciled yourself to your son's decision?'

Paulette cast an agonised glance at her sister. Nicole said, in her most authoritative tones, 'Let me speak to your superior, my man.'

'The captain? Oh, sorry, madame, but he's busy.'

'Go into that office and tell him I wish to speak to him. Either you do so, or I'll see you reduced to private by the end of the week.'

He started back almost visibly. For a moment he looked as if he might even salute. 'A... Well... I'll just pop in and see if he can spare you a minute. Er... Who shall I say?'

'Tell him La Veuve Tramont wishes to speak to him.'

His mouth fell open in a gape. He swallowed hard, then rushed into the inner office. A moment later the captain, in a fine dark blue uniform frogged with red, appeared in the doorway. 'Madame de Tramont! Pray come in! What an honour!'

She swept past the startled sergeant, taking Paulette in her wake. The inner office showed signs of a handsome cafe-tray lunch, which the sergeant removed at a gesture from his superior. The captain set chairs for them.

'Captain Lenoir, at your service!' he said, with a smart salute before he sat down behind his desk.

'Captain, my sister came the day before yesterday to inquire after her son, Robert Paul Fournier, who volunteered for military service on Monday. She informed the sergeant that the boy didn't have her permission to volunteer. Moreover, he's only seventeen years old. She wishes to have him returned to her care.'

'Oh,' said the captain, with a smothered smile in Paulette's direction, 'I see. You're the lady who cried so hard–'

'That your sergeant didn't take her seriously. Nevertheless, you see now that he should have done so. My nephew was just about to enter L'École Centrale des Arts et de Manufacture. His mother wishes him to pursue his studies.'

'I quite see your point, madame. All the same, the boy enlisted in proper form.'

'But surely he has to have parental permission?'

'He said he had it.'

'And you believed him!'

'Why not? In any case, madame, we can't go running to families asking for confirmation every time a young man comes to enlist.' He saw that his manner was drawing a frown from the great Madame de Tramont, and amended his remarks with: 'He signed the papers and took the usual oath that all he had affirmed was the truth. We believed him.'

Paulette clasped her sister's arm. 'Nicole, we've got to get him back!'

'Exactly. Captain, I want you to send for Robert and ... what's the phrase?'

'Muster him out? Well now, madame, that's not so easy. In time of peace, of course, you could buy him out quite simply. But we've a war to fight.'

'My God, if you need boys of seventeen to help you fight the Prussians, I recommend you to sue for peace at once!'

'Madame, that's almost treasonable!' he cried in indignation.

'Oh, rubbish! What possible use can an untrained boy of seventeen be to you? By all accounts you expect to be in Berlin by the end of August. He'll scarcely have learned to handle a gun by then!'

Captain Lenoir allowed himself a little smiling bow. 'In that case, ladies, you need have no great fears, need you? Once the victory is achieved, you can apply for the young man's release. I'm sure there will be no problems then.'

'Nicole!'

'It's all right, Paulette, I'm not accepting that. Captain, I wish you to set in motion whatever routine is necessary to have the boy released and returned to his home. Is that clear?'

'I deeply regret, madame, that's quite impossible. My work is to recruit soldiers, not arrange for their release.'

'So to whom should we apply? To the commander of the Strasbourg barracks?'

'Good God, the lad isn't there, madame! As you yourself have just said, he hardly knows one end of a gun from the other. He's been sent to training camp.'

'Where?'

'I'm not at liberty to reveal that!'

'Oh, don't be absurd! Where is my nephew?'

By now the captain was thoroughly annoyed with this pretty, elegant but angry lady. Who did she think she was? A wine-maker – did she really believe she could give orders to the French army?

'I have no idea which camp your nephew has been sent to, and if I knew it would be against military regulations to tell you. I'm sorry, mesdames – there's nothing I can do for you.'

He rose, expecting them to do likewise. Paulette got up, but Nicole drew her down again. 'Captain, I apologise for my bad manners. You must understand, his mother and I are very worried. Robert has had ... a blow to the heart, if you understand me. We're afraid he has joined the army in a kind of despair.'

'Ah...' This was different. He was a romantic at heart, despite all that six years in the army could do. 'I understand. He's gone for a soldier because life seems empty. Poor fellow... Well, Madame de Tramont, I really can't help you. I'm not just being obstructive – army regulations forbid me to help you. However, if you were to see a good lawyer...?'

'That would be the best step?'

'I think so.'

'Captain Lenoir, I thank you from the heart. Perhaps in due course you'll be good enough to accept a case of champagne I will despatch to you.'

'Oh, madame, you're too generous...'

With an appearance of goodwill on both sides, they parted. Outside Nicole almost threw her fists in the air, she was so angry. 'Self-important fool! Army regulations forbid him to tell us which camp Robert has gone to! Well, never mind, we'll find out. Paulette, we'd better go to your lawyer.'

But he was a gentleman who knew how to deal only with the making of wills and the buying and selling of property. He recommended them to an agent of insurance, because insurance companies had gone into the business of getting young men out of the army during the days of the first Napoleon. If a substitute could be found for the young man being called up, the army had no objections: thus a business grew up whereby agents found and paid substitutes. Under the new Napoleon they still found plenty of work to do.

Monsieur Clarent was such an agent. A heavy, elderly man, he listened with sympathy to their account of events. 'Well, ladies, the young man has caused you a great distress, I can see that. But as to not being able to say which camp he's gone to, that's nonsense. I can find that out within a day or two, and get word to the camp commander.'

'And he'll be sent home?'

'We-ell … we can get his case started, at least. I take it, since you don't know where he is, that he hasn't written?'

'Not a word.'

'Ah, that seems to mean he hasn't changed his mind. Often, you know, these romantic young volunteers come to their senses after a taste of army life.'

'Robert won't change his mind,' Paulette said with a tremulous sigh.

Monsieur Clarent began to think it was

rather a pity they wanted him out of the army. He sounded the kind of youngster the military forces could do with. He had heard rumours that the Prussians had a million men under arms, whereas the French army was somewhat less than half of that. A rushed mobilisation and training programme was now in being but it would be a long time before the two opposing armies were equal in strength or ability.

But of course by that time the war would be over and the Emperor Louis Napoleon would be in Berlin. Monsieur Clarent quite believed that. The legend of the Grande Armée was still strong, blotting out the perception that lassitude and inefficiency were rife in it.

'Leave it with me, ladies. I'll set everything going. I've no doubt I can make a good case. Only son of widowed mother…'

'No,' Paulette said, 'I have another son.'

'Oh? That's a pity – at least, of course, I don't really mean that–'

'But it would have been easier had Robert been an only son?' How ironic. Robert was in fact Nicole's only son – but that was not a fact that could be mentioned.

'Never mind. It's not a bad case anyway, since he's so young and his mother wants him at home. And … you know … a little money expended in the right way can work wonders, eh, madame?'

'Quite so.'

'In a few days I'll be able to tell you which camp he's in, and then after that we'll enter a plea to have him released.'

'When will he be let go?'

'Oh, a couple of months, I suppose – three at most.'

'Months?' wailed Paulette. 'I hoped to have him home next week!'

'Oh, dear lady, that's quite out of the question. You see, if he himself doesn't wish to be mustered out, then it has to go through the army's legal procedures – parental rights, all that kind of thing. In the end you'll win, I imagine, because he's so young…' And because, he added internally, he's the nephew of La Veuve Tramont.

Further discussion yielded no greater hopes. Nicole and Paulette left, Paulette on the verge of tears yet again.

'Darling, you'd better pack up and come back to Tramont with me,' Nicole urged. 'You're not fit to be left on your own.'

'No, no! If they *should* decide to let him go, I must be at home to welcome him.'

'But, Paulie, it may be weeks and weeks–'

'It doesn't matter.' She shook her head stubbornly. And since Nicole thought that she would have felt much the same in Paulette's place, she gave in.

When she got back to Tramont, her daughter came rushing to greet her.

'Mama!' She seized Nicole's hands urgently.

It was the first time since the frustrated elopement that she had used the name in addressing her mother. Nicole felt a gush of emotion – relief, gratitude, love, pity. She took her daughter in her arms.

But Delphine struggled free. 'No, no – tell me – it was about Robert, wasn't it? The day after you left I suddenly felt – I knew – something's happened to Robert, that's it, isn't it? Tell me!'

Disappointment was like a stab at Nicole's breast. But she said, 'It's all right, don't be afraid. He's fit and well, so far as we know.'

'So far as–?'

'He's enlisted.'

For a second her daughter gaped at her, totally taken aback. There was a moment when tears seemed ready to spill over onto her cheeks. But she forced a proud smile.

'How like him!' she cried. 'How brave and fine! Oh, I might have known he would find something fine to do with his life!' She turned away. There was bitterness in her voice as she added: 'He's luckier than me. I can only stay here and be unhappy.'

'Child, there's nothing lucky in offering yourself as a target to enemy bullets!' Nicole said angrily.

That brought Delphine round with a jerk. The true facts struck at her. Robert hadn't gone into a peacetime army to take part in pageants – he had gone to war. 'Oh,' she said, on an indrawn breath. 'Of course – the march to Berlin!'

'With God's help, he won't go on that,' Nicole said, 'I'm arranging to have him released. It may take a month or two but we'll get him safely back. But Delphine, dear … I beg you, put him out of your mind. You must, in the end.'

Delphine nodded. 'I know that. I'm trying, Mama. But … oh, it's so hard.'

This time, when Nicole put an arm about her, she accepted the embrace. Together they went into the drawing-room. It was the first time in weeks they had been close.

Monsieur Clarent wrote to say he had found Robert. He was in a training camp of the 7th Army Corps at a village a few miles north of the great fortress of Sedan. 'I have had a clerk seek him out and speak with him. When he discovered the reason for Masson's visit, he walked away. He seems adamant that he wishes to remain with the army. Masson spoke with the major in charge of recruit-training who told him he had singled out your nephew as officer-material, so that it may well be that he will be moved on after basic instruction to an officer-training corps. Unfortunately, that may make it more difficult to get him out.'

After some inner debate, Nicole let her daughter read the letter. It was, after all, about a family matter. The time must come when Robert could be mentioned in front of Delphine without causing her to go pale with hurt emotion.

Almost at the same time came a letter from Edmond, who had heard from his mother about Robert's enlistment. 'I must confess to you, Aunt Nicci, I'm amazed. He's the last man I'd have thought would do a harebrained thing like that. Never mind, if he wants to help give those Teutonic oafs the hiding they've been asking for, good for him! Only Mama is very upset so, dear Aunt Nicci, if you can get him out, I suppose it would be best. Though why she's so perturbed I don't know because according to what they're all saying here in Paris, King William will be hiding in his cellars in Berlin in a week or two.'

The news, when one could get any, didn't bear out that optimistic view. Far from the French army invading Germany, it seemed the German army was in France. What was more, it wasn't behaving as if it were made up of stupid oafs. Quite the contrary.

At first it appeared that a French army under Frossard had taken Saarbruck, a town on the German river Saar a few miles inside the German border. Glorious reports of the victory appeared in the Paris papers and were repeated in the provincial: the German army had been annihilated.

But if that were true, how came it that the Germans were reported at Weissenbourg on the French side of the Rhine? Moreover, what were they doing there? Could they possibly be going to attack Strasbourg?

In the midst of rumour and counter-rumour, Nicole became very anxious for her sister. That anxiety was relieved when Paulette herself arrived in a hackney coach from Rheims.

'Oh, Nicci!' she cried, falling into her younger sister's arms. 'Oh, you've no idea how terrible it's been!'

'What, darling? What's happened?' For the first few moments Nicole thought it was bad news about Robert.

But no. 'The Prussians are outside Strasbourg! I only just got away in time! I was on the last train out!'

During the following week it was rumoured that the Germans had taken first Brumath, then Strasbourg. Some believed it, some did not. But the truth of it was shown as refugees from Alsace and Lorraine began to trickle into the Champagne region. Communications had totally broken down: the postal system was gone, the railway by means of which letters and newspapers were distributed was largely out of action. Provincial papers issued broadsheets consisting of what they had gleaned from occasional copies of Paris papers and from news sent by telegraph – but nothing seemed certain, no one knew what was happening except that some great disaster was taking place.

All hope of getting Robert released from the army was acknowledged as lost. The agent charged with the task had fled from Strasbourg under the German bombardment, as had Paulette herself. Besides, in the midst of this chaos, who would trouble himself over a young volunteer about whom his relatives were anxious? Mothers and sisters throughout France were in grief and concern for their menfolk, struggling wearily hither and thither under commanders who seemed scarcely to know what they were doing.

On the 22nd August Alphonse the postman trotted up, but with no letters. Nicole was called from the vine rows to speak to him. She'd been discussing with Compiain how soon the grapes would be ready for picking or if, this year, they ever would be.

'Madame, the French army under General Macmahon is in Rheims.'

Compiain, who had accompanied her to the courtyard, gave a grunt of surprise. Nicole said: 'Are you sure of this?'

'I saw them myself last night. Listen, madame, you can be sure the general isn't there to conduct a victory parade. He's there because he expected the Boches.'

'But the Germans would never attack Rheims! My God, think – if the cathedral should be damaged–!'

Compiain said: 'Never mind the cathedral – what about the people? What are they doing?'

'Well, those of them that can, are leaving. Like me.' Alphonse made a grimace and a shrug which lifted his shoulders expressively.

'You're leaving?'

'You bet! No sense in staying to be hit by mortar shells when the attack begins. No, I'm off.' He jerked his head towards the little mail cart.

'That's government property,' muttered Compiain.

'Really? Which government is that? If you ask me, there's nobody in charge, so I'm taking what I can use to get out of danger. And, madame, I advise you to do the same. Everything's really bitched up–'

'Alphonse!' Compiain rebuked him.

'Sorry, madame. But it makes you use bad language! "To the Rhine!" they cry when they start this damned war, but now it's "Every man for himself!" If I were you, I'd pack and go.'

Nicole shook her head at him. He was a foolish old man, well-known as a spreader of gossip. All the same, to steal the mailcart...

410

He must really have seen soldiers in Rheims.

A couple of days later news came that the army had moved out of the city. It was said Macmahon was going to join General Bazaine at Sedan, though whether this was true in any part, no one was sure.

'Sedan!' gasped Paulette. 'That's where Robert's training camp is!'

'Don't distress yourself, Paulie. There's no certainty in any of this. Oh, if *only* one could get hold of the true facts!'

These were supplied from, of all places, London. A messenger arrived in a post-chaise with a letter to Nicole from Lord Grassington.

'My very dear Nicci. Since the postal service between London and Paris is all but suspended and in any case I shouldn't like this letter to fall into the hands of a postal censor, I am sending it by a confidential clerk.

'His instructions are to wait while you pack and then escort you and your family to Switzerland, where a house of mine in Bienne is at your disposal. I beg you not to wait, but to leave at once.'

'Despatches from the British Ambassador in Paris speak of misgivings over the Emperor's reign – no one, he reports, speaks loyally of him. The series of defeats suffered by the French is not likely to be halted by a change to Republican government and it seems inevitable that the German army will continue its march south and east, relatively unchecked, so that Metz, Nancy, Chalons, and perhaps even Paris itself will fall.

'This means that your estate will lie directly in the path of the advance. You are in great danger. You must get out before it is too late.

'Your loving and anxious friend, Gerrard.'

Nicole felt the blood drain from her heart as she read the letter. The clerk, standing respectfully in front of her desk, watched with sympathy. 'I am to wait and arrange for your removal to Bienne, madame. When do you wish to leave?'

'Not so fast!' She folded the letter, laid it on her desk. 'I have to confer with my manager.' She rang the bell and when the butler came, sent the clerk to have a meal in the kitchens. She also sent for Compiain, who arrived soaking wet and covered in mud.

'This confounded rain! It's the worst season I can remember. God knows when we'll be able to pick, madame–'

'It's not about that, Arnaud. I've had a letter from a friend, with reliable information about the war. He says the Germans will be here soon.'

'Here?'

'On their way south and east, to Paris–'

'Huh! They'll never let the Germans get to Paris.'

'Perhaps not. But as they try to prevent them, they fight their battles – and we seem to be on the route the Germans are taking.'

Compiain cocked an eyebrow. 'Well, madame?'

'My friend recommends that we should pack and go.'

Compiain looked surprised. 'Go where, madame?'

'I am offered a sanctuary in Switzerland.'

'Oh, then, I think you should go, if you're worried.'

'But you?'

'Where would *I* go?' Compiain said, running a hand through his shock of upstanding hair. 'This is my home, my wife and children are here, my father, my aunts and uncles…'

'But, Arnaud! This friend of mine–' she touched the letter – 'a very well informed man – says there will be battles.'

'Oh, well, a few cavalry troops riding down the vines and hacking at each other–'

'No, no, war isn't like that any more, my friend! They have great guns, that can destroy a house with one salvo. They say that Strasbourg is in ruins after the bombardment there.'

'Huh,' said her chief of cellar, 'well, we'll just go down in the caves, then, eh? There can be the worst thunderstorm in the world up above, but you don't hear it in the cellars.'

Nicole stared at him. He was, as Jean-Baptiste had once said, like a thistle – skinny, wiry, with a bush of strong coarse hair that stood up like the purple petals of the flower. Nicole respected him thoroughly for his knowledge of the wine and his devotion to his work. She had never thought of him as heroic, however.

'And how long do you imagine we could stay down there?'

'Oh, indefinitely, I s'pose. There's light and water – it'd be cold, of course, we'd need lots of blankets. But so long as we took woollens and plenty of food, we could hold out for days, weeks even. Then we'd come out when the Germans had been chased away.'

'You don't want to move out until things quieten down?'

He shook his head. 'But you go, madame. It's different for you.'

How was it different for her? She was a native of the village of Calmady, just as Compiain was. She had loved and married the owner of the great house that belonged to the village. There she had borne his children, survived the first griefs of widowhood. Jean-Baptiste had lived and worked here.

The wine that had given her prestige and money belonged here. It was as much part of the countryside as the people who tended the vines. Its elegance and sparkle were the pride of the Champagne region.

So now she was to run away? Leave it all to the invaders? She pictured German lancers riding over her vineyards, drunken soldiers knocking bottles open to pour the rich champagne down their thirsty throats...

'Thank you, Arnaud,' she said. 'I don't think I'll be going anywhere.'

He nodded. 'No, best not. You want to be here to keep an eye on things, eh?'

But she felt it her duty to convey the contents of the letter to her sister and her daughter. 'If you want to leave, I think now is the time to go. Lord Grassington's messenger will escort you.'

'But where to, dear?' Paulette quavered.

'To Bienne, in Switzerland.'

'Oh no! No, no! I couldn't possibly leave France! My sons are here.'

'Perhaps you'd rather go to Paris to join Edmond? I'm sure you'd be safe in Paris.'

Paulette hesitated. She'd had no word from Edmond in over two weeks. 'I'm not even sure he's still there. The last time he wrote, he spoke of joining a student corps to go to the front...'

'What about you, darling? Would you

rather leave Tramont?'

'You're staying?' Delphine inquired.

'Yes, I want to try to make at least *some* wine this year – otherwise it will be a total loss.'

'Then I stay too,' Delphine said, her chin coming up.

They talked about it long into the night. The decision was that they would stay, relying on the fact that the Prussians were more likely to be fighting in the towns than in the countryside. Battles, if any – and after all Gerrard's prediction might be wrong – were more likely to be at Chalons or Rheims.

Nevertheless, it was good sense to make provision. Nicole had food taken down to the cellars: hams and smoked sausage and fish, potatoes, biscuit-bread, anything she could think of that would keep several days. The chill of the caves was ideal for such provisions. She also sent down all the spare blankets from the manor house.

This was done rather than attempt to carry out the grape harvest as yet. The weather might yet improve. There might be a burst of sunshine to put some plumpness on the fruit. Such things had happened before: a poor outlook until the very end of August and then, in the first week of September, glowing sunshine and a sudden improvement in the grapes. The thinning of the leaves was carried out, to let what light there was help to sweeten the small bunches.

In a way, it was a help to have the 'siege preparations' to take her mind off the disastrous harvest. But we're not going to need any of this, she kept telling herself.

She was wrong. Three days later, as the last week of August began, horsemen could be glimpsed scouting in the thickets along the road to Epernay. Then, in the distance, there was a sound like thunder.

'The artillery!' said Nicole.

'My word, you were right, madame! They do sound as if they could knock a house down.'

There were skirmishes between scouting parties on the outskirts of Calmady. The gun batteries were coming noticeably nearer. In the middle of the following night, shells began to shriek across the village. French infantry were marching along the road to the east; they were the target for the gunners, but it was difficult to find the range. The first shell that landed in Calmady destroyed four houses in the main street, killing most of the occupants.

The villagers began to stream out of their homes. Safety for them lay in the cellars of Madame de Tramont. The women and children were quickly taken down in the lifts which Nicole had installed the previous year. The men had to go down by the steep staircases.

Compiain decided not to take cover. 'A few of us are going to be a welcome committee,' he explained. 'We've got some rifles the infantrymen have abandoned–'

'Arnaud! You're not a soldier!'

'Right, madame. All the same, we can't just let them take our homes, now can we?'

Deep in the caves, nothing could be heard. From time to time one of the boys was sent to the entrance at ground level to find out what was happening. The reports for four days were of extended warfare, a regiment of infantry dug in at Calmady trying to hold up the German advance, Uhlans and cuirassiers in cavalry clashes, flames visible on the skyline from other villages besides Calmady.

On the fifth day the gas supply was cut off. It came from Rheims by way of great pipes laid in the Champagne clay. Either the pipes had been fractured by mortars or the supply-station at Rheims had gone out of action.

'Never mind, we've plenty of candles,' Nicole said. She knew the passages and vaults of her cellars as well as she knew the Villa Tramont; she knew the contents of all the store cupboards as well as she knew the contents of the carefully stacked champagne bottles.

Another day and a night went by. Young Jacques Lessouet went up to reconnoitre. 'It's gone quiet,' he said when he came down again. 'There's flames still to be seen to the east – I think it's Pernigort burning. But I didn't see any soldiers or hear any horses, and the guns are further away.'

A sigh of relief ran through the cold, huddled crowd in the cellars. 'Is it still raining?' called a waggish old man from the back of the vault.

'Yes, still raining!'

In the morning they went up the stairs, by twos and threes. The pulleys that worked the lifts had been damaged, so it took a long time to help the old people and mothers with children up to the surface.

It was a little after dawn. The sky had a watery brightness, the breeze was chill. A strange smell hung in the air – carbide, gunsmoke, mingled with another they later learnt to know as the reek of dead horses.

A goldfinch was fluttering round the ruined gantry-house, chirping as he picked seeds from a dock-plant. Otherwise there was a strange silence. Cautiously the villagers of Calmady began to move away from the entrance to the cellars. No one appeared to bar their way.

'They've gone!' cried a joyful voice.

At once the young and able-bodied began to run for the estate entrance, to hurry back along the road to their homes. The servants of the Villa Tramont looked towards it, uncertain. Its high slate roofs could be seen above the trees. They appeared to be quite undamaged – no holes to be seen.

'Come along,' Nicole said, and with either arm about her sister and her daughter, she set off. The housekeeper and the butler fell in behind her. She was amused to see the phalanx took up position strictly according to rank.

They came to the house via the office of the chief cellarman and the out-buildings. Nothing stirred. Still they felt no desire to break out into loud talk; everything seemed caught in a web of quietitude.

One of the grooms said under his breath, 'I believe they've taken our horses, damn then! I can't hear a sound from the stables.'

He moved off to take a look. The rest of the servants filtered slowly to their appointed places. Some went into the house by the back door.

'Oh, how I long for a bath!' murmured Delphine.

'Go along in, then. They ought to get the stove going again soon, if the coal hasn't been stolen. You go too, Paulie – you look as if you could do with a good hot bowl of soup.'

They left her, the girl with an arm about her aunt's shoulders.

Nicole stood looking at the house. How wonderful – it seemed to be truly undamaged. She walked across the courtyard to the path leading round the house. At once she saw that some of her trees had been cut down – presumably to allow line-of-sight for gun placement. She bit her lip.

But if that were the only thing they'd lost, she had nothing to complain of.

She came to the front court. The door of the house, she noticed, stood open. Looters? Perhaps. But before she went indoors, she would go out to the drive for a look at the rest of the park.

She went across the courtyard, under the porte cochere. It was shadowy there, the morning sun shining at an angle across its openings. She walked out into the drive, momentarily blinded by the light.

She blinked.

Sitting his horse with perfect composure, a Prussian cavalryman in a spiked helmet was regarding her with interest.

Chapter Twenty-two

'Good morning,' said the officer.

'Good morning,' Nicole said, too taken aback to do anything but respond.

'May I know your name?'

'I am Nicole de Tramont.'

'Ah, The Widow Tramont herself? How delightful to meet you. I am Lieutenant von Kravensfeldt.' He was speaking fluent though accented French. Now he called a command in German, and a corporal detached himself from a group standing by their horses further up the drive, to take his reins. He dismounted.

'I was about to go indoors. Shall we enter together?' He offered his arm.

Nicole stood still. Was she being asked to play hostess to the enemy?

'Come,' he urged. 'I must inspect the house. I'm attached to the staff of Duke William of Mecklenburg, who must soon move out of his quarters in Rheims to accommodate His Majesty. I thought perhaps he might take up residence here.'

'Rheims?' faltered Nicole. 'You've captured Rheims?'

'Rheims surrendered without a fight,

422

madame. Unfortunately some madman blew up the powder magazine as we were taking over from the French garrison, killing and injuring a great many. Your General Theremin himself has been badly wounded – I tell you this so that you will not believe the rumour now circulating, which is that we Germans wickedly blew up the town when it had accepted occupation.'

As he spoke he was gently leading the way to the front entrance of the manor house. He went in ahead of her. She noticed that none of his men followed – it seemed they expected no trouble, and they were right, for thought the servants were startled into protest at his appearance, they at once obeyed when he asked to be shown round the house.

Nicole waited until he returned. 'I shall recommend the house to His Grace. It remains to be seen whether he will take it. He may prefer to remain closer to Rheims–'

'I don't wish to have German officers in my home!' Nicole said, having recovered from the first astonishment.

'No doubt. Rest easy, madame.' He was smiling, almost in sympathy. 'We shall not be here long – the King of Prussia and his staff will be moving to Versailles very soon.'

'Versailles?'

'Oh yes. He wishes to be closer to Paris to direct the–'

'It's a lie! You haven't taken Versailles!'

The officer made a little grimace. He was very young, scarcely more than a boy – tall, fairskinned though his hair showed dark brown under his spiked helmet.

'Madame, few people have ever called me a liar. But I make allowances for your natural bewilderment. To explain your situation to you, let me just say that our forces are in possession of most of the north of France and are about to take Metz and Sedan–'

'Sedan... I have a son – I mean, my sister has a son...'

'At Sedan?' He smiled. 'My congratulations, madame. It will be a fine fight, I assure you. Well, thank you for your hospitality. I will make my report to the Duke.'

He gave a little stiff bow and saluted by touching the rim of his helmet. He turned smartly about and was gone. She heard him ride out, accompanied by his escort of cavalry who had come into the courtyard to await him.

Delphine and her aunt came running down to the hall. 'I saw him from the windows!' Paulette cried. 'I hid in a cupboard!'

Nicole was almost angry. 'And you, Delphine? Did you hide?'

'No, Mama, I was in my room when he

424

was shown in – I simply turned my shoulder on him, he apologised and backed out.'

'Why was he here? Does it mean our troops are gone, Nicci?'

'It seems so...'

In the days that followed they pieced together the story of what had happened to Calmady. Fourteen men of the village had been killed trying to defend the place after the French troops had withdrawn to Pernigord – among them Arnaud Compiain. 'I don't understand it,' his father, now a very old man, said in broken tones. 'Arnaud was never a lad to enjoy a fight...'

Many of the houses had been destroyed in the course of close fighting. The vineyards had been trampled down or ploughed up by shells, or sometimes cut to pieces by shrapnel. The smashed red Pinot grapes lay like clots of blood on the white clay.

Now, it seemed, the German forces were following the course of the Marne and the Seine, on their way to Paris.

'Edmond is in Paris!'

'And so is Old Madame.' Nothing had been heard from either of them in weeks, but with the postal system and communications generally in such a bad state, it had caused no special anxiety. As for the news about Sedan, Nicole kept that to herself.

But not for long. On Monday the 5th September the *Journal de la Marne* came out with a single-sheet newspaper. It was of course officially allowed by the occupation force, yet somehow the news it contained had the ring of truth.

Sedan had been taken, after a battle lasting through the 31st August and the lst September. The entire army of General McMahon – eighty-four thousand men, two thousand seven hundred officers, thirty-nine generals – had capitulated. With them went the general himself and the Emperor Napoleon III.

When the copies reached Calmady, groups gathered to read them in what remained of the inn, and on street corners. 'It's not true! The Emperor a prisoner? The army would never allow anyone to take the Emperor!'

There was no way of knowing. All the information they had at present came from sources permitted by the German army. Yet Nicole had a terrible feeling that what they were reading was the truth.

A party of Uhlans was quartered on the Villa Tramont. No officer, only two sergeants in charge. 'What about the Duke?' Nicole asked.

'Duke? What duke?' They spoke very poor French, and Nicole very poor German. When she at last mentioned the name Mecklenburg, they laughed. 'Versailles!' they said, pointing eastwards.

They took up their domicile in the stables and outbuildings. They were no trouble. In fact, they made themselves useful carrying baskets of grapes to the weighing points and helping to push them down the slope to the press.

For although most of the harvest was lost, Nicole had determined to do what she could to save the vintage of 1870. A bitter vintage it would be, and never likely to be raised in a toast at a happy event. The harvest was small, the grapes of poor quality, the resulting wine was below the high standard of the Champagne region. But Nicole was determined to put it into her cellars. That was her business – the production of wine.

'How can you be so heartless!' Delphine cried. 'All this time, no news of Robert – he may be dead, he may be a prisoner in enemy hands! And all you can think of is the wine!'

'Delphie, there is nothing I can do about any of that. But at least I can make wine.'

'It's disgusting, obscene! I wish every single vine had been cut to pieces!'

Nicole merely shook her head. It was useless to reason with her while she was in this state.

The Uhlans received orders to move on. They said a polite goodbye. One of them kissed one of the housemaids heartily and gave her a button from his tunic as a keepsake. Nicole presented them with some bottles of the newly made still wine. 'You're giving them our wine?' Delphine cried in fury.

'It's all it's fit for – to give away to invaders,' Nicole said with a grim smile.

New soldiers appeared to take up residence at Villa Tramont. These were older men, foot soldiers. By and by it emerged they were territorials from the state of Baden, just across the Rhine from Alsace. They spoke passable French and seemed very pleased to have such comfortable quarters as warm stables and grain stores. These were to be the long-term occupation force, allowing the attack regiments to concentrate on Paris.

Paris was now under siege. Rumours came and went: that the Germans had bombarded the city, that Notre Dame was in flames, that no, the Germans had agreed to respect the holy cathedral, that they had allowed a certain number of Parisians to leave, that they had taken them prisoner, that they had sent them on to Evreux under safe-passage, that a Republican government under Gambetta was now carrying on the war with a new army...

The last rumour at least seemed to be true. After the capture of the Emperor everyone had expected a peace to be signed, but the war still went on. Paris had refused to surrender: Paris was the symbol of French pride and resistance.

On the last day of September a gentleman in a small closed carriage drove up to the manor house. The butler announced him as Dr Charles Percival of the Red Cross Ambulance Corps. When he was shown in he proved to be wearing a dark blue uniform braided and frogged with black, and a white armband bearing a red cross.

'Madame de Tramont? Forgive my intrusion. I believe you have your sister, Madame Fournier, staying with you?'

'That's perfectly correct. Please sit down, doctor. Can I offer you some refreshment?'

'Thank you, a glass of wine and a little something to eat would be very welcome. I've been travelling for days now...' He spoke French with a strong American accent.

Nicole nodded at the butler to bring food and drink. Dr Percival said: 'May I see Madame Fournier? I've news of her son Robert.'

Nicole went cold. Her throat seemed to seize up. The doctor, who had taken a chair across from her, sprang up. 'Madame! Are you ill?'

'No – no – you surprised me– Please, what is the news of Robert? Please tell me! Please!'

'Should the news not be given first to his mother?'

'Is it good news? Is Robert alive?'

'Alive, yes. Otherwise … perhaps the news is not good.'

'Oh God!'

She bowed her head, put her hands over her face, and for a moment let the hot tears gush between her fingers. Then she straightened, wiped her cheeks with the palms of her hands. 'Please tell me, doctor. My sister is of a very timid disposition. If the news is bad, it has to be broken very gently.'

'I see.' The American looked a little puzzled but went on: 'Your nephew was taken prisoner at Sedan with all the others. He was badly wounded – there had been some rashly courageous act to take out a gun-post threatening one of the city gates. My unit was active in the city of Sedan. After the cease-fire we went round collecting the wounded.'

The butler returned with a silver tray bearing bread and cheese and red wine. The visitor seized the glass eagerly, drank deeply, chewed at the crusty bread. Meanwhile Nicole waited, scarcely daring to breathe.

'News has of course been scanty. You perhaps are aware that one of the conditions of the cease-fire was that the entire French army must go into prison in Germany?'

'Yes.'

'My unit went with the wounded. You understand that we tend both sides dispassionately, cooperating with the army surgeons. Resources on the march into Germany were strained and moreover, disease had taken hold. We lost many to dysentery.'

'And Robert?'

'He is still very ill and weak. His wounds have been slow to heal and I'm afraid...'

'What? Tell me!'

'He may not walk again. He received very severe injuries to the spine. It's too early yet to tell, but I feel it only honest to give you the facts.'

Nicole could say nothing. She sat at her desk, staring at the man.

'May I?' he said, and swallowed bread and cheese voraciously. 'I've been on the roads for seven days. I've messages for many a mother still to deliver.'

'The Germans allow you to travel unhindered?'

'Oh yes, I have a laissez-passer signed by Bismarck himself. But it's the devil! – food's short, the roads are a quagmire, and often the families have moved from the addresses I've been given, due to the excesses of war. Your sister's house in Strasbourg, for instance – it doesn't exist any more. The local prefect told me she had probably gone to stay with you, and as I had other families in this direction to visit, I made a slight detour to come here.'

'I'm very grateful,' Nicole said, keeping her voice steady by a searing effort. 'I'll pass on the news to my sister. Do I gather you have yourself spoken to Robert?'

'Robert, yes, he was under my direct care.' He got a list out of the inner pocket of his uniform jacket to consult it. 'I see I have no written message – he was too weak to hold a pen.'

Nicole gave a gasp.

Percival looked up. 'I'm sorry, madame, but haste makes one tactless. Your nephew is in a prison camp near Elberfeld. He's in the camp hospital, of course. In due time an exchange of letters and parcels may be arranged under the auspices of the Red Cross – I will see that you get news of the facility if it is allowed.'

'Will he – can he be allowed home soon?'

'Negotiations for the exchange of wounded are taking place, but I must tell you your nephew is not in a condition to travel again.' The doctor put the paper back in his pocket, shaking his head. 'I tell you, madame, I served in our Civil War back home and I never saw wounded worse than those I've had to deal with in this war. Those damned modern guns...'

'Is there anything we can do at present? Any representations we can make?'

'I hardly think so. While the Republicans remain so obdurate and Paris holds out, there cannot be a peace. Meanwhile the Prussians – quite understandably – refuse to negotiate lesser matters. I assure you, the wounded are receiving good care, but it's not the same as having them in a city hospital with a full nursing staff.'

She pressed him to stay overnight, but he pleaded other business. 'I hope to make Chateau Thierry by nightfall. Thank you for the food – much appreciated.'

'Thank *you!*' Nicole said with fervour as she shook hands.

She didn't at once tell Paulette and Delphine. She needed time to accustom herself to the news before she shared it with anyone else. She snatched up a shawl and went out, to walk by the lake where she used to take her daughters when they were children.

It was greatly changed, from a swampy pond restored to a handsome stretch of water where the leaves of water-lilies still floated. The water-birds came up as usual to be fed. She had brought nothing for them, so they paraded reproachfully in front of her on the dark grey surface.

'Robert is alive!' she whispered to them. 'He's alive!'

Later, when she nerved herself to convey what she had learned, the reaction wasn't what she expected. Paulette didn't break down in tears. At first, when Nicole warned that she had news of Robert that wasn't entirely good, she threw out a hand in terror. But Delphine caught it and held it tight. She heard her sister out in silence, motionless.

'I knew it,' Delphine murmured, 'I sensed he was still alive. If he'd been killed, something would have told me.'

'You must understand that the American doctor says he's still very sick.'

'Because of being dragged all the way to a prison camp in Germany.'

'Yes, I'm afraid so.'

'I hate them!' Delphine burst out. 'I hate them! They march into our country, destroy our village, take our men–!'

'Delphine–'

'I hate them! It's their fault that Robert is a cripple! Oh, if I were only a man – I'd show them how much I hate them!'

Nicole shook her head. 'My dear, don't take it like this! Be thankful instead – Robert is still alive–'

'Oh yes,' whispered her sister, stars in her eyes. 'I thank God for it. I promised Him, you know – that if only He would save my son for me, I'd give every penny I possess to repair the roof of Strasbourg Cathedral...'

Nicole nodded at Delphine to lead her aunt upstairs to her room. Perhaps in its privacy Paulette gave way to tears, but for once Nicole was spared the need to comfort her.

But, as the days went by, it seemed Delphine really meant what she said. She refused to talk to the German troops, although she spoke their language fluently. The mayor of Calmady, charged with numerous duties by the occupation force, had relied on her to act as interpreter; she now refused this office. Whenever a Badish infantryman crossed her path on the Tramont estate, she turned her back.

'Delphine, what *good* does it do?' Nicole begged. 'We have to live with them–'

'Oh yes, and sell them our wine – that's all that matters, isn't it!'

Winter came. It was one of the worst in living memory. The cold was so great that the trunks of oak trees in Tramont's park burst asunder. There were problems with fuel supplies for the machinery of the wine-making processes, but Nicole comforted herself with the thought that this was in any case the resting period for the wine – not that it mattered much, for the *cuvée* was uninspired to say the least. She made the blend with the newly promoted chief cellarman, Compiain's assistant, Rodrigue. He was nervous and uncertain: she had to make all the major decisions alone – but once again it hardly mattered, for nothing she could do would make this a great wine.

At last news came from Paris, by an extremely round-about means. A balloonist managed to fly out of the beleaguered city, bringing with him sacks of despatches and letters. The letters then went south; some were delivered easily in the unoccupied territories. A letter from Edmond to his mother went by way of London to Le Havre and at last, under the safe-conduct of the British Embassy, reached Paulette at Tramont.

'Dearest Mother, I hope this letter reaches you. Much has happened since I last wrote. I intended to join a student corps but everything was such a muddle that we never left Paris. The blockade is severe and food is very short but, thank God, the enemy haven't as yet used their guns – I dread to think of the results of cannon-fire in Paris's great blocks of houses.

'For the moment I am staying with Old Madame, at her invitation. The cold has been very hard on her. I fear she is feeling the effects of her age. I asked her the other day how old she was to which she said, with some of her usual spirit, "None of your business, young man!" But in general she is quiet and has a bad cough. She is depressed because she expected the monarchists to make some coup when our great Emperor was led off to prison. She was greatly disappointed when the new Republic was proclaimed.

'Dear Mother, I hope you are well and safe

– we heard Strasbourg had been destroyed but there are so many lying rumours it's impossible to know what to believe. What news of Robert? I got your letter telling me he had joined up, but since then, nothing. I hope he is fit and well – he would be too recently trained to be sent to the front.

'Give my love to Aunt Nicole and Delphine. I hope you can read this – I have had to use the thinnest paper possible so as to lighten the load of the balloonist who is taking the mail out. I don't expect a reply although there is now some talk of a truce to allow the Red Cross Corps to move out some sick and wounded. Your loving son Edmond.'

Paulette was in seventh heaven as she pressed the letter to her breast. 'Oh, how lucky I am! Oh, I thank God! Both my sons are alive! Nicole, I am the luckiest woman in the world!'

'Yes, my dear,' agreed Nicole, hugging her. It was good news indeed, and all the more welcome because life in the Champagne region was so grim – the harvest almost a disaster, German uniforms everywhere, food scarce, the cold bitter and unrelenting.

Christmas was not a time for celebration that year. There was the usual midnight mass in the wrecked church of Calmady, Ste Anne's. There were carols sung by the children – thin, white-faced, large-eyed children who didn't receive the usual bon-bons and candied fruits. There were carols also by the German troops, unexpectedly beautiful: 'There is a rose new-born, Within a stable laid...' Nicole, hearing the strong, tuneful harmony, laid her head on her office desk and wept.

She was impelled to go out later to thank them for their singing. An officer in the spiked helmet and highly-polished boots of the Uhlans was coming out of the stables as she approached.

'Good afternoon, Madame de Tramont.'

'Why, it's Lieutenant von Kraven...' She sought for his name.

'Von Kravensfeldt.' He gave his little bow and salute, with a click of the heels. 'How flattering that you remember me!'

'I'm never likely to forget you! You were the first enemy soldier I ever saw!'

'Madame,' he said in reproach. 'The German army is not an enemy to civilians.'

She could have asked him how he explained the siege of Paris in that case, but had learned to guard her tongue. Instead she said, 'What are you doing here, lieutenant? I thought you had gone on to Versailles.'

'Quite so. But I have been sent with a small detachment to the headquarters of Count Walderne at Rheims. At the moment I am visiting my men.'

'Yours? But you are a cavalryman–?'

'Quite so. I have been given the role of welfare officer to the local occupation force. I am here just to check that the men have had an agreeable Christmas. They tell me they have nothing to complain of here.'

She understood that this was a compliment so she smiled and nodded. It was cold in the stableyard. She turned to go back to the house. He accompanied her.

'Do you remember that I was here to requisition your house last time we met?'

'I do indeed. Nothing came of that.'

'No, events moved so rapidly.' He pulled his cloak about him. 'By heaven, it's cold! In Prussia we call this iron-fist – the earth is grasped by a frost as hard as iron.'

He had reached the back door. The early dark was gathering. She heard the clatter of his escort in the driveway beyond the house. She felt an impulse of sympathy – a long ride home in the bitter weather before they could have anything.

'Would you care to come in for some hot punch?'

'Oh, thank you, but my men–'

'I'll send some out to them – in fact I could send it to the stables as a thank-you to your troops for their singing. They could all drink it in the warm.'

'That is most kind, madame. Thank you.'

He followed her indoors, looking about

439

with curiosity. The last time he was here, the place had been covered in dust. Now, the house was warm with the burning of pine logs, scented with their resin, bright with polish.

In the hall she rang for the butler. 'Tell Cook to make a big bowl of rum punch and have Jacques take it to the escort. Tell him to send them to the stables with it.'

'Yes, madame.'

'And bring some into the drawing-room.'

'Yes, madame.'

Delphine was reading by the light of one of their precious candles: gaslight had still not been restored. She turned her head idly at her mother's entry, then sprang up at the sight of the uniform. 'Mama!'

'I want you to meet Lieutenant von Kravensfeldt. This is my daughter, Delphine.'

'My respects, mademoiselle.'

'The lieutenant is here to see to the welfare of the men. I've asked him in for a hot drink.'

Delphine was stricken to silence. Her eyes carried a message of angry reproach.

Lenhardt von Kravensfeldt began a stilted conversation about the weather. He got very little response from this startlingly pretty young lady. She sat with her eyes bent upon her book, as if that was the most important thing in the world. Only Nicole replied to his remarks.

The hot punch was quickly brought, providing a new topic of conversation. Delphine got up. 'I won't have any, thank you, Mama. You'll excuse me–'

'Delphine, please sit down and have some punch with our guest.'

'No, Mama, you know I don't care for rum.'

'Delphine, it's Christmas. Sit down and drink some punch.'

The butler offered the glass. Delphine accepted it, set it by on a table beside her chair.

'We should have a toast,' suggested Lenhardt, eager to bring about some relaxation of the tension he could feel in the air. 'What shall we drink to?'

'To peace and goodwill,' offered Nicole, with a frown at Delphine.

'Excellent! To peace and goodwill!' He raised the glass in its little silver holder. He waited politely until Delphine did likewise.

They all drank simultaneously. Delphine made a startled sound, slapped down her glass so that it spilled half its contents. 'Oh, I've burnt my mouth!' she cried.

With that excuse she leaped up and ran out.

'Oh, mademoiselle–' began Lenhardt.

Nicole gestured to him to sit down. 'It's nothing, she'll see to it in a moment. Tell me, lieutenant, where is your home?'

He talked to her comfortably for ten minutes about Trakehnen, where his family owned large tracts of land on which they raised 'the finest horses in Prussia'. They had always had connections with the cavalry regiments: his father had been in the personal bodyguard of the King. His mother seemed to play only a small part in his life but then he was the youngest of a large family brought up mainly by nursemaids.

When the punch in the glass had sunk to a mere spoonful he rose to go. 'Thank you, madame, for a most enjoyable interlude,' he said. She was about to ring for the butler to show him out when he added, rather sadly, 'We seldom have such friendly contacts, alas.'

'I understand,' she said, going with him into the hall. 'You must realise – it takes time to see that enemies are merely men...'

'May I hope to see you and your family when I visit this detachment again?'

'Perhaps.'

He bowed and saluted.

Strange to say, his duties as welfare officer brought him back only three days later. Nicole was amused when he was shown into her office, having asked for her. 'Well, lieutenant, are you here to buy my wine?'

'That might not be a bad idea,' he said. 'But that would be the duty of the commissariat. I've been looking at the bedding my men use. I've decided they need extra blankets.'

Those infantrymen were going to have a very agreeable increase in comforts for the foreseeable future, thought Nicole. She wasn't the least surprised when Lenhardt said, 'Is your daughter indoors?'

'She's taken a walk to the lake – the poor birds suffer greatly when it is iced over.'

'Have I your permission to join her?'

Nicole hesitated. 'I have no wish to forbid it. But, lieutenant...'

'Yes, madame?'

'My daughter has strong patriotic feelings.'

'I should think the less of her if she hadn't,' he said, saluted, and went out.

Poor boy, thought Nicole. So young and decent, and about to fall in love with a totally unreceptive girl...

Chapter Twenty-three

If there had ever been the slightest chance that a friendship might develop between Lieutenant Lenhardt von Kravensfeldt and Delphine de Tramont, it was done away with by news that began to filter through in the middle of January. Count von Moltke, weary of waiting for the Parisians to surrender through hunger, began the bombardment of the city.

Many country-dwellers refused to believe it when they heard the news. 'Bombard Paris? No one would do that!' There was much talk of the 'sacred soil of France' and the 'holy home of Notre Dame' – but, Nicole asked herself, why is the soil of France sacred and Paris untouchable when we were proposing to march straight through Germany to Berlin?

Her daughter wouldn't even listen to thoughts such as those. Her stifled anger against the occupation force grew.

An attempt was made to break out of Paris on the 19th January, but it was a shameful failure. The Parisians held out for another week while their city was methodically destroyed by the long-range German siege guns. Then Jules Favre went to Versailles to arrange the longed-for armistice. Though it was granted, there were still problems – Favre and his colleagues represented only the city of Paris, there was no government of France proper.

So during the three-week armistice a National Assembly was set up at Bordeaux. Meanwhile, the citizens of Paris were allowed some freedom of movement: transport began to function in and out of the city, food supplies were taken in and news came out.

Edmond Fournier wrote giving sad news. Old Madame had succumbed to the rigours of the siege in the week after he had written his last letter. 'She didn't seem to want to live. If the royalists had seized power in Paris she might have felt some hope – she'd have wanted to live to see a Bourbon on the throne again. But when Favre and his group got control, she just lost interest in life.'

He told them he himself wasn't unwell physically, but the news he'd received in a long letter from his mother – his brother's injuries and imprisonment, the total loss of their home in Strasbourg, the occupation troops in control of the lands of Tramont – had had a bad effect on even his cheerful disposition.

He had no money and couldn't get transport to bring him home. He ended by sending his love to all but felt he might not see them for months yet because the German army were being very difficult about allowing men of military age to move about.

'You see?' cried Delphine in angry resentment. 'Nothing can ever be right, nothing, while these people hold sway over our lives! Oh, how I loathe them!'

'Delphie, can't you just take them as you find them? The men we meet are decent enough. And Lenhardt–'

'Lenhardt! You mean Lieutenant von Kravensfeldt, I take it – one of our conquerors?'

'He's a nice enough lad–'

'He's a Prussian!'

'Never mind,' sighed Nicole, 'they'll be gone soon now that the peace negotiations have begun.'

She was quite wrong. The hasty French elections returned a body of representatives from whom they wanted a peace settlement at almost any cost. Had Old Madame lived, she would have seen an Orlcanist, a supporter of the monarchist cause, at the head of government. Adolfe Thiers undertook the negotiations with Germany, which was now no longer a union of separate German states but an empire with William of Prussia as Emperor. His Chancellor, Bismarck, had no intention of making a gentle peace settlement.

Newspapers were now in production again, so the information about the agreement reached at Versailles on the 26th February was quickly known. A gasp of horror went up at the terms. It must be a mistake. France couldn't be humiliated like this.

Yet it seemed it must be true because, in protest against the terms, the citizens of Paris rebelled. They set up a commune declaring independence from the government which had given in to Bismarck's demands. By the end of March, Paris was once again a besieged city.

'Oh, God,' moaned Paulette, 'and Edmond is still there...'

'Be thankful at least that someone has some pride!' cried Delphine. 'Oh, Mama, if only I were there! I'd fight like a man–'

'Delphine, stop talking nonsense,' her mother said, her voice very sharp, and with a glance of pity at Paulette. 'If you insist on hating the Germans, I can't stop you. But if you really believe that Paris can impose its mad ideas on the rest of France, you're out of your mind! What this country needs is peace so that–'

'So that we can export wine – oh yes, I quite understand! I'm sorry I got my priorities wrong. I should have known that trade comes before honour!'

'God help me!' exclaimed Nicole. 'Daughter, you may be a grown-up young lady, but if I hear one more word from you about patriotism and honour, I declare I'll slap you!'

'Mama!'

'Oh yes – look shocked because I lose my temper! What do you think *I* feel when I hear you getting angry about the "invaders"? We were ready enough to invade their country, weren't we? "To the Rhine", everyone was crying last year. Well, we've had the tables turned on us with a vengeance and it seems to me...' Her anger gave place to regret. 'It seems to me, dear, we ought to learn from that. War is wrong, hatred is wrong. I want to live in peace with the Germans.'

Delphine didn't reply, as she might have done a moment ago, that her mother only wanted friendship with the Germans for reasons of commerce. But she couldn't resist saying, 'I don't think it's as easy as you imagine, Mama. Turning the other cheek only invites another blow.'

It proved she was right, for the treaty eventually imposed at Frankfurt could hardly have been more insulting. France was forced to sign away all rights to the provinces of Alsace and Lorraine, which were to become part of Germany. The great fortresses of Metz and Sedan were to be given up. An indemnity of five milliards of francs – a sum impossible to visualise – was to be paid by the French nation to Germany.

Worst of all: until this sum was fully paid, German troops were to remain in occupation of northern France.

Delphine said, with a grim triumph Nicole couldn't gainsay: 'So much for turning the other cheek.'

'Delphie, France will gather the money. It will soon be done and the troops will go.'

'The sooner the better! I can't bear to see them swaggering about–'

'They don't swagger, Delphie! Try to see them honestly!'

But for some weeks the easy relationship that had grown up between the people of Champagne and their conquerors received a decided check.

Now that the war was won, the German Kaiser had no particular wish to make enemies. He sent instructions that his commanders should make themselves agreeable to the local populations. So a programme of band performances, displays of horsemanship, choral concerts and balls was set in train.

The mayor of Calmady came to see Nicole. 'Madame, I need your help. The local commander, Colonel von Jarburg, is pressing me to get influential people to support his efforts of friendship.'

'You wish *me* to help in that?'

'Madame, I am approaching everyone of standing.' He didn't add that he'd been told to do so in no uncertain terms.

'Monsieur Le Maire, you are an optimist! I had one nephew wounded and taken prisoner into Germany. I have another cooped up in Paris. My mother-in-law died there of privation. And you ask *me* to support you?'

'We can all tell tales of that sort,' Loudandet said dolefully. 'It makes no difference to the fact that the indemnity may take years to collect – and during that time we have to live with these people.'

'I don't see why we can't just go on as we have before – they in their world, we in ours.'

'Madame, it's because the occupation troops *need* our friendship. They're lonely...' He sighed. He had a son interned in Switzerland, part of that last despairing French army which had refused to surrender to the Germans but had chosen internment in a neutral country instead. He couldn't help picturing that son, lonely in a foreign land.

'Besides,' he added more practically, 'if we don't help them to amuse themselves, they'll get up to mischief. You know what young men are like, madame – they'll drink too much and gamble and start fights and

450

get angry with the women when they keep saying no. It will only end in a state of continual unrest. It's really better if we collaborate with them, madame. It really is.'

Nicole wasn't sure if it was true. She promised to think it over.

Meanwhile she had many other matters to occupy her mind. There was news yet again of the movement of the phylloxera insect: it had been noted on the banks of the Rhone in the previous year but because of the upsets of war, the information hadn't become generally known. Nicole had her own vines carefully examined but so far they seemed safe enough.

Nevertheless, the vines weren't doing well. There had been a sharp frost in May just as the blossom was setting. She walked the vine rows with Rodrigue, trying not to listen to his sighs of anguish. She rode in her little phaeton to visit other vineyards, black bonnet tied firmly under her chin against the breeze of her own passing.

Sometimes, such were the vagaries of frost, other districts might have good blossom safely opening. She might be able to buy good grapes from someone else. But no – everyone told the same sad tale. There would be a small grape crop this year.

On the 23rd May came a terrible shock. The Paris Commune had been defeated two days earlier after a series of battles between the citizen-army and the troops of their own country. The whole of France was divided on the subject: some said it served the bastards right, mad revolutionaries as they were. Others said it was a stain on the honour of France that French troops should attack their own people.

Yet the Communards seemed to have behaved with horrific callousness. In their retreat before the forces of the government they set fire to the Tuileries, the Palais Royal, the Town Hall, the Law Courts, and many churches.

That was how Edmond was killed. He was burned to death while seeking shelter in a church.

Paulette took the news with dull stolidity. 'I prayed too much for Robert,' she told Nicole, dry-eyed. 'I should have asked Him to protect Edmond – I could easily have offered my jewellery as well for the re-building of the cathedral–'

'Dearest, you can't make bargains with God,' Nicole protested, holding her close and rocking her.

'No, you're wrong. You see it worked for Robert. I still have Robert.'

Delphine was too shocked to be able to say comforting words to her aunt. Like Paulette, she'd thought only of Robert. Edmond – carefree, sunny Edmond – had seemed the kind of man who would always survive and do well.

She repented bitterly of her thought-lessness. But she couldn't help thinking that it was all because of the war. If the Germans hadn't driven like a sabre-thrust into her country and besieged Paris, the Commune would never have arisen. There would have been no wild resistance-fighters to set Paris alight.

Nicole's lack of enthusiasm for the programme of Franco-Prussian friendship hadn't gone unnoticed. To help matters along, Colonel von Jarburg from his head-quarters in Calmady's Town Hall decided to billet some of his officers on her house.

'My dear Kravensfeldt, you've built up some relationship with the family, I believe?'

'Yes, colonel. I've visited several times.'

'And been well received?'

'We-ell...' Lenhardt couldn't complain of Nicole's attitude. She was always polite, sometimes positively friendly. The aunt, Paulette, seemed somewhat scared of him. The daughter, Mademoiselle Delphine, said little. When he sought her out he let him talk though he always felt she tried to put an end to any *tête-à-tête* as quickly as possible.

But that was what any wellbred young lady would do.

'I think they're disposed to be friendly, sir.'

'Very well, you shall be billeted there. You'll be a damn sight more comfortable than in these poky little cottages in the village. I'll send you, with Rheinmann and Krum–'

'Oh, colonel – do you think Krum?'

'He's a good enough fellow. Just keep him sober at mealtimes, that's all.'

'I think it's indelicate to send him to a household of women, sir.'

'You do, eh? All right then, I'll send Palbech. You're the senior lieutenant, I leave it to you to see they behave well. We pay, of course, for everything we eat, and for any extras we commandeer. Improve on what you have already, von Kravensfeldt. I need these people to like us if we're to stay here two or three years.'

'Very good, sir!' With a smart salute and a singing heart, Lenhardt went out to tell his batman to pack his traps.

The household at the Villa Tramont were divided in their reception of their guests. Nicole took it philosophically: she felt she'd brought it on herself by not being active in the friendship programmes. Paulette scarcely noticed: she'd withdrawn into a temporary religious fervour, having masses said every day for the soul of her dead son.

It was her own daughter that Nicole was worried about. She summoned Delphine to her boudoir after a week of having the officers in the house, and gave her an outright warning. 'I know how you feel

454

about the occupation troops, Delphie. Don't think I'm without sympathy. But I forbid you – do you understand? – I *forbid you* to antagonise these officers. You mustn't think only of your own feelings. There's a whole household of servants and estate workers to consider. You mustn't bring down the anger of the German commander upon them. Have I your promise to be polite to them?'

'I'll be polite.'

'Delphine! Being polite means not sitting in complete silence when they speak. It means acknowledging their acts of good manners. It means not reading a magazine when one of them gives us the pleasure of his talents on the piano.'

'I hear you, Mama.' She shrugged. 'Don't ask me to simper at them, that's all.'

'I only ask ordinary decent manners. You promise that? Very well. You may go.'

News had come from the Red Cross that parcels and letters could now be received for transmission to the wounded prisoners of war in Germany. The able-bodied had started to come home by now. It hurt Delphine to see young men she knew, safely home and about their business, whereas Robert was still lost to them in a land of strangers.

Nicole began negotiations to have Robert brought to Paris. Her plan was that Paulette should go there to live for the present while Robert would be in a civilian hospital. It was difficult to get information about his condition: red tape seemed to tie up the reports they needed.

Meanwhile, the Prussian officers weren't difficult to live with: they had military duties that took them on horseback to Calmady most days, and often they dined in mess, which was in an assembly hall at the *maire*.

All the same, it was uncomfortable. Certain topics had to be avoided. The youngest of their guests, Ernst Palbech, was as good and friendly as a puppy, but utterly without tact. He would describe battles in which he'd made 'a good tally', meaning a large number of Frenchmen put out of action by his sword or pistol.

But always Lenhardt von Kravensfeldt could be relied on to smooth everything over. Nicole began to feel a genuine affection for the young man. Lenhardt, who wasn't without perception, was encouraged by it. He felt a lady who liked him was more likely to further his ambitions concerning her daughter.

He was by now head over heels in love with Delphine. The strange thing was, he had never known the real Delphine, the gentle, laughing girl of two years ago. He loved this slender, silent maiden with the soft light hair. He loved her serious gaze, her young dignity. He even loved the way her glance would grow absent, travelling past him to some scene he couldn't envisage.

With a little string-pulling and some help via Lord Grassington in London, Robert Paul Fournier was at length released from the hospital at Elberfeld into the care of his mother. She went with a Red Cross Ambulance Corps officer to collect him, then travelled with him in a specially-hired train compartment to Paris. There he was taken into the Hospital of the Hotel Dieu.

'Let me go and stay with Aunt Paulette in Paris,' Delphine pleaded. 'I could be a great help to her.'

Nicole shook her head. What good could possibly come of it? She doubted whether her daughter would be able to resist the temptation of visiting Robert in hospital. And that would only harm both of them.

Paulette wrote regularly. The need to be active had summoned her back from her religious enthusiasms. But the news she sent wasn't optimistic. Robert was in a wheelchair now, and the surgeons were conducting various tests and trying various treatments. The fact seemed to be that they didn't really know whether he would walk again.

Robert wrote also, short duty-letters to Nicole. He expressed his grief for the death of old Madame de Tramont, sent his sympathy over the occupation of the house by the Prussian officers and the district by German troops. He ended usually with: 'My regards to Cousin Delphine.'

Another Christmas came – another Christmas with Badish infantrymen in the stables and outbuildings. This time the season was more festive: there were parties given by the troops for the local children. Food was more plentiful.

The months rolled on. The year changed its name to 1872. Money piled up for the indemnity to the German government, yet it still wasn't enough to make up five milliards.

The regime of the vines and the wine-making went on. New earth was laid on the roots of the vines. In the cellars the blending of last year's wines into the *cuvée* took place. A poor wine... In March the vines were pruned. In April the stakes were renewed and the growing branches were tied in. There was a shortage of bottles that year but it didn't matter, the bottling could be delayed because the *cuvée* was small in any case.

The time came for the party on the estate to celebrate the end of bottling the vintage. There was nothing much to celebrate, for it was a poor, scanty wine. Yet tradition demanded the party should be held, and certainly it would give spirits a little lift.

It was impossible not to invite the billeted

officers. To have shut them out would have been a downright insult. Besides, the company of infantrymen who had turned the stables into a little German village were sure to take part, because they had girlfriends by now among the families of the locality.

Thus it came about that on an evening at the end of June, Delphine found herself waltzing with Lieutenant von Kravensfeldt in the decorated shed at the far side of the estate. The atmosphere was lively. A little band from the infantry company was playing German and Viennese tunes. Pretty coloured globes had been put over the gas jets, the gas supply having been restored. The scent of new wine and flowers was in the air.

'It's very hot in here,' suggested Lenhardt. Indeed, for him it was very hot, in stiff-collared dress uniform and white kid gloves. By contrast Delphine looked cool in her gauzy crinolined gown of light blue.

She submitted to being led outside to the arbour of vines which were allowed to grow for decoration outside the main shed. Other couples were sitting on the benches, however. Lenhardt led her on to the shadows of the oak trees. It was about ten o'clock. Beneath the oak boughs there was almost complete darkness.

Lenhardt took the gloved hand that had

been resting on his sleeve. He raised it to his lips.

'Mademoiselle Delphine,' he murmured, 'you are the most exquisite creature I ever saw...'

Delphine frowned in the darkness. But he couldn't see her expression. Since she made no sound, he went on: 'You must know how much I admire you. I beg leave to tell you that I have chosen you for my wife.'

'Your wife!' It was pure startlement. She had never been more than coolly polite to the young man. What could he mean, speaking in this fashion? Had he drunk too much?

'Certainly. You couldn't think my feelings for you would lead me to offer less than the most honourable alliance? I believe your mother will give her consent. Say I have your agreement to ask her.'

'Not at all!' Delphine cried, twitching her hand from his grasp. 'You must be insane! Marry a Prussian?'

'Oh, if that is your only objection, then all is easy,' Lenhardt cried, totally misled by his own preconceptions. 'Your mother doesn't feel any enmity towards us, I am certain–'

'But I, sir! I feel enmity,' Delphine broke in. She turned to run back to the party. He seized her arm.

'Oh, wait!' Then, shocked at his own bad manners, he drew back. 'Forgive me,

Delphine. But I can't let you run off without giving me your answer. May I look forward to offering you my hand and heart?'

'Please do not,' she said. Her chin came up. 'I have to accept that you are living in my home, in unavoidable proximity. But never speak to me again on this subject.'

'But, Delphine – why not? You like me, don't you?'

'Whether I like you or not has nothing to do with it. I could never marry a Prussian.'

This time she made her escape. She went back to the party and ensured her safety by dancing with one after the other of the men from the wine-house. She withdrew early, so that she was in her own room when the celebrators at last straggled homeward and the German troops, singing harmoniously to the last, fell into bed.

Lenhardt was puzzled by Delphine's attitude. She had been perfectly polite and complaisant since they took up residence in the house. Of course, she hadn't encouraged him, but he hadn't expected encouragement: that would have been improper.

Next day he consulted his commanding officer. He warned him first that it was a personal matter, then set out his wishes concerning Mademoiselle de Tramont.

'Well, well... When I told you to build up good relations, I didn't quite foresee this.'

'But you have no objections, sir?'

'None at all. In fact, I believe there have been one or two engagements and marriages already, elsewhere in the occupation zone. Well, von Kravensfeldt, when is the happy day?'

'*Herr Oberst*, Mademoiselle de Tramont did not give me much encouragement. She … her mother had already mentioned to me that Mademoiselle Delphine has very strong feelings of patriotism. She seemed unwilling to entertain any offer from a member of the occupation force.'

'What nonsense! In a year or two this war will be quite forgotten! Oh, my dear boy, don't let that stand in your way. What does the mother say about the match?'

'I haven't yet approached her, sir.'

'Well, do so, do so! You won't get any further until you have her approval.'

'The point is, sir… I'm not very good at this kind of thing. I should be quite at a loss if Madame de Tramont upheld her daughter's viewpoint. I never thought of myself as ruled out of court simply because I'm a Prussian'

The idea was to him almost incredible. He was a professional soldier. He had done his duty when his country went to war. The war was now over. Everyone could now be friends. No one, surely could hold it against him that he had fought for his country?

'My dear Lenhardt, what do you expect

462

from me, then? Nothing can happen until you've spoken to The Widow Tramont.'

'No, sir... As a matter of fact...'

'Yes?'

'I wondered if you would speak to her, sir? You're so much better than me at this kind of thing. And of course if we were at home, it would be my father who would speak to the parents.'

'Aha! You wish me to act in loco parentis?' Von Jarburg was amused. 'All right, I see no objections. I'll call on her tomorrow.'

'Thank you, sir! Much appreciated!'

Colonel von Jarburg was quite a young man, who had risen quickly in his career after distinguishing himself with the Prussian army in the Battle of Sadowa. He had got himself just the wife he wanted, with a handsome fortune attached. He had good looks, ability and confidence: he was sure there was nothing he couldn't do.

His message to Nicole brought forth only consternation, to his astonishment.

'But, dear lady, why do you react in this way? I assure you, von Kravensfeldt is an excellent match. He's a younger son, it's true, but his maternal grandmother has left him a very handsome property north of Berlin and he has a fine career ahead of him in the army. True, he's only a lieutenant at present, but his promotion is in the pipeline already for good service in the war.'

Nicole managed to recover herself.

'This is most unexpected, colonel. My daughter hasn't mentioned any approach from the lieutenant.'

'Waiting to have it done in proper form, as is only right. Normally Baron von Kravensfeldt would be discussing these matters with you–'

'Has the Baron been informed of his son's intentions?'

'I believe not. But there can be no problem there. Baron von Kravensfeldt is hardly likely to object to a match with the daughter of The Widow Tramont.'

'I see.' Nicole was searching wildly for a good excuse to dismiss the idea.

'I gather from the lieutenant that there is already a rapport between himself and your family. He seemed fairly certain you had nothing against him as a suitor?'

'Oh, not in the normal way,' Nicole said, floundering, and annoyed with herself as a result. 'But you see ... my daughter...'

'He mentioned to me that she had some objections on nationalist grounds. But, dear lady, those can hardly be taken seriously when weighed against the attractions of the match. Von Kravensfeldt – the father, I mean – was a member of the bodyguard of our Kaiser when he was King of Prussia. The son is likely to follow in the father's footsteps. And think how advantageous, madame – when the husband receives royal notice, the wife does too.'

'I don't think that is likely to be an attraction to my daughter–'

'I think you're wrong there, madame. There's something about being at court that is very appealing. And you know, von Kravensfeldt himself is a very good fellow – doesn't drink or gamble more than he should, goes to church regularly...'

'I'm sure what you say is true. I have found him just as you describe. But then you see, it is my daughter who would have to live with him. And she isn't likely to want to.'

'But why not? Apart from the nonsensical reason about his being a Prussian?'

Nicole hesitated.

'The young lady is not already promised elsewhere?' the colonel asked sharply.

'No... But there was a young man...'

'There was marriage in view?'

'Certainly not!'

'Then what about this young man?'

'She is still grieving for him.'

'Ah? He's dead? I understand! Well, really, the sooner she gets over that, the better, don't you agree? Unless you plan to allow her to become an old maid?'

'No, that was not my plan,' acknowledged Nicole. She was vexed with herself at not having pursued a match for her daughter, but so many other things had claimed her attention. Besides, she'd sensed that for some time Delphine would still say no to everyone she proposed.

The same remained true of Lenhardt von Kravensfeldt.

'I really feel it's no use to press the matter with her, colonel. Delphine is not of a mind to accept an offer of marriage.'

Colonel von Jarburg frowned. He was a little put out to find he wasn't winning this argument. Moreover, what was the lady thinking of, allowing her daughter to say yes or no as she pleased to suitable offers?

'Allow me to speak to the young lady,' he suggested. 'I could perhaps lay arguments before her–'

'Oh, no, colonel – really – and besides, Delphine is out at the moment.'

'Ah, too bad. Well, let me invite her to tea one afternoon. We could have a little chat. I'm sure I could persuade her.'

'I think not, colonel.'

'Please, madame. I must insist,' said von Jarburg. He wasn't accustomed to having civilians say no to him. He softened it by adding, 'I promised Lenhardt to do my best for him. I really feel I must put his case earnestly to the young lady.'

There seemed no way out of it, short of telling him he was an interfering young ass. Nicole sighed and bent her head.

'I shall expect her … let me see … the day after tomorrow? Afternoon tea *à l'anglaise* – it's quite the fashion at the Prussian court.'

'At what hour shall we call?'

'At about four? But please, madame – I should like the young lady to come alone. I'll send a carriage for her.'

Delphine, given notice of this appointment, went pink with annoyance. 'What can he imagine he'll achieve? I've already told the lieutenant it's out of the question!'

'I think the colonel is a man who needs to have it said to him in person,' sighed Nicole.

The appointed day was a Thursday. On that morning a letter arrived from Paulette for Nicole. She had clearly written it when extremely depressed after having had the results of Robert's latest tests.

'My dearest sister, I wonder whether it is worth your while spending any more money on the fees of specialists. They are agreed that Robert is likely to spend the rest of his life in a wheelchair. I have decided to reconcile myself to the fact and wonder if you shouldn't do the same. God knows I have prayed for some miracle to intervene, but without result.

'As to Robert himself he is, naturally, very low in spirits. He told me this morning that he wished the Prussian guns had finished him off instead of leaving him only half a man.

'I believe, Nicci, it will be best to take him to some quiet retreat where he can live without upsets. We cannot return to our home in Strasbourg without having to live as Germans, which I suppose would make him miserable. I think it would be best to sell out my business interests in Rethel, such as they are, and settle in a healthy sea-side town.

'Let me have your views on this. If you *insist* on his continuing to see other doctors, I will of course obey, but I think it is useless. Yr. affec. sister, Paulette.'

Nicole folded the letter hastily and put it by on her desk. It was imperative not to let Delphine see it without first preparing her for the news. Unfortunately Delphine, coming in later while her mother was out in the vaults, saw her aunt's handwriting and as usual took up the letter to get the latest news of Robert.

Was she read was like a blow to the heart. So when, later that day, two Uhlan troopers arrived with a gig to take her to her appointment with their colonel, she was in no mood to be respectful.

'Well, dear young lady,' said von Jarburg when she was shown into his office in the *mairie*, 'it is charming to have your company.' In her dark green afternoon costume of fine silk, she was a delightful sight. He didn't blame young Kravensfeldt for wanting her.

He waved at his servant who, sparkling like a diamond in his polished buttons and small white apron, poured tea into porcelain cups. 'Milk or lemon? Lemon, Hans. Sandwich? No? I think I will have one.'

He waited until the manservant withdrew. Then he said, 'Dear young lady, with your mother's permission I address you on behalf of Lenhardt von Kravensfeldt—'

'You needn't bother,' Delphine said, the picture of Robert before her eyes. 'Nothing you could say would make me accept him.'

'But why not? Here is a young man, a good career in the making, chances of a post at the Imperial court, a fine fortune in his own right—'

'I'm aware of all that. I'm also aware that he is a member of the army who wrecked someone very dear to me—'

'Put all that behind you, mademoiselle,' urged von Jarburg in what he thought was a winning tone. He smoothed his moustache before adding, 'War is of course cruel. That is why men fight the battles, dear young lady. Women should not think too much about such things. I gather that you have strong feelings about the late war, but I must insist to you that patriotism, though a manly virtue, is not something ladies should take too much to heart when a good marriage is in consideration.'

Delphine put by her tea-cup. 'I am entitled to my opinions,' she exclaimed. 'I didn't come here to be lectured on such a topic!'

'Well, well... Certainly it is about the lieutenant that I principally want to speak. Since I gather you are not promised to someone else, it is your duty to consider him seriously. Over-sensitivity about the past can never be healthy. You should overcome it. I'm surprised your mother permits it.'

She leapt up, disregarding the fine porcelain cup which slopped its tea all over the little gilt table.

'How dare you!' she cried. 'Who are you to tell me how I should feel and what I should think? I find you impertinent!'

On the pavement outside the *mairie* the guard was being changed. The sergeant marching the new sentry to his post glanced up at the sound of a woman's voice raised in outcry from the open window above. He made an inquiring grimace.

'Fine young lady with the colonel,' explained the sentry going off duty. 'Brought in with a two man escort. Oh, she's a looker, I can tell you!'

'New light o' love for the colonel?' asked the new sentry.

'More likely a spy, if you ask me,' joked the man going off duty. Salutes were exchanged, the sergeant took the old guard off to smoke a pipe behind the guardroom.

Upstairs in the headquarters office, the colonel was trying to repair the mistakes he'd made. That was the problem about trying to do diplomatic things in a foreign language: you weren't quite sure if you had the words exactly right. 'Mademoiselle, please don't take what I say amiss. I speak for your own good. Why, back in Berlin, young ladies would give their eye-teeth for a young man like Lenhardt–'

'Then let them have him, by all means! He means less than nothing to me!'

'But joking apart, mademoiselle, you ought to think about it. Besides, the poor fellow's mad after you.'

'That is his misfortune. I have already told him I don't wish to hear any more on this subject.'

'But your mother is quite willing to have you consider him. She tells me you aren't engaged–'

'My affairs are not a matter for discussion between other people!' cried Delphine, beside herself with vexation at having a stranger meddling in her private life. 'And why you should take it upon yourself–'

'But Lenhardt asked me to–'

'Good God, does he really think I would listen to a silly little man like you?'

'Mademoiselle!' He was affronted.

'Oh, don't open your mouth and look astonished. What did you expect if you interfere where you haven't been invited?'

'Nevertheless, one doesn't expect abuse–'

'Oh, be quiet!' She made for the door.

Surprised, he got in her way as she attempted to leave. She tried to go round him. He put out an arm. She pushed it aside. 'Don't dare to stop me. I'm leaving–'

'Mademoiselle, please – don't leave in this hysterical–'

'Hysterical? I'm not hysterical! Just because I don't want to listen to your patronising nonsense–'

'Mademoiselle!' He was hurt and angry. So this was what you got for trying to talk sense to a high-strung young French girl. 'I demand that you stay and hear me out!'

'I shall do nothing of the kind! You may command the army post, but you don't command *me!*'

'But I'm speaking to you about marriage – about a chance to make a brilliant match–'

'A brilliant match! The only man I ever wanted to marry is beyond my reach – no strutting Prussian will ever take his place!'

She darted under his outstretched arm and out of the door. She was halfway down the stairs before he recovered his wits. He rushed after her. 'Mademoiselle! Mademoiselle!' His cry echoed in the stone staircase.

She ran down, little soft slippers slapping the stone steps. The sentry outside heard her come, and looked into the doorway.

She pushed him aside and ran out. There was no carriage for her. For a moment she looked about, at a loss.

'Mademoiselle!' shouted Colonel von Jarburg. 'I beg you, come back – we must talk!'

The sentry heard his colonel shouting after her in French, which he himself scarcely knew. He was a country boy, only recently called to the colours. All he could make out was that his colonel – who to him was the Voice of God – was angry, because the young lady was running away.

And Josef had said she was a spy!

'Stop!' cried the sentry. 'Stop at my command!'

Delphine didn't hear him, or if she did couldn't believe he was addressing her. She ran towards the side of the building, hoping to see the groom who had led away the carriage.

'Sentry,' shouted the colonel from above, in German, 'stop that young woman!'

'Stop!' cried the sentry to Delphine. 'Halt or I fire!'

Still it never occurred to Delphine that he could mean it for her. She was at the corner, saw the carriage with the shafts resting on the roadway, knew there was no conveyance ready for her. She glanced back to the high street, hoping to see a passing cart.

The sentry raised his long rifle, sighted,

and fired.

Delphine was aware of something slamming into her between the shoulder-blades. She was thrown forward, on her face on the cobbles of Calmady's main street.

The colonel had reached the doorway. 'What was that?' he cried. 'Who fired?'

'I did, *Herr Oberst,*' said the sentry, and pointed.

Delphine was lying face down on the stones. Von Jarburg gave a terrible cry and raced to her. He knelt on the muddy cobbles, heedless of his fine white trousers. He stretched out a hand to touch the stain that was making Delphine's dark green jacket darker yet.

'My God,' groaned the colonel to the white-faced sentry, 'you've killed Delphine de Tramont!'

Chapter Twenty-four

General Stiemendorf descended stiffly from his carriage. His escort had stayed respectfully the far side of the porte cochere, but he regretted their presence. It was months since a German officer had needed an escort for his safety in the occupation zone.

His adjutant was already raising the crepe-wrapped knocker. Menecque the butler had heard their approach. He opened the door at once, presenting the silver salver for the card of condolence.

'The general would like to speak with The Widow Tramont.'

'Madame de Tramont is unable to receive visitors.'

The general waved his aide aside. 'Pray tell Madame de Tramont that it is very important I see her. I want to prevent bloodshed.'

Menecque blenched, backed off, bowed, and went off down a passage without inviting the visitors further into the hall. After some delay a black-clad figure appeared from the same direction.

General Stiemendorf, in his bright uniform, felt gaudy and disrespectful beside this sombre dignity. Madame de Tramont wore a crinoline gown of stiff black silk unrelieved by any touch of colour. The soft white cap trimmed with ribbons which she normally wore had been replaced by a scarf of black veiling tying back her rich brown hair.

She indicated her drawing-room, without speaking. The general followed her in, with his adjutant at his heels. Both men now regretted the decision to come in summer uniform of light blue tunic and white trousers. But it had been deemed essential to appear as representatives of the military authority.

'What do you wish to say to me?' Madame de Tramont asked, without inviting them to sit down.

'Madame, first I must express the bitter regret of the German High Command over this terrible accident–'

'Accident!'

'It *was* an accident. The infantryman who fired was under a complete misunderstanding–'

'And will go scot free!'

'No, madame, there will be a court martial. I assure you, everything will be done to show our respect for your tragic bereavement. Colonel von Jarburg will be removed from his post. He has received official censure for meddling in the private affairs of the civilian population. Lieutenant von Kravensfeldt will be sent to serve elsewhere; his promotion has been deferred.'

'None of this will bring my daughter back,' Nicole said in a low voice.

'Madame, we are only too bitterly aware of that. For the past, we can only express our regret. But for the future there is something we must do – and in this we need your help.'

'You ask me to help you?'

'You are the only person who can prevent unrest in the district. Already our intelligence officers are reporting arms being smuggled in from elsewhere. The villagers of Calmady and nearby have got hold of some garbled account of what occurred. They intend to take reprisals.'

She looked at him, eyes heavy with tears long shed. 'Well?'

'Is this what you want, madame? Do you think it will achieve anything except the death or wounding of some dozen or so angry country folk? My men are fully trained and armed – and my orders are to prevent any kind of uprising. I shall see those orders carried out with efficiency, but it will mean casualties.'

It seemed to him that some gleam of concern showed in her expression. He went on quickly, his tone serious: 'I have the greatest respect for the French fighting man. I believe this war was lost by France through ineptitude in the leadership. So if your villagers begin a campaign of revenge, I expect them to do it with vigour. But it only means more deaths. Surely, madame, there have been enough deaths.'

She moved to the window and stood looking out at the courtyard, so as to have time to compose herself. She was easily overset now. Since her daughter's murder four days ago, her hold on her emotions had become tenuous. Tears, never easy with her, would rush to her eyes. Her vision would blur, she would find herself growing cold and faint. And the slightest thing could bring it about – it needed only a mention of some flower that Delphine had loved, or a muted question about the funeral arrangements, and she would find herself losing control.

When she turned back, she had herself in hand. 'Please sit down, gentlemen.'

Thankfully they did so. It was a warm July day. Their uniforms were stifling them. An old war wound of the general's was throbbing painfully.

'You said that you needed my help.'

'Yes, madame. I am here to ask you to make a gesture of ... of forgiveness.'

She made a faint sound, threw up a hand in protest.

'Hear me out! I don't ask you to forgive – if such a thing had happened to a child of mine I should want the perpetrator strung up!'

The adjutant coughed respectfully. His superior must really not damage the prospect of reconciliation by uttering phrases like that. Taking the hint, General Stiemendorf drew a deep breath and began again. He was angry with the men to whom he'd entrusted Calmady: by their stupidity and carelessness they had put the German High Command in the position of having to ask favours from the civilians. He was angry, too, at the waste: a young life extinguished, two good careers brought to a standstill.

'Madame de Tramont, I ask you to let the German troops take part in the funeral service—'

'No!'

'Please!' He held up a white-gloved hand. 'Listen to what I have to suggest. The men stationed here on your estate have become friendly with the local people. They tell me they want to show their respect and distress by taking part. We have considered the request at Rheims HQ and we feel it would be a good way to demonstrate the fact that you do not hold us responsible for your daughter's death.'

'Her murder, you mean.'

He shook his head. 'That is too harsh a name. The boy who fired the shot is overcome with grief. Whether or not he is exonerated at the court martial, we shall have to muster him out – he's quite unfit for service now. You must surely know, madame, that a nineteen-year-old boy newly arrived from Feilburg could never wish any harm to Mademoiselle de Tramont.'

'I have spoken to the boy myself, madame,' the adjutant put in. 'I can tell you, he has had a severe breakdown. It's useless to tell him he did what he thought was his duty – all he does is weep and cry out that he is a murderer.'

Nicole closed her eyes and tried to withdraw herself from the pain of his words. But she could see the young soldier in her mind's eye – a bent figure in a prison cell, rocking to and fro, keening his despair.

The general felt they had scored a point. He pressed on. 'I assure you that our participation in the funeral service would be dignified. The Badish infantry company beg you to let their choir sing at the service. We would like to supply a military band–'

'A band!' she protested.

'To play the Funeral March in the procession to the family vault. The instruments would be draped with crepe, the bandsmen would have black armbands.'

'Oh, for the love of God! What kind of comedy do you want to stage here?'

'It's no comedy, it's in deadly earnest. We hope by showing our wholehearted grief in this way, it will mollify the understandable

480

anger of the menfolk. And if you could bring yourself, madame, to allow a party of officers to walk behind you to the grave–'

'No.'

'I won't urge it further at the moment. I only beg you to consider what we are trying to achieve. So far, during our occupation of the north, there has been very little unrest. I think the population were weary of war. But a little time has gone by since the peace treaty and there are hotheads who might seize an opportunity to raise a standard. Who knows what spark might ignite a further conflagration?'

'The Herr General would also like to mention that a heavy compensation will be–'

'Richdal!' snapped the general. 'This isn't the time!'

'I regret, Herr General. But,' went on the adjutant, greatly daring, 'times have been hard for the champagne industry these last two years or more. Madame de Tramont is a businesswoman. I thought it only right to mention that the German authorities will take account of the injury her family has endured.'

'Blood money?' Nicole said coldly.

'Let us leave that,' Stiemendorf said. 'It's more important to preserve lives than to pay compensation for those that have been lost. I hope you agree with me there, madame.'

'Yes, I agree with you. I shouldn't want another drop of blood shed over Delphine.'

The old general felt a surge of pleasure. He knew he had won. She would agree to his plans. She would modify them, of course – that was her right. But she would allow the demonstration of regret by the German troops stationed in and around Calmady. The villagers would be appeased. He had solved his problem.

They stayed only moments more. He knew when it was time to beat a retreat – it was what had made him a good field general in his younger years. As he was helped into his waiting carriage by Richdal he said through gritted teeth: 'Damned shame! If the daughter was anything like as pretty as the mother – what a waste!'

Nicole sat in silence long after they had gone. The butler came in at last to ask if there was anything she needed. The whole house was very attentive and gentle with her.

'No, thank you, Menecque. I'm just … letting time go by. How long before we can expect Madame Fournier?'

He glanced at the elegant gilt clock. 'Any moment now, madame. Shall I have refreshments prepared against her arrival?'

'You may as well.'

They heard the carriage trundle into the courtyard about half an hour later. It had been sent to Rheims that morning to await Paulette's train. She heard the servants hurry into the hall to open the front door, fetch in the luggage, do anything at all to show their eagerness to serve.

Slowly she got up. She went to the drawing-room door, to wait for Paulette to appear in the hall. But there was some delay. She crossed the shadowy floor towards the brightness shining in from the big entrance.

Two of the menservants were lifting something down from the carriage with infinite care. Paulette stood by, holding a small lap-rug.

Tears welled in Nicole's eyes at the sight of her sister. Yet she saw clearly enough still to understand what was being lifted out of the carriage.

A wheelchair.

'Robert...?'

It was a croak of inquiry. Her throat seemed to have seized up. But the sound brought her sister whirling round. Paulette ran to her, threw her arms about her, embraced her with savage love, and whispered: 'Oh, my poor Nicole! Oh, my poor sister!'

When at last they turned to the bustle at the doorway, the invalid chair was set down on the polished floor, but hidden by the two men stooping over it, arranging the lap rug.

'He insisted on coming, Nicole,' whispered Paulette. 'I told him he wasn't fit for the journey but he wouldn't listen.'

Nicole detached herself from her sister's grasp and moved slowly to the front of the hall. The two footmen, hearing her approach, removed themselves.

Sitting in the chair was a scarecrow figure – very thin, with his suit jacket and soft shirt loose about his torso. The bones of his face were prominent. The dark eyes seemed huge, the dark brows seemed to sit like slashes of pitch on his white forehead.

And he was still so like Jean-Baptiste...

'Robert,' Nicole said, kneeling by the chair. 'I'm so glad you came.'

He took her hand in both of his. It was like having a skeleton cradle her fingers.

'I had to come, Aunt Nicci. You understand?'

'Of course.'

A male nurse appeared from outside bearing a valise of medicines. He urged that his charge should be taken to his room to rest after the rigours of the journey. 'He's a treasure,' Paulette told Nicole, 'very strict, far stricter than I should be if I were in charge of Robert alone.'

'Paulette, he looks wasted away to nothing.'

'Darchier says he's sure that can be changed. Darchier says he thinks Robert should have been trying to walk – he thinks the surgeons were wrong to keep him abed so long. I half think Darchier knows more about it than some of the doctors. He's worked with about four other disabled men and achieved a great improvement.'

It was quite clear that Paulette felt she'd been lucky to find this male nurse to help her bring her son to Calmady. Alone, she could never have done it. She was full enough of this story to help them over the first hour or two after their meeting.

Nicole had dreaded her sister's arrival. Paulette's ready tears, she felt, would encourage her own. But it wasn't so. Paulette seemed less ready to weep than in days gone by. Moreover, the mere fact that Robert had made this great effort, had insisted on travelling from Paris to the Villa Tramont, was a good omen. And that next morning he seemed little the worse for the journey cheered her even more.

Robert insisted on attending the funeral, though both women counselled against it. 'Darling,' urged Paulette, 'it will only distress you–'

'I didn't come here just to sit at home while Delphine is laid to rest on the other side of the village. I want to go to the funeral.'

Nicole took Darchier aside to ask what he thought. The nurse, a burly middle-aged man with arms like a wrestler, merely shrugged. 'I think the patient should be encouraged to do whatever he feels he can do.'

'But if it's too much for him?'

'Then he'll have to recover from it next day.'

'You don't think it would harm him?'

'No doubt it will harm him. He may be exhausted physically and mentally. But what would you prefer – that he lives out the rest of his life like a peaceful cabbage?'

She was shocked at his bluntness, and looked it. He grinned. 'Sorry, madame, but I've dealt with so many anxious relatives in my time! The worst enemy of a wheelchair patient is the protectiveness of his relations.'

Nicole had faith in his judgement, as had Paulette. On the day of the funeral they had Robert's wheelchair lifted into the carriage that was to take them to Ste Anne's behind the black-plumed hearse.

The de Tramonts had always charged themselves with the upkeep of the village church, but Nicole hadn't been able to supply funds for its complete repair after the damage of the war. It would have been unable to shade its usual congregation under its patched roof, but today there was no question of containing the mass of people who had come.

Every villager from the surrounding countryside seemed to be there. They stood

486

in black rows under the July sun. As the carriage drew up there was a rustling murmur of sympathy. Nicole descended, then Paulette. Then the footman and Darchier set the wheelchair on the church forecourt. A whisper of puzzlement arose. Darchier went into the carriage, to emerge with Robert in his arms. As he set the young man in the chair, a faint cry seemed to lift in the air, of pity and admiration.

'It's Monsieur Robert... It's the cousin... It's Madame Fournier's son...'

Behind their carriage in its slow progress to the village had marched the troop of Badish infantry quartered on the de Tramont estate. A growl was heard as they appeared.

Nicole mindful of the reason for their participation, turned to make a little gesture of welcome to the sergeant martialling them. He saluted smartly, then gave low-toned orders to his men. They filed in under the scarred porch of the church.

Inside, every bench was full. The priest had been overwhelmed with offers of flowers and expensive candles. The local gentry were there in force. At the back, as inconspicuous as possible, a row of officers sat.

The funeral mass was longer than usual, enriched with the singing of the infantry choir. Even the local people who had come determined to hate the soldiers were touched by the simplicity of their music. They sang two old German hymns and a folksong whose last verse asked: 'Oh what is contentment, what is peace? Listen only to the voice of God to learn that secret, and having learnt it, take it to the grave.'

The coffin was lifted on the shoulders of the bearers. The cortege moved off on foot to the far side of the village where the graves were dug in the unrelenting clay of Champagne. The small military band fell in behind the mourners. The sound of their slow, sombre strains seemed to lie on the heavy summer air. To Nicole it had a dreamlike quality: she seemed to be sleepwalking in an unreal world to music too heartrending to bear.

The family vault of the de Tramonts was on the highest slope of the graveyard, surmounted by an elegant small mausoleum erected in 1714. Here the priest completed the funeral service. Some of the village women knelt as the door to the vault was opened. The bearers prepared to go down the six shallow steps with the bier.

'Help me up,' said Robert suddenly.

'Oh, Robert – no!' gasped Paulette.

'Help me up,' her son said through gritted teeth. 'I want to be on my feet to say goodbye to Delphine!'

Paulette's hand had been on his shoulder,

restraining him. Now it fell away. Darchier and the footman lifted him up. He stood between them, shoulders hunched by their grasp on him, but on his feet.

Afterwards, when they were home, Darchier said to Paulette, 'You see? A time comes when a move has to be made. That time came today. It's a beginning, at least.'

'You think he'll be able to do it again?'

'I think so. And do it without help in the end.'

'He'll walk?'

The male nurse hesitated. 'I can't be sure of that. But I hope so. If he works at it, and the paralysis retreats ... who knows?'

General Stiemendorf made one more visit, at the beginning of August, to thank Nicole for her cooperation in damping down the incipient resentment over her daughter's death. 'It seems there were a few further meetings between plotters who wanted to make some sort of vengeance attack, but support had leaked away.'

'Then I am glad. But I didn't enjoy all the trappings you added to the funeral, monsieur. I would have preferred to say goodbye to Delphine more simply.'

The general had lived a good many years. 'She is always with you, I am sure. You haven't really said goodbye to her.'

She said nothing.

He handed to her an envelope containing

an order on the Bank of Hanover for a very large sum in marks.

She took it unwillingly. 'This won't bring back my daughter, General.'

'No, madame. This has been a tragic episode. But war *is* tragic. I say so, even though it has been my profession.'

He saluted, bowed with a click of the heels, and left.

All billeted officers had been withdrawn at the time of the tragedy and now the infantrymen in the outbuildings put their haversacks on their shoulders and prepared to march out. *'Ade, nun ade,'* they sang tuneful as ever, waving and accepting kisses from the girls as they left.

The Villa Tramont was left to itself again. Only the family and the servants occupied it now. The work of the estate picked up. It was August, time to spray the vines again to protect against insect damage and mildew, time to hoe for weeds among the roots. In a few weeks Nicole would have to begin making choices about which grapes to pick first, which to leave for another burst of sunshine, which to buy from neighbouring vineyards.

She shouldered the tasks with a strange weariness this time. Her spirit seemed held back by the chains of Delphine's death. Why had she worked so hard all these years, except to hand it on to her children? And now Alys was in some foreign land, cut off from her, and Delphine was in her grave.

For the time being Paulette and Robert were staying on. At first there had been much private discussion between the two sisters about whether it was wise to keep him in the country, so far from the surgeons and specialists of Paris.

'But he's made more progress in this last month than he ever did all last year,' Paulette murmured. 'Perhaps he's better off here.'

Darchier, when consulted, stated that he was quite happy to handle the patient on his own if the ladies had enough confidence in him. 'You understand I've no medical qualifications, ladies. But I've seen men get better almost despite the opinions of the doctors. It's a matter of character and determination now, if you ask me. And he's shown he's got determination.'

It seemed he was right. At first Robert was helped to his feet twice each day, morning and afternoon. By September he was able to walk, supported on either side, across the drawing-room. Darchier declared that by Christmas he'd be walking on his own, 'with walking sticks, of course, sir – but you'll be on your own legs.'

'Christmas it is, then,' said Robert.

Nicole found him one October afternoon sitting in a sunny spot on the terrace overlooking the croquet lawn. He had a book on his lap, but it was forgotten as he gazed out at the smooth green grass.

'Do you remember how we used to compete against each other out there?' he murmured as Nicole sat down beside him. 'Alys and Delphine, Edmond and I...'

'Old Madame said you were a handsome quartet.'

He made a little gesture that took in his bony body. 'Not so handsome now... Ah well, who cares about that.'

Nicole took his hand. There was more flesh on it than when she had first held it on his return.

'Do you ever hear from Alys?' he asked.

She coloured. 'I found a letter of condolence from Alys's husband, Monsieur Hopetown, among the correspondence that piled up after Delphine's death.'

'Have you replied to it?'

She sighed. 'I don't know what to say.'

'Say you're sorry you disowned them. You ought not to be separated from her, Aunt Nicci, now that Alys is your only remaining child.'

She pressed his hand. '*You* are my child, Robert.'

'I never forget that. But it's not the same, is it? It can never be acknowledged. Whereas Alys is the daughter of the de Tramonts.'

After a pause she said: 'Robert, do you

blame me for what has gone by?'

She found she was waiting with bated breath for his response. She had often felt an intolerable burden of guilt for the unhappiness she'd caused.

'Blaming people is no use, Aunt Nicole. Delphine is dead and I'm not the same person I was three years ago.'

'It's true you've changed, Robert – changed greatly.'

'That's because I've had to choose whether I would live or die.' He smiled, tolerant of himself. 'I thought I wanted to die, but it seems something inside me had a different view – for here I still am.'

'Darchier says you have determination.'

'I also have Darchier. Perhaps, if he hadn't come along in answer to Mother's advertisement for a nurse to help me travel to the funeral, I'd have joined Delphine in the grave–'

'Robert! Don't!'

'It's all right. That man has changed the world for me. He's shown me I can have back my independence.' He gave a little laugh. 'Two sticks by Christmas! That's the slogan!'

'I know you'll do it, dear.'

'Yes, and then what?'

'What do you mean?'

'What am I to do with my life, Aunt Nicci?'

She hesitated for a long moment. 'You could help me, Robert.'

'Here? But I know nothing about making wine!'

'There's more to running Champagne Tramont than making the wine. I need help to run the financial side. Times are very hard in the champagne trade – we've had two bad years and look like having another, with nothing worthy of our label coming out of the presses. And then there's the constant dread of the phylloxera...'

'But that's stayed much further to the south, Aunt Nicci. The bug doesn't like cold climates, it seems.'

'So far, so far...'

'Come now, it's not like you to be pessimistic.'

She burst out suddenly, 'Sometimes I get so tired of being the moving spirit of this place, Robert! I need someone to whom I can talk... I need someone to lean on a little.'

'No use leaning on me as yet,' he said, smiling. 'I'd only fall over.'

'But if you would stay, Robert? If you would think of that as something to do with your life?'

'I'll think about it,' he said.

Lord Grassington arrived at the end of that week. By pulling strings in London, he had managed to have himself accredited as neutral observer to the court martial of the hapless private from Feilberg.

The death of a daughter of La Veuve Tramont had been reported in the London newspapers, causing much interest. On the whole the British had been pro-German at the outbreak of hostilities but the siege of Paris followed by the harsh peace terms had made them rather pro-French. This report of a tragic incident involving one of their favourite French families made everyone watchful; diplomatic sources were interested.

The trial of Hans Gibblich had been put off from week to week because of the mental condition of the accused. The German High Command weren't displeased: it gave time for hot feelings to cool and public interest to lapse. On the other hand, it gave time for the wildest rumours to grow, the chief of which was that Colonel von Jarburg had made improper advances to Mademoiselle de Tramont, she had defended her honour and escaped, and the colonel had ordered her shot to prevent her proclaiming the insult.

Nicole had no way of knowing the facts. But Lenhardt von Kravensfeldt was allowed to make one visit to her, to report his colonel's side of the story.

He was rigid with suppressed despair, white-lipped, determined to be an officer and a gentleman to the last. 'I assure you,

495

madame,' he said, 'the *Herr Oberst* would never intentionally have done anything to distress the mademoiselle. He tells me, and I believe him, that she ran out in a state of high emotion after some unkind remarks about Prussian officers.'

'And he tried to stop her.'

'No, he called after her, the sentry misunderstood and thought she was an enemy agent under interrogation. There you have it.'

Nicole knew the curt words for the truth. She could find nothing to express her sense of waste and loss. She sat looking blindly at the lieutenant.

'Madame,' he said in a hoarse voice, 'tell me you forgive me.'

Still her mind refused to function, her voice was crushed to silence in her throat.

'Madame!'

She managed to focus upon him. Tears were sliding down his white cheeks. He was standing to rigid attention all the while, one thumb touching the side-seam of his breeches, a glint of sunlight reflecting off the helmet he held under his arm.

'I forgive you, Lieutenant von Kravensfeldt.'

She thought for a moment the military façade would crack. For one dreadful, chaotic moment she thought he was going to fall on his knees and grasp her hand. But then military discipline reasserted itself. He saluted, bowed, wheeled about, and marched out.

Nicole had been informed she could attend the court martial if she wished – a great concession, since it was supposedly a military matter only. She thanked the adjutant who brought her this news but refused.

Now Gerrard came from Rheims with the result. 'The poor lad was declared unfit to plead through "mental debility" – a regimental surgeon and a civilian French doctor certified the condition. He's been discharged.'

'And now what happens to him?' Robert asked with a weary shake of the head.

'God knows. He'll go home to his father's farm in the State of Baden and try to live with what he's done.'

'What else happened?'

'Von Jarburg was severely censured and removed from his post. Von Kravensfeldt was held to be less blameworthy having consulted his superior officer on a personal matter as he was entitled to do. But it's a blot on his career. I don't think he'll ever reach the Emperor's bodyguard now.'

Nicole looked at Robert, to see how he was taking this news about the man who had loved Delphine. He was sitting quietly, his expression unreadable. Afterwards he said to Nicole: 'I don't hold it against him. If I could have offered for Delphine's hand honourably, I'd have done everything I could to win it.'

'The awful thing is, Delphine was scarcely aware of his existence. She was polite to him because I insisted on it – but he was no more to her than a fly on the wall.'

Robert drew her down towards him and kissed her lightly on the cheek. 'Don't grieve too much. There's been enough grief.'

'I keep trying to tell myself that. It's time to think about the future, such as it is.'

'Aunt Nicci, I've decided to accept your offer to stay and work for Champagne Tramont. That's if you haven't changed your mind.'

'Of course not!' She clasped her hands together in thankfulness.

'I'd like to start learning what I can, even while I'm still not totally on my feet. You could let me have the records and the books to study, couldn't you?'

'Yes, at once. I'll have my clerk Lebel put together a useful packet of records – perhaps we could start with a study of our markets?'

'Very well.'

Lord Grassington was pleased when Nicole told him the news. 'I think it's time you began sharing your burden, dear. It's a shame you and de Tramont didn't have a son, but a nephew is still family... He's a decent lad, bears up well despite his state of health.'

'He'll get better,' Nicole said with conviction.

'Do the doctors say so?'

'Darchier says so, which is more important!'

'Oh, Darchier...' Grassington found the male nurse amusing. He reminded him of the kind of tough, kindly trainer one saw around London boxing rings. 'Let's hope he's right. Now listen, my dear ... I can't help seeing signs that you're hard pushed for money–'

'Oh, Gerrard – does the place look so neglected?'

He laughed. 'I'm a land-owner myself, Nicci. I can see the little signs. What I wanted to say was – now don't take this amiss – if a loan would help, you have only to say so.'

She gave a little gasp. 'Take money from you?'

'Dear, it would be strictly a business transaction. Good business, too, because these poor grape harvests can't go on forever. Next year or the year after, you'll make good wine again and plenty of it.'

'I keep telling myself that. But sometimes, Gerrard – I get frightened...'

'Who doesn't?' he said, putting a friendly

arm about her.

He had to return to London to report on the court martial to the Foreign Office and then take part in a debate in the House of Lords on farming policy. He took his leave reluctantly. 'Shall I see you in London soon, Nicci?'

'Perhaps, but it isn't easy getting permissions and passes while the occupation force remains in command. I think they have a suspicion that any movement of any kind means you're smuggling your money or yourself out of their reach – and we still have to pay off that accursed indemnity.'

'But the balance left to gather is getting less all the time. Only about one milliard to go, I hear.'

'Well, if we pay it off next year and the Germans depart, I may start travelling again, Gerrard dear.'

'I look forward to that.'

After he had left, for a few days Nicole felt strangely lonely. Dearly though she loved her sister and Robert, she couldn't talk to them about business matters in the easy mixture of love and good sense that Gerrard brought her. Robert would learn, it was true – one day he would be able to speak up in a debate about what to do over future policy. But otherwise there were only the employees of the firm – Emile Rodrigue with his understandable uncertainties, old

Leboilean who was now so set in his ways that almost nothing might be changed in the vineyards without a fight.

But it was November, the wine was 'resting', time to start making experiments for the *cuvée* of next February. She went to inspect the samples that Rodrigue had assembled in the laboratory of the chief of cellar, the room where Jean-Baptiste had once held sway.

As she came in that first morning, a sense of loss struck at her like an actual physical blow. Once, she would have been able to turn to Jean-Baptiste. But he was gone, and even Robert who looked so like him could never take his place.

She worked hard that morning, sipping, making notes, listening to Rodrigue's suggestions, reading measurements of sugar content and sediment. She knew already that they would make a poor champagne this year – poor, that is, compared to the wine that had made her famous. The grapes had been small and sharp, the juice had looked dark, the new wine lacked vigour.

At lunch she found Robert eager to discuss something he'd found in the records of wine shipments by barge. 'Do you realise, Aunt Nicci, that you are paying out a fortune in transhipment charges? It would pay you to have your own dock on the river Marne from which to send the barges down to Paris.'

'Robert, that would take a fortune. We'll do it one day, perhaps, but not for the foreseeable–'

In the distance came the loud rumble of the wheels of a heavy coach. Paulette cried, 'Someone's coming in under the porte cochere! Are you expecting anyone, Nicci?'

Nicole shook her head. It must be a travelling coach to make so much noise, for they were eating in the dining-room round the east side of the house. Who could it possibly be?

Everyone stopped eating. Robert turned his wheelchair to look at the door of the dining-room. It opened. Menecque came in, flustered, pink with excitement.

'Madame!'

'Yes, what, Menecque?'

'It's Mademoiselle Alys!'

'Alys?' Both Nicole and Paulette jumped up.

From the hall could be heard the sounds of trunks being set down, servants running, a baby crying.

'Alys!' shouted Nicole, and ran like a deer to see her daughter.

Standing inside the big entrance were several people. Alys was a little to the fore, holding by the hand a toddler in a thick white flannel coat and buttoned boots. Behind her, gesturing at one of the footmen to take care, was a tall fair-haired young man. One glance from him to the toddler told Nicole that this was the father. At his side, holding a baby wrapped in many shawls against the chill November weather, was a dumpy girl in a dark blue serge, the nursemaid.

Mother and daughter stood for a moment staring at each other. They had not met for three years. Alys saw a still slender, vigorous figure clad entirely in black, with scarcely a thread of grey in the brown hair held in check by the black silk cap. Nicole saw a dark-eyed young woman in a dark grey travelling costume, her skin lightly tanned, her lips parted with a greeting yet unspoken.

'Mama...?'

'Oh, darling! Darling Alys! Oh, my angel, my dove – how I've missed you!'

They were engulfed in each other's embrace. Gavin Hopetown found his sleeve being wept over by a lady who bore a distinct resemblance to his mother-in-law. The toddler staggered over to a gentleman in a chair that moved and gravely leaned against his knees.

'Gramma's house,' she told him.

'That's right. You're home in Grand-mama's house.'

So it proved. After a chaotic half hour, in which everyone talked at once in loud voices over the baby's crying, Nicole heard their explanation.

'There's a big English community in Portugal,' Gavin told her. 'We got the London papers regularly. As soon as we saw the report of Delphine's death...' He hesitated, but his mother-in-law seemed able to stand mention of the name. 'Alys said at once that we must go to you. I immediately started trying to get permission. It's been hell! – beg pardon,' he added apologetically.

'You've no idea, Mama,' Alys put in, dangling the toddler on her knee. 'German bureaucracy and French bureaucracy! At first I was going to write to say we were coming, but it kept looking less and less likely that we'd get permission. Then all of a sudden, they said yes.'

'So I handed in my resignation–'

'You've given up your job?' Nicole cried.

'Oh yes, of course, Mama! I knew you'd need us. Of course I didn't know about you, Robert–' Her little gesture took in his invalid chair.

'This is only temporary,' he replied.

'Good for you,' Gavin said. 'Well, at any rate, here we are. We weren't sure of our welcome but as Alys said, if you turned us away we could always go on to London. I have an offer of a post there now – a couple of steps up the ladder.'

'Do you wish to take it?' asked Nicole, feeling a trembling of the heart at the

504

thought of losing them again just as she'd had them given back.

'No, no, darling Mama, how can you be so silly!' Alys cried. 'That's only what we'd have done if you'd closed the door on us. I wasn't sure if you'd forgiven me for being disobedient.'

A sudden silence fell. Gavin drew in a breath. 'Madame, I never asked for your permission to marry your daughter. It would ease my conscience if you'd give us your blessing now.'

Nicole, smiling, said nothing. Words weren't needed.

'The next point is, can you use my services?' It was a relief to turn from emotional matters to practical points. 'I've no experience of making champagne, of course, but I know the business side of import-export, and I've had three years helping to run a sherry vineyard.'

'Sherry,' Nicole said with a shudder.

'Well, everyone to his taste, of course. I won't talk about sherry if you'd rather not. I'll soon learn how to talk about champagne. I wondered if you could use me on the estate? If you'd let me be assistant to the present chief of vineyard–?'

'You're a godsend,' Nicole told him. 'Leboilean is so *old* and such a curmudgeon! He's got rid of two likely young men I brought in, but he can hardly get rid of the owner's son-in-law, can he? And you can learn from him – he knows all there is to know about Pinot grapes.'

'It would be an honour.' He hesitated. 'Robert ... am I treading on your toes here?'

'Not at all. I hope to take over some of the business side during the coming months – I believe I can see how to improve the movement of the wine from cellar to market.' He gave a little sound, half laugh, half sigh. 'Once, in what seems another life, I wanted to study architecture. It's something of an architectural problem, this business of getting the right warehouses and freight depots for wine. I've already got some ideas – but they'll take money.'

'Which we haven't got. Well, never mind. So long as we have a roof over our heads, bread to eat, and grapes to grow, we have something to work for.'

Nicolette, the toddler, had been given soup and a crust of bread to stay hunger pangs after her long journey. Now she had fallen asleep on her mother's lap. 'I had better put her to bed for her afternoon nap,' said Alys. 'Which room should I take, Mama?'

'Your old room, of course. And you could have Delphine's room...' her voice trembled but she went on... 'Delphine's room next door as a nursery.'

'Yes, thank you, that will be lovely. Come,

506

my precious ... it's time you were snuggling down.'

The house began to organise itself after the furore of their arrival. Lunch, which had been interrupted, was resumed with a larger table. Afterwards, while Alys with Paulette's help set about unpacking, Nicole showed Gavin Hopetown round the estate.

There was little to be seen, indeed. The vines were dormant, scarcely more than little pieces of crooked stick in the wet Champagne clay. The sky was dreary with misty clouds. Rain had fallen, more threatened. Their breath made steam before them as they walked. She glanced at her son-in-law anxiously. How would he see this, accustomed as he was to the sunshine of Portugal?

'I hope I shan't have to do any of the actual digging,' he said teasingly as he kicked at a ridge of unrelenting clay. 'It's terrible stuff, isn't it? Who would ever believe it produces such wonderful wine?'

'It's a mystery, Gavin. That's why I feel it's such a ... a responsibility, an honour.' She fell silent, embarrassed. She seldom spoke of her feeling for the land which had given her her wine.

But he understood. 'I thank you for allowing me to take part in it,' he said. 'I'll try never to let you down in any way.'

'I know that, Gavin.'

As they were trudging back to the house, Robert came out to meet them, walking in his strange stork-like fashion with Darchier on one side and a walking stick the other. 'One-man-one stick!' he called as they approached. 'Two sticks by Christmas!'

Nicole ran to give him a kiss of congratulation. 'It's wonderful, Robert. Who would ever have thought, when you arrived in July...'

They fell silent at the mention of that month, that awful time.

Then from the house came the faint wail of the baby, Philippe, waking up hungry for his evening feed.

'Your grandson is calling for attention, madame,' Robert teased.

Nicole ran indoors. She wanted to get to know the baby. She wanted to knit up the old relationship with Alys.

Oh, there was so much she still wanted to do.

The publishers hope that this book has given you enjoyable reading. Large Print Books are especially designed to be as easy to see and hold as possible. If you wish a complete list of our books please ask at your local library or write directly to:

Magna Large Print Books
Magna House, Long Preston,
Skipton, North Yorkshire.
BD23 4ND

This Large Print Book, for people
who cannot read normal print,
is published under the auspices of

THE ULVERSCROFT FOUNDATION